COURAGE & CALLING

EMBRACING

YOUR

GOD-GIVEN

POTENTIAL

Revised
and
Expanded

GORDON T. SMITH

An imprint of InterVarsity Press
Downers Grove, Illinois

InterVarsity Press
P.O. Box 1400, Downers Grove, IL 60515-1426
World Wide Web: www.ivpress.com
Email: email@ivpress.com

Revised and expanded edition ©2011 by Gordon T. Smith
First edition ©1999 by Gordon T. Smith

InterVarsity Press® is the book-publishing division of InterVarsity Christian Fellowship/USA®, a
movement of students and faculty active on campus at hundreds of universities, colleges and schools
of nursing in the United States of America, and a member movement of the International Fellowship
of Evangelical Students. For information about local and regional activities, write Public Relations
Dept., InterVarsity Christian Fellowship/USA, 6400 Schroeder Rd., P.O. Box 7895, Madison, WI
53707-7895, or visit the IVCF website at <www.intervarsity.org>.

Scripture quotations, unless otherwise noted, are from the New Revised Standard Version of the
Bible, copyright 1989 by the Division of Christian Education of the National Council of the Churches
of Christ in the USA. Used by permission. All rights reserved.

While all stories in this book are true, some names and identifying information in this book have
been changed to protect the privacy of the individuals involved.

Cover design: Cindy Kiple
Interior design: Beth Hagenberg
Images: Nicolas "Kipourax" Paquet/Getty Images

ISBN 978-0-8308-3554-6

Printed in the United States of America ∞

Library of Congress Cataloging-in-Publication Data

Smith, Gordon T., 1953-
    Courage and calling: embracing your God-given potential / Gordon T.
Smith.—Rev. and expanded.
        p. cm.
    Rev. ed. of: Courage & calling.
    Includes bibliographical references (p.   ).
    ISBN 978-0-8308-3554-6 (pbk.: alk. paper)
    1. Vocation—Christianity. I. Smith, Gordon T., 1953- Courage &
calling. II. Title.
    BV4740.S63 2011
    248—dc22

                                                        2011006805

P   18   17   16   15   14   13   12   11   10   9   8   7
Y   26   25   24   23   22   21   20   19   18   17   16

*The place God calls you to is
the place where your deep gladness
and the world's deep hunger meet.*

Frederick Buechner

To my sons,
Andrew and Micah

CONTENTS

1

STEWARDS OF OUR LIVES

Navigating Change with
Grace and Courage

God calls people. Whether it is the calling of Abraham to leave the land of Ur and go he knew not where, or the calling of Moses, confronted with the burning bush, or the calling of Isaiah who encountered the glory of God, or the calling of St. Paul to bring the gospel to the Gentiles, an awareness of call is both mysterious and powerful. A calling is always a demonstration of the love and initiative of God, but through vocation we also come to an appreciation that God takes us seriously.

It is helpful to understand the call of God in three distinct ways. First, there is the call to be a Christian. The God of creation invites us to respond to his love. This *call* comes through Jesus, who invites us to be his disciples and to know the Father through him. To be Christian is to respond to this call to know and love God, and to love and serve others. It becomes, then, the fundamental fact of our lives; everything about us is understood in light of this call. Every aspect of our lives flows out and finds meaning in light of the fact that we are a called people. And the church is made up of "called" ones. Nothing matters more to us than that we are called. It is sheer gift—an invitation offered to us in the mercy of God to become his people and walk in faith and obedience to his Word. It is, essentially, a call to God's salvation.

Second, for each individual there is a *specific* call—a defining purpose or mission, a reason for being. Every individual is called of God to respond through service in the world. Each person has a unique *calling* in this second sense. We cannot understand this *second* meaning of call except in the light of the first. When we fulfill our *specific* vocation, we are living out the full implications of what it means to follow Jesus. Therefore, while we all have a general call to love God and neighbor, we each follow our Lord differently, for though he calls us all to follow him, once we accept his call we are each honored with a *unique* call that is integrally a part of what it means to follow him. The second experience of call is derived from the first.

Third, there is the call that we face each day in response to the multiple demands on our lives—our immediate duties and responsibilities: the call to be present to my sons when they are involved in an athletic competition, or to help out in my local church, or to respond to some specific and important need before me. These are *my* tasks— not in the sense of burdens but as those things that are placed before me today by God. It may be nothing more complicated than helping my son repair his car. But that is what God has for me today. It may be to teach a class or be present for a committee meeting. I would not speak of these as my *vocation* (which is closer to the second meaning of call), but they are nevertheless those duties and responsibilities God calls me to today.

All three distinct meanings of "call" need to be understood together.

Called of God: The Three Expressions of Vocation

- The general call—the invitation to follow Jesus, to be Christian
- The specific call—a vocation that is unique to a person; that individual's mission in the world
- The immediate responsibilities—those tasks or duties God calls us to today

This book will focus on the second of these three aspects of our calling, and this is the primary way I will be using the word *calling* or *vocation*—not as an occupation or "line of work," but something that nevertheless speaks of our engagement with the world in response to God. But we must consider this second sense of call in light of the other two dimensions noted. Our vocation is a critical means by which we fulfill the call to be a disciple of Jesus. Part of what it means to follow Christ is to accept his specific and unique call on our lives.

But we must consider the immediate duties and obligations we have as Christians, as members of families, as spouses and as friends. The daily demands on our lives are not necessarily threats to the fulfillment of our vocation—the second meaning of *call*. They are all part of what it means to be called of God.

Because vocation, in the second sense, is part of, but only part of, what it means to be a Christian, we must see our specific and unique vocations within the context of *all* that it means to be called to be Christian. This will require that we move away from compartmentalization of our lives. We are whole people, complex people, people who fulfill our callings within the whole setting of circumstances, problems and relationships that constitute what it means to be a Christian. I, for example, fulfill my vocation as husband to Joella, father to two sons, and grandfather to three grandsons and two granddaughters. This is an unavoidable and vital dimension of my life, and I cannot consider and think constructively about my work in the world apart from these realities.

What follows is a guide to thinking about calling—in the second meaning described earlier. But when thinking well about calling or vocation in this sense, we do so within the context of all three dimensions of what it means to be called by God.

NAVIGATING TRANSITIONS

Transition is one of the givens in our lives, and we only live well, we only manage our lives well, when we manage these transitions well.

Our world changes; the circumstances of our lives change. The economy changes and forces change in our lives. For those of us who work in the church, the dynamics around us change and we either adapt and respond or we lose our moorings.

If we are facing a transition, it is often due to one of three factors.

First, inevitable transitions flow from the normal course of a human life. We grow up; we leave home; perhaps we marry. If we marry, we may have children; if we do, this brings us yet another transition. Indeed, many parents note that it is not merely the experience of *a* child; having a second or a third brings yet another transition that calls for a faithful and hopeful response.

The transition into early adulthood is but the first of a series of changes that will intersect our lives as we make the pilgrimage through life. We grow up and grow older, and move through midlife. As young adults there are many things that we might have taken for granted that in midlife we no longer view as a given or an assumption of our lives. The biggest assumptions that are challenged may include coming to terms with our limits. On the one hand, we know ourselves better; as we grow older we come to a deeper appreciation of what matters most to us.

The transitions through our early and midadult years are but the first rounds of what for many will be the biggest challenge of our lives: the transition into our senior years. Perhaps it could be said that we only truly live well, in the end, when we graciously manage this transition into the last season of our earthly lives. Speaking of vocation, work and career necessarily means that we consider how the diverse chapters of our lives reflect new challenges, opportunities and circumstances. And there is no other way to speak of calling but in a recognition that these inevitable transitions call for a mature and generous response.

Some will no doubt read this book hoping to find guidance and wisdom for the early adult years—the transitions out of their parents' home and into the marketplace; for others this book will be helpful as they navigate the changing circumstances of their middle years.

And yet guidance is just as needed for those moving into their senior years. These are surely some of the most important years of our lives, and one of the signs of strength for both our culture and for the church is that we are a community and society that effectively empower senior members of our society to embrace the calling of God on their lives. I will speak more to this in chapter four, "The Chapters of Our Lives."

Second, another kind of transition comes with the inevitable changes in our work world. Many will be unemployed or, better stated, unwaged at some point in their lives. Some will have been let go due to problems in the workplace. Others will be released from their employment because their employers could no longer afford to keep so many on the payroll. Some farmers can no longer afford to farm because the crop they have been cultivating is now available elsewhere at cheaper prices; thus they can no longer compete given their own labor costs or other circumstances. Others, in different sectors of the employment world, have not been able to keep up with the information and technology developments, and have been replaced by a computer or are being replaced by someone younger and seemingly quicker, or who has the technological savvy to make it in the new work environment.

We can no longer assume that we will have a single job throughout our adult years. Even if that was the case a number of years or a generation ago, it is certainly not the case now. No one, regardless of vocation or line of work, can live with that kind of assumption.

We can think about our context in this way: the economy is changing. Wendell Berry describes the *economy* as "our way of making a living," that which, "connects the human household with the good things that sustain life."[1] And this economy—the "way we make a living"—is changing. The changes are permanent; this is not a temporary blip on the screen. These changes will affect all of us. Everyone, literally everyone, will have job changes and transitions as a matter of course. Whether we fulfill our vocation in the church or in the world will make little difference. The organizations we work for will reflect the turbulence in our economy with downsizing, outsourcing, a "just in time" labor force and the growth of temporary agencies. But employment will be just that—temporary!

We will only thrive in this new economy when we accept this reality—turbulence and change—and then embrace what it means for us, that is, embrace it as an *opportunity* rather than a threat.

Third, some transitions come about as a result of changes in our own hearts. In many cases this transition reflects the simple fact that we are growing older and wiser, and so perhaps have a better read on ourselves and what really matters to us. This merits separate mention because for many this reflects a different dimension of their experience.

One of the things that causes my heart to ache is meeting people who simply hate their work. In some cases the workplace itself is toxic. Others may feel they are involved in an industry that cuts deep into their own personal sense of what is good and right and true. This may be because of something obvious: they simply cannot in good conscience continue to work for a casino, which they know erodes the lives of those who gamble as well as the local economy that depends on the taxes that come from the gambling. They recognize that it is no way to build a life or an economy.

Others may feel that the product they sell or the service they provide, while good in itself, no longer fits their own personal passion and commitment. They may have for many years been glad to have a job that paid the bills, but increasingly their heart is telling them they no longer feel a congruence with this company and its values.

Something very similar could emerge in the heart of those involved in religious work. They might realize that they can no longer in good conscience identify with the mission agency they work for. This could be for any number of legitimate reasons: perhaps they are concerned that there is a one-dimensional concern for personal religious experience and no concern for social justice, or perhaps they can no longer enthusiastically participate in the work of the agency because of theological concerns.

I realize that there are many people who simply have no choice;

they are "slaves." For any number of reasons—economic, social, marital—they do not have control of the basic elements of their lives and their careers. They cannot resign; they cannot walk into the managers office and say "I quit!" How they would love to do it. But they are trapped in role and responsibility that violate their human worth and dignity. Whenever the products we use, the food we eat or the benefits we experience are the fruit of this kind of work situation—shoes made by forced labor, food served by underpaid wait staff—we need to have the courage to say "no more!" And we need to be advocates on the national and international levels for just forms of labor. In the meantime the following is written to those who do have the capacity to respond to what they know is right and true, which they increasingly recognize needs to be reflected in their work.

It is important to note that this transition of the heart often comes slowly. We look back and in retrospect see that something has grown gradually in our heart, perhaps a holy discontent, and we know that in good conscience we need to ask how best to navigate this transition with a faithful and hopeful response. It will require courage; making a move might disappoint a whole host of people and lead to greater financial insecurity. But increasingly we recognize that we have no choice; we need to initiate a change. In other words, some of the transitions we experience are the natural result of growing older; some are the result of external factors that force us to respond; and some are the kinds of transitions where we take the initiative, step out and courageously inform the corporation or the organization that we are moving on. I hope that this book can be a resource to you if you are in this position; may it give you the spiritual and emotional tools to navigate this transition with faithfulness and hope.

A CRISIS OF CONFIDENCE

When transition is so much a part of our lives, one of the inevitable features of our work will be a crisis of confidence. We change and enter into a new set of opportunities, or the world or the circumstances around us change; the familiar is gone and what we once felt we might have been able to do well is no longer assumed to be part of the equation.

Robert Kegan has published a fine book that is well worth reading, but its title alone captures something that merits repeating: *In Over Our Heads*. The distinct impression we get in this new economy is that we are all in over our heads. Regardless of our line of work or responsibility, whether in business or in the task of raising children, whether it is pastoral ministry or the challenge of public education, the changing circumstances leave us with a lack of confidence that we can accomplish what we are called to do. In this new economy we could easily conclude no one can say she is the *master* of her field or that he is a leader in his discipline. Not anymore.

I serve as the executive director of a nonprofit agency. I enjoy my work and come to it with a sense that on the whole I do it well—that I have the experience, the expertise and the determination to be effective. But what regularly impresses me and others in this line of work is that we can never keep up with all that we need to know in order to do our jobs well. The complexities of managing nonprofit organizations are such that it almost seems like sheer presumption to suggest that *anyone* can do this job well.

The wonderful word *master* used to describe the person who is at the top of his or her craft, whatever the profession. It was a title that one could work toward and with some degree of confidence ascribe to the person who was very good at what he or she did—whether it was watch making, shipbuilding, teaching or business management. But in the new economy we are all "in over our heads." Just when we think we might have mastered our craft, the circumstances and expectations have changed. The field I work in is developing so quickly that I always feel one step behind.

In some cases this has meant that individuals have experienced failure, setback and disappointment. They did their work to the best of their abilities but were not deemed to have done it well enough, and the change in their employment situation shattered their sense of competence and even their confidence in being able to do any job at all.

While perhaps still employed, others have faced criticism or a lack of affirmation and support, which has left them with little if any confidence to be able to press on in the midst of the changes in the economy and their work situation. In some of these circumstances the political pressures of their occupation have taken the wind out of their sails.

Still others have moved out of the waged workforce for a time, perhaps as mothers to raise a family, and now it may be as much as fifteen years later and things have changed so much that they lack the confidence to pick up their careers again or return to the roles or responsibilities they once had.

There are those who have gone into pastoral ministry, and in midlife come to a realization that congregations are changing so rapidly, especially in the way they are governed and what they are looking for in pastor, that they wonder if they really have what it takes to provide effective religious leadership.

Some have chosen a line of work or a career as young person, but now they have come to midlife, perhaps into their fifties, and have found that what they had envisioned is no longer there. The land they hoped to farm for life is no longer theirs. Or maybe an anticipated career is gone; they trained for a particular line of work only to discover that people in that field are no longer needed in the workplace.

Yet others face retirement and struggle deeply with what it means to let go of their careers; it is so easy to feel like they are being dismissed by the organization they have worked with for many years. There are few things so painful as the feeling that we have been pushed out, and that pain in many cases strikes at the heart of our self-confidence.

Finally, for some the crisis of confidence comes from the dashing of grandiose ideals—the young woman who was certain that by her midthirties she would have her own successful business and have made her first million, or the young pastor convinced that in no time at all he would master what it takes to have a congregation that is the envy of all other pastors, or the team of individuals who longed to do great deeds for God in the inner city only to discover that the very ones they longed to serve actually rejected their help. These kinds of ideals often need to be set aside, and sometimes there is nothing to do but accept the disappointment and honestly see that our illusions about ourselves are just that, illusions. We were trying to be heroes, and the sooner we let that dream go, the better. But however much we needed to face up to our illusions, it still is painful, and we are still experiencing a crisis of confidence. Sometimes it hurts so much that we wonder if we can ever do anything well again.

STEWARDS OF OUR LIVES

Part of the reason why we feel these transitions so keenly is that we know that our lives matter. Yes, there is the obvious: we only have one life to live, and so we naturally want to live well. But we need to probe this more deeply.

Living well, surely, is a matter of taking seriously the life that has been given to us—the opportunities and challenges that are unique to us, to our lives, our circumstances. Taking our lives seriously means that we respond *intentionally* to these circumstances and the transitions of life. But we will only do so if and when we recognize three things. First, our lives are of inestimable value. Second, living our lives to the full is precisely what it means to be good stewards of our lives. Third, we live fully by living in a way that is deeply congruent with who we are.

The worth of human life. In the Scriptures there is a clear proclamation of what it means to have human identity—a person created by God, with worth and significance. But it is also the case that the field or discipline of psychology has enabled many to appreciate the full significance and weight of this scriptural insight. Erik Erikson helps us appreciate more fully what it means to become an adult—mature in one's personal identity. Viktor Frankl effectively argues that deep within the psyche of each person is a longing for meaning that needs to be expressed in hopeful work and purposeful activity. Rollo May, recognizing the essential worth of each person, appreciates the power of crisis and stress to undermine personal identity. He helps us see that the resulting emptiness and anxiety can only be overcome through the power of love, which enables us to live with freedom and courage. And Abraham Maslow gave us the language of "self-actualization"—as the ideal or goal toward which each person strives, to realize our potential in our work and relationships, and to be able to do so even in environments and contexts that threaten our capacity for inner strength, authenticity and courage.

Yet what is so significant in all the profound insights of these writers is that so much of what they are saying lies within the ancient text of Holy Scripture. The Bible affirms the essential worth and significance of each person, created in the image of God, chosen and elect of God, and thus as having incomparable worth and significance in the eyes of God.

No lives are dispensable; of none can it be said that their lives or work do not matter. Each person brings beauty, creativity and significance to the table. And in this I am speaking specifically of the individual. Yes, we must speak of community. And yes, we need to always speak of the individual as only truly flourishing insofar as he or she is in community and an integral member of society. All true. And yet what must not be lost is the inherent value and potential of the individual person who is loved, called, and equipped or empowered by God to do good work.

Thus, when we speak of calling we do so with the appreciation of the extraordinary potential of each person to make a difference for good. By this I do not mean that everyone needs to be a hero, but rather, in the midst of the simple ordinariness of everyday life, the work we do has the capacity to be good work that has profound worth and significance.

Living our lives to the full. There is an oft-quoted line from the church father Irenaeus: "The glory of God is the human person fully alive." The perspective captured in this simple declaration must be affirmed: the human person brings glory to God, not by self-abnegation but rather precisely through the affirmation of the human person. Yes, we must speak of denial—the negation—of all that is not of God. In particular we need to affirm and actually insist that the human person is not God; as persons we live in radical dependence on God. But when God is seen as clearly and wholly God, humans are free to be precisely who they are called to be.

To put it differently, we are not the center of the universe! Children as often as not assume that the world revolves around them, but part of growing up includes the growing realization that they are but a thread in a tapestry, one member of the team, an integral part, no doubt, but still only a part of the whole. Thus it is sad to meet those adults who still assume they are the center of not just their parents' world but everyone else's too. The observation is often made that children in a one-child family struggle most with coming to appreciate this; they missed out on having siblings to keep them in their place! But we all need to learn this as an essential part of moving toward personal and spiritual maturity.

Archbishop of Canterbury Rowan Williams observes that the biblical ideal is not so much that we need to deny the self as to decenter the self: To see the self in truth, as an integral member of a community and society in which the only indispensable one is God.

May God grant us the grace to not be overly taken with ourselves.

But then, with this as the essential context in which we view the human person, we rightly must ask: how then, in the economy of God, can this person flourish, thrive and succeed, and we ask this precisely because we long to see this life, this person, be a living witness to the glory of God. In other words, the flourishing of the human person is not a threat to the glory of God; to the contrary, God longs for us to be, precisely, all that we are called to be.

Further, the Scriptures unequivocally affirm the significance of the *actions* of each human person. Our work and our actions make a difference to God. God called Adam to name the animals and till the earth, and since then God has continued to take seriously the actions of each person. From beginning to end the Scriptures affirm the all-encompassing glory of God and his work. But this is never portrayed in such a way that it reduces human activity to meaningless or even to mere robotic actions that have no inherent value or significance. For many Christians, the human person is nothing and Christ is everything. They speak of themselves as "channels only." They insist that they are only a means of grace, and the ideal is that the Christian should be but an "instrument" in the hands of God. The repeated emphasis is captured in the notion that as Christians we should become less and less, that we would "decrease" so that God can work. The less of us the better, so the work of God can be magnified. By implication, you and I are an obstacle to the glory of God.

But is this really what is reflected in the accounts found in Holy Scripture? When I watch Abraham and Jacob contending with God, wrestling with God, when I see the dynamic personal communion of David with God, when I watch the prophets and see their capacity even to confront God, it is clear that we need to rethink this understanding of human persons. Contrary to the view that denies the significance of humans and of human actions, the Scriptures have a different message. They speak of the human person as a coworker, a partner with God—even an ambassador for God (2 Cor 5:20). Human actions matter greatly; our choices and decisions make a difference. St. Paul urges Timothy to fan into flame the gift of God, quite simply because if *he* does not do it, the gift will not flourish (2 Tim 1:6-7 NIV)! Timothy is urged to be proactive, to take responsibility for his life and his actions, and he is urged to see the significance of these actions. The patterns of his life would make a difference in the church and in the world.

Those who argue that the ideal is for the human person to "decrease" often do so on the basis of the text in John 3:30 where John the Baptist speaks of his own joy in the coming of Jesus and affirms that "[Jesus] must increase, but I must decrease." Unfortunately, to extrapolate from this that humans therefore have little significance misses the point. John was speaking *vocationally*. His work was that of a friend of the bridegroom, not that of the bridegroom, and so, naturally, when the bridegroom appears, it is only appropriate that the friend of the bridegroom step aside, and this is his joy (and surely that of the bride as well). This principle is valid, though, in the affirmation that we are called to lose our lives if we are to gain them, that if we are to be great, then we must be servants of all. But do not fail to note that implicit in these affirmations is the recognition that we have a life to give, and that in giving our life we gain it, and that through this giving we achieve greatness. The assumption is that the individual human life, before God, has the potential for greatness. When the disciples wondered who would be great in the kingdom of God, Jesus' response was not to scold them for desiring greatness but rather to point them to the way of service. And Jesus called his disciples into his service precisely because of his confidence that in his grace and in the fullness of his Spirit they would make a difference. Further, in John 15 Jesus makes the remarkable statement that his disciples are not merely servants; they are friends, for his work with them includes the extraordinary reality that he is making known to them what the Father is doing (Jn 15:15). We are not merely "channels" or "instruments in the hands of God." We are, in the language of Paul in 2 Corinthians 5, *coworkers* with God in the work of God in the world, knowledgeable and informed participants in that which matters to the Creator.

In the chapters that follow I am making a basic assumption: that each person is responsible for the choices he or she makes, and that these choices are meaningful and significant. They make a difference. Without God, such a thought would only lead to despair—as it has for many twentieth-century existentialists. But *with* God and with faith in God, we are empowered by the thought that our actions are meaningful and that our lives can make a difference. We make our choices in response to God, and we make our choices knowing that God is Lord of the universe.

Our only hope for a genuine and full response to our current life circumstances is a theology of the Christian life that takes our full humanity seriously, which means that we have an intentional theology of human actions and human responsibility. I cannot help but wonder if the fear of Pelagianism—the doctrine which suggests that human beings are capable of obedience to God through their own strength and will power—while understandable, actually undercuts our capacity to embrace human responsibility. We must affirm the priority of divine action and grace, but we also need to do so in such a way that both calls and enables us to respond fully to God's grace. As Gary Badcock aptly puts it, "a theology of response does not need to be Pelagian; it need only be a theology in which the reality of the *human* is taken seriously."[2]

To take humanness seriously is to recognize the power and destructive reality of sin, and thus the fact of what St. Paul calls the "old self," which is corrupted and deluded (Eph 4:22). But it also embraces the *new* self, which has been "created according to the likeness of God in true righteousness and holiness" (Eph 4:24). We are called to deny the old self, but to live in congruence with the new self, which finds its origin in God's creative act. This is the true self, created to respond to God: the self that is given generously in service and is found in community. It is estimated that over 80 percent of the books published in any given year are about the self. We could easily say that we are consumed with our "self." And for some, what follows will merely be another book on the self. But there is a critical difference. We will be absorbed with ourself if we cannot, in response to God's grace, find moral grounding, a clear sense of authentic identity and, in the end, clarity regarding our own vocation. Only then can we turn from self-absorption and self-centeredness, and know the grace of generous service to others. This book is designed to enable us to make that turn, that is, to become fully converted, to move from self-absorption to becoming selves that are centered in God and true to our own identity and call.

Intentional stewards of our lives. Notice then the sequence here: If each person is of inestimable worth, and, further, if we can ask how each person can flourish, it naturally follows that we recognize all of this requires intentionality: we need to ask, what can we do to be good stewards of our lives, of the gifts, talents and opportunities that God gives to us? This book provides guidance for this kind of intentional stewardship. We can rightly ask, What does it mean to take responsibility for my life in response to the way God has made and called me? The response to this question is that we learn how to work with the hand that we have been dealt. The card-playing metaphor really captures the point: We are not being asked to take responsibility for anything other than the hand that has been dealt to us—including, well, everything! Our gifts, talents and potential, of course. But also the range of setbacks, disappointments and limitations that have been thrust on us. I like the way that golf handicaps a player so that in the end I am not actually playing against my sons (whom I would love to beat, though the chances of that diminish each year), but against myself. All I am being asked to do is to take responsibility for what I have the capacity to bring to this stroke, this hole, this round of eighteen.

By implication, then, I am not responsible for the lives of others. Yes, of course, we look out for others, we encourage others, we teach and equip others, and we live in a way that allows as many as possible to flourish. But in the end we are not God to them, and we cannot take final "adult" responsibility for the other. Indeed, the wise course of action is to stop trying to run or manage others' lives. Rather, we must ask, In this situation and set of circumstances, what is my particular calling which, yes, might be for the sake of the other but is still only what I am being called to do.

This principle applies to my sons; I am there for them, but in the end they are responsible for their own lives. Of course, my work and responsibility also includes supporting, encouraging and equipping others in their lives and work. But in the end they will only flourish if they learn how to take personal responsibility for their lives. This is part of what it means to be an adult; we live in mutual interdependence in society and community.

When we speak of being the steward of our life, something else must be stressed. We are called to be the steward not of some ideal life or even the life we wish we had; rather we are called to be steward of the life that we have on our hands.

What follows is a study for people who are prepared to think honestly about their lives—willing to acknowledge the gifts and abilities that they have from God, willing to be honest with themselves, willing to make some tough choices, and willing to do so in partnership with others. One of the temptations that will arise as you read will be to have regrets about the past. All of us can identify things that we would have done differently—mistakes we made, choices that were not wise decisions and so on. But we cannot confidently face the future if we are locked in regret. This book is for people—young and old, in college or in midcareer, or even facing retirement—who want to make an honest appraisal of their lives, but more, who want to look to the future and be all that they can be, to the glory of God and for the well-being of Christ's kingdom. Without regret we will look to the present and the future conscious of the tremendous potential that we have because of the grace of God. This book is for people who, in hearing the parable of the talents, want to invest their talents— whether it is one or ten—for God, and to do so in a way that recognizes that our point of departure is not the ideal life but our actual life, with all its complications.

GOOD CONVERSATION

We talk about our work all the time. It is rare that a conversation with a person we have recently met does not at some point lead to the inevitable question, What do you do? by which we mean, how do you spend your life and days. What is the work that this person does, that, ideally, God has given him or her to do?

But this is only a point of departure in our conversations with others. When I meet with friends, we of course speak of family and the joys and sorrows of children, grandchildren, the well-being of our favorite sports teams and whether the coming national election will lead to a change of government. Sure. But then, as a rule, the bulk of our conversation is about our work. This is not inappropriate; indeed, in chapter two I will speak of the significance of our work. Consequently, it is no wonder that we talk about it. It matters.

But it is crucial that in our conversation we learn how to speak well about our work, with new acquaintances, but more, with those who are closest to us—with our spouse if we are married, with our children and parents, with friends and associates, colleagues and neighbors. If we are speaking regularly about our work and the joys, sorrows, setbacks and successes of our work, then it only follows that we long to speak well about our work. We want to speak about our work in a way that is deeply informed by a biblical and thus Christian vision for doing good work.

We need this conversation. We need conversation that is marked by wisdom and hope. It is so easy to speak of work in a way that disparages it—thanking God that it is Friday—and thus speak of work through a posture of complaint. Yes, work is difficulty. Yes, there are significant points of stress, difficulty and setback. But what we urgently need is conversation partners who know how to speak of work in a way that is deeply and thoroughly informed by grace.

This book intends to foster this kind of good conversation. You will certainly find it helpful to read this book on your own; I am confident of this. But you might find it of greatest value if you read it in the company of another, so that together you cultivate a way of speaking of work in a manner that is informed by a biblical theology of work and is marked by grace and hopefulness.

I will speak of conversation more at the conclusion of this book (see chap. 12). But for now consider this: When it comes to our work we likely need at the very least three conversation partners. Two of these should ideally be peers—perhaps one who is in a similar line of work (e.g., a fellow nurse who knows the unique challenges of this profession), another who is from another line of work (e.g., the pastor who is strengthened and encouraged by regular conversation with a person in business). The third person, ideally, is someone a generation older; or, as we move into our senior years, someone who is at least ten years older than we are.

If you have these kinds of people in your life, you have a huge gift and extraordinary resource—a source of wisdom and encouragement. If you don't have this, then find it, work at it, cultivate these kinds of friendships and community. For, indeed, our work is our work. No one else will do it for us, and at many times along the way we will feel the inevitable loneliness that comes with doing good work: the athlete who trains alone for hours, the preacher who spends the required hours in solitary preparation, the businessperson who knows that there is no making this business work without many days of diligent engagement with his or her own enterprise, the artist who works alone on a quilt that in the end will be enjoyed by many, but no one will fully appreciate the lonely hours of tedious work that lies behind the completed project

But though we work alone, in the end we will only be faithful and good in our work if we have the grace that comes from others: their wisdom, support, guidance and encouragement.

And so we join the conversation; we talk about our work. But let's seek to do so as those who learn from others who have gone before us. This book is an invitation to join a fascinating conversation about vocation, work and career—a conversation that draws on the accumulated wisdom of a number of threads of conversation as they relate to this topic. In what follows, as much as possible, I have summarized this wisdom. I have been impressed time and again by how pertinent all of this is for everyone. For missionaries and pastors, but also men and women in every walk of life. For young adults but also for those in midlife and in their senior years. For women as well as for men. The principles outlined in the chapters that follow are universal— equally applicable to all people, regardless of their religious or faith orientation. In other words, my perspective is Christian and my outlook will come from the vantage point of Christian faith with an outline of implications for Christian experience. However, individuals of all faith persuasions should find this helpful.

We long to find and do work that is meaningful, that makes a difference and needs to be done. Further, we long to find a balance between work and leisure, between our responsibilities in the world and in the home, between the church and the society in which we live. We need to be able to manage competing demands and in so doing manage our lives, our time and our priorities.

We also long to make sense of the organizations we work in—to know when to accept a position and when to resign, to know the grace of being engaged with our work in an organization without being married to the company.

We all want to grow in our capacity to work with others—with people of other cultural backgrounds and with the opposite gender, as well as with people who are both older and younger than we are.

Finally, we earnestly long to be able to manage the transitions of life as we move through the different chapters of our adult careers.

For each of these points of longing, the way forward is by a conscious reflection on what it means to have a *vocation*, based on a good theology of work, of vocation and of self. What follows is meant to encourage that reflection and conversation. The biblical foundation for this study is the assumption that we are called to be stewards of the gifts and abilities and opportunities that God gives us. In the language of the second epistle to Timothy: "Fan into flame the gift of God" (2 Tim 1:6 NIV). This study endeavors to do that by considering the question How can we, individually and in community, be all that we are called to be? How can we fan into flame that gift of God that enables us to respond with creativity and strength to the opportunities before us?

THE MEANING OF
OUR WORK

A Theological Vision
for Engaging Our World

We will be best able to discern and respond to our calling—our vocation—if we have a deeper appreciation for the meaning of work. If vocation is about responding to the call of God to be in the world and to do work that reflects this call, then we naturally need to ask about the meaning and purpose of work, and what constitutes good work, work that is congruent with God's purposes in our lives.

We are living with a crisis of the "active" life. The life of engagement with the world is for many, if not most, marked by a hectic, busy and bewildering pace. We have a remarkable capacity to live overworked lives, caught up in hectic activity that "has to be done." This is one of the sins of modernity and of life and work in urban, industrialized societies. In our disturbed passion to accomplish so much and to accomplish it as soon as possible, we have lost a sense of true leisure and also of what it means to be reflective and contemplative.

Yet this frenetic, unfocused approach to life and work is but one side of the greater crisis of our day: a loss of *meaning*—in our work, our relationships and of our own identity (but for our purposes here, it is especially about our work).

The identity of some is wrapped up in their work, and the loss of employment or a forced retirement has left them feeling hollow, with little sense of purpose, or perhaps they are still on the job but are just floating from one assignment to another without focus or direction. For others the problem is that they are trying to do so much—running around caught up in hectic activity. The busyness often makes us feel important, but we know that that is all it is, busyness. And we know we are mistaken to assume that if a person is busy he or she must be important or, to turn it around, that if an individual is important than he or she must be busy. Underlying all of this lies an inevitable aware-ness, if we are honest, that in our busyness we begin to lose a sense of what our actions mean and ultimately what our lives mean.

As a result, people of all religious persuasions are trying to find answers, solutions and meaning. Well-written books on work, career, career transitions and career development are best-sellers. There is a palpable sense within our communities that we need to be able to resolve this crisis and come to terms with both our identity and our work so that we can find meaning, joy and purpose in that work.

While various helpful resources are available, it is critical that we think deeply about a *theological* response to this crisis. Many may consider this idea either strange or perplexing because they have not given intentional theological thought to *anything*. But when a crisis looms in our lives, we often have to ask the most critical questions. And here is where careful theological reflection can provide us with a way forward.

A THEOLOGICAL VISION FOR GOOD WORK

The huge assumption of our social context is that work is bad and leisure is good. Our only hope for a transformed vision for vocation, work and career, and for navigating the transitions of life, is to engage our world with a theological vision for *good* work—to redeem the very idea of work.

The revolutionary message of the Bible is that work is precisely that: *good*. Central to the biblical description of the formation of the first man and woman is the mandate they received to till the earth and name the animals (Gen 2:15, 19-20). They were created to work, and their work was meaningful. God made them workers so that they could be co-creators with him—not in the sense that they are creators of the earth, but that their work was a part of God's continual re-creation, and as such it was important, significant and valued by God.

With the Fall and with sin, work becomes *toil* (Gen 3:17-19). And thus a crucial part of the Christian mission in the world is to seek and declare a recovery of meaningful and joyful work. Work is a central expression of what it means to be a Christian believer, a critical component of our spirituality. Indeed, in many respects our work is a central context for living out our Christian identity. In this, then, we can and must affirm that not all work is good. Work can be destructive, hurtful and a disservice to Christ and to others. We can violate the very meaning of work whenever, through the skills and energy God has given us, we exploit or injure others or merely gratify our misguided desires. Consequently, our longing for meaningful work must be framed in the context of that which is good, noble and excellent—that which enables us to bring pleasure to our Maker, that which we can with genuine passion say that we do "as unto the Lord" (Col 3:23 KJV).

Unfortunately, we have been deeply influenced by the notion that work is bad and to be avoided, and many people live with the longing to be released from work, looking forward to retirement, when they will no longer work. While retirement does mark an important transition, our ultimate joy is not to be released from work. Jesus promised his followers that if they were diligent and careful in small things, they would be rewarded with *more* work to do (Mt 25:21). The hope of the new kingdom is not that we will be released from work but rather that our work will be in perfect partnership with God, in the kingdom that is yet to come. The prophet Isaiah spoke of the new heavens and the new earth as a time when we would build houses, plant vineyards and enjoy the work of our hands (Is 65:21-22).

One of the most powerful depictions of good work in the Scriptures is found at the conclusion of the book of Proverbs. Proverbs assumes and demonstrates that we are not wise unless and until we are wise in our work. This theme of good work as the sphere in which we live in wisdom is found in threads throughout this book of the Bible, but it is particularly instructive to consider the theological vision of work that is implied in Proverbs 31.

Many tend to think of Proverbs 31 as the celebration of a woman and a wife. And it is. But implicit in this celebration is another: the affirmation of her *work* and of thus of work as something we engage with energy, passion, joy and diligence. All of us, both women and men.

Could it be that one of the most helpful ways of reading Proverbs 31 is not to see it so much as an addendum or epilogue, as is so frequently done, but rather as a capstone to the collection of proverbial sayings found in this book of the Bible? What is instructive is that the woman described in this chapter is clearly an embodiment of the wisdom that emerges throughout the book of Proverbs, and further, this wisdom she embodies is most evident in the quality of her *work*. While there is surely more to wisdom than our work, this chapter celebrates a person who is wise in doing good work. And what is implicit in these verses of Scripture is the contours of a biblical theology of work that has profound relevance for us as we seek to make sense of our lives and recover a theological vision for work.

A capable wife who can find?
    She is far more precious than jewels.
The heart of her husband trusts in her,
    and he will have no lack of gain.
She does him good, and not harm,
    all the days of her life.
She seeks wool and flax,
    and works with willing hands.
She is like the ships of the merchant,
    she brings her food from far away.
She rises while it is still night

and provides food for her household
and tasks for her servant girls.
She considers a field and buys it;
with the fruit of her hands she plants a vineyard.
She girds herself with strength,
and makes her arms strong.
She perceives that her merchandise is profitable.
Her lamp does not go out at night.
She puts her hands to the distaff,
and her hands hold the spindle.
She opens her hand to the poor,
and reaches out her hands to the needy.
She is not afraid for her household when it snows,
for all her household are clothed in crimson.
She makes herself coverings;
her clothing is fine linen and purple.
Her husband is known in the city gates,
taking his seat among the elders of the land.
She makes linen garments and sells them;
she supplies the merchant with sashes.
Strength and dignity are her clothing,
and she laughs at the time to come.
She opens her mouth with wisdom,
and the teaching of kindness is on her tongue.
She looks well to the ways of her household,
and does not eat the bread of idleness.
Her children rise up and call her happy;
her husband too, and he praises her:
"Many women have done excellently,
but you surpass them all."
Charm is deceitful, and beauty is vain,
but a woman who fears the LORD is to be praised.
Give her a share in the fruit of her hands,
and let her works praise her in the city gates.

Consider then the biblical vision or theology of work implicit throughout this text of sacred Scripture. And in passing I would note that perhaps in cultures that have a one-dimensional view of women, who are only judged by their physical appearance or sexuality, this chapter is a powerful corrective and a dramatically different articulation of what it means to be a woman. But for all men and women, we have a vision for good work.

HOME VERSUS MARKETPLACE

First, we note that this woman is celebrated as she moves between the domestic sphere (caring for the household) and the public sphere of the marketplace (buying and selling real estate). What strikes us is the ease with which she moves between these two worlds.

Contemporary society assumes that we make a choice: one member of a household will be the "homemaker" and the other the "breadwinner" (i.e., in the marketplace generating income to sustain the home). The assumption is that a person cannot be ably engaged in the world, perhaps in a career, if he or she is managing a house or raising children. We have to choose: Will I raise a family or develop a career?

While there certainly are challenges and tensions that come in the interface of each dimension of our lives and work, the woman of Proverbs 31 is clearly engaged on both fronts. And by implication it is important to observe that there is no inherent tension between them. Indeed, perhaps the two are essential to each other, authenticating or legitimizing the other, each a counterpart to the other.

Thus, there is a need to beware of a temptation to claim a higher calling to our work—perhaps our work in the world—and in attending to this dimension of our lives, neglect our basic, mundane, ordinary responsibilities in our home and in the needs of family, neighbors and community.

In 1 Timothy we find a list of qualities and capacities that are to mark those who serve as elders or overseers in the church. The point is made that a person cannot be expected to play a role of leadership in a congregation if the person cannot manage his or her home (1

Tim 3:5). I wonder if this speaks to the inevitable continuity between home and marketplace: our calling and our work inevitably call us to manage the affairs well on both fronts. The two are not then necessarily in tension. And the genius, at least in part, of discerning and living in a way that is consistent with our vocation is that we do not isolate the diverse spheres of our lives, personal and professional, home and office, but live out of the deep connections between these. Yes, there are boundaries; we do need to maintain the sanctity of home and beware of conflicts of interest in the professional world (e.g., the dangers of nepotism). But the main point here is to insist that we are called to live faithfully on each front, including both the domestic sphere and the public and professional spheres of our lives.

RELIGIOUS VERSUS SECULAR

Deep within the religious psyche of most Christians is the assumption that religious work is inherently more sacred than all other activities—whether at home, in the garden or in the marketplace—and that the very best work we do is religious in nature and, many would insist, is either focused on the life and ministry of the local church or can be described as a direct participation in church mission.

Consider how easy it is for most Christians to assume that teaching a Sunday school class has more weight and significance than repairing a broken chair, or that a short-term missions trip to Haiti carries more inherent value that the long days of getting a new business started. Or imagine the response of a church community when they hear that a young couple has decided that rather than managing the local bookstore, they are going to assume a pastoral appointment. We assume that the second has more kingdom value and therefore it merits higher affirmation.

Yet, what strikes us about the woman of Proverbs 31 is that she is celebrated—there is a doxological character to these verses—for the work of buying and selling fields, managing a home, working with fabric and with her hands.

I will speak to this more directly later in this chapter, but for now the following needs to be stressed: while the Christian spiritual and religious tradition has always struggled with this question and has consistently split sacred and secular, and generally assumed that religious work is more sacred, this faith tradition has consistently been at its best and has its greatest and most consistent impact for the glory of God and for the reign of Christ when it has affirmed that women and men are called into each sphere and sector of society. The underlying assumption of this book is that religious work or church-related activities, while very important, do not inherently have more weight or significance than the work of the gardener, the business-person, the public school teacher or the pharmacist.

WITH OUR HANDS AND OUR HEADS

It is a typical assumption within every society I have lived in for any length of time (Latin America, Asia and North America) that manual work is *menial* work: that the ideal form of work is "professional" rather than manual, that there are two classes of work—white collar and blue collar, professional and labor—and that professional work is to be more highly valued and esteemed.

Even if parents have been active in the so-called trades as plumbers, electricians and carpenters, they often wish that their children would be doctors, lawyers and senior managers in corporations. And when they become doctors, lawyers and managers they hire other people to do the manual work, including everything from carrying their bags to repairing the broken window in their home.

The Christian religious tradition does not share this more negative view of manual work. Indeed, in 1 Thessalonians 4:11 the apostle Paul actually encourages his readers to work with their hands. This is why the text of Proverbs 31 is quite fascinating. Here is a woman of some financial means: she buys and sells fields, works with fine fabric, has servant girls, supports a husband who serves in the governing council of the land, and makes it a point to look out for the poor. She is a wealthy woman. And yet we cannot miss that she works with her hands.

- She works with willing hands (v. 13).

- She puts her hands to the distaff, and her hands hold the spindle (v. 19).

- She reaches out her hands to the needy (v. 20).

In the space of very few verses, her hands are mentioned four times. We cannot help but wonder if this is intentional. It seems the biblical author is making a point that wise people work with their hands, that they are not above doing menial labor. Consequently, just as the Christian tradition at its best celebrates the potential sacredness of all work, even so this is a tradition that refuses to pit head and hand against one another in speaking of good work.

One of our urgent needs is to find ways to celebrate the work of those whose work takes them into nursing, carpentry, auto repair and farming. There is something profoundly un-Christian about the family that pushes their son or daughter into a so-called profession because it brings them more wealth or prestige. How sad and what a loss when young people cannot pursue the longing of their heart, especially when that longing is to work with their hands.

Thus I celebrate the publication of Matthew Crawford's book *Shop Class as Soulcraft*, which is an extraordinary reflection on the beauty and power of manual labor.[1] Crawford, a trained philosopher, probes the deep meaning of working with our hands and writes from the vantage point of a motorcycle repair shop. He does not write as a Christian believer per se, yet his way of speaking of work, with our hands, is very Christian.

The woman of Proverbs 31 is praised as one who worked with her hands. Our Lord himself is traditionally viewed to have been a carpenter; St. Paul was a tentmaker. There is probably truth in the suggestion that only as we learn to work with our hands—and master a craft—whether as a means of employment or as a form of recreation, are we truly integrated with our bodies. When we live entirely in our heads we miss out on a major dimension of good work and thus of a good life.

WAGED WORK AND THE WORK OF THE VOLUNTEER

I write these words shortly after the conclusion of the Vancouver 2010 Winter Olympics. One of the things that marked these Games in the minds of participants and observers is the remarkable contribution of an army of volunteers. The event was tremendously successful, but that was only possible because women and men gave generously of their time to host the athletes and visitors from around the world, and to work with the organizers to assure that each event was managed well.

When we come to the text of Proverbs 31, it is clear that the woman described here is successful in business: she buys and sells fields, she manages the production of a vineyard and assures that her merchandise is profitable. She is not running a nonprofit. She is the wage earner or, as some put it, the breadwinner of her home.

So where is her husband? Many come to the end of the chapter and read that her husband "praises her," and with a chuckle they insist that he had better praise her! He did very well in marrying this woman. But what is *he* doing? Verse 23 speaks of the city gates—the place where the town council met to discuss civic affairs—and there he sat with the elders of the land. It is likely that he did not receive remuneration for this work. It is good and necessary work, but it is not likely *waged* work.

This indeed speaks of a major assumption: those who go into public service should not do so for financial benefit. The state of New Mexico, for example, provides no salary for its state legislators, and those who work in the world of the nonprofit as charities, mission agencies and religious ministry could all likely make a higher salary if they worked in business. But they go as volunteers—paid nothing or at more modest wages to do their work.

I make this point in order to make another. Some within our society do good work that has direct remuneration; they have, as we read in Proverbs 31, "profitable merchandise." But many are called into work where they will receive either no direct compensation or they receive a wage so they can do their "volunteer" work full time. And they can only do so if they are supported by those whose merchandise is "profitable"—whether it is those of us in the nonprofit work who depend on the financial support of those in business, or those within a family system who do volunteer work and depend on another member of the household to sustain the house financially. The point is that both are good; both are necessary and are worth celebrating. Therefore, we do not judge the value of anyone's work by the wage they are paid. We do not make a one-to-one correlation between good work and the amount of a person's salary. Indeed, perhaps we should all find a way to volunteer—to do work on a board or committee or local community center or orphanage—where all we do is give our time and expect nothing in return but the joy of having been able to serve. Indeed, during our senior years many of us will do good and necessary work with no remuneration. We will pour ourselves into our work without a thought for compensation or wages, but merely a joy and passion to do good work in service for others.

PUBLIC WORK AND PRIVATE WORK

There is something else that catches our attention in this description of the wise woman. She is clearly a public woman; she is in the marketplace buying and selling fields. But she is also just as clearly a private woman, private, that is, in her work. Indeed the text highlights this: while others are asleep, she is up early and attending to her responsibilities as the manager of the home.

This speaks to us something fundamental about the work we do: the quality of our work depends, in large measure, on the integrity of the work we do when others are not watching. This is true of all work, all vocations. Our work is marked by quality, integrity and beauty when we are faithful behind the scenes, when no one is overseeing or affirming or praising us. We either learn to work in obscurity or we do not learn how to work at all; many kinds of work—whether teaching, governing, performing as an athlete or entertainer, or sales—have a public character. But for each of these and many others, the quality and integrity of the work depends on the diligence with which we work behind the scenes: the careful research of the salesperson who knows everything there is to know about the product on the shelf, the professor who comes to class thoroughly prepared or the government official who spends extended hours in the thankless work of writing and rewriting legislation that constituents hope to see passed in the city council.

Often when we think about roles or occupations and good work, we are struck by the public side and often overlook the simple fact that what we see is likely but the tip of the iceberg; most of the work is done with little affirmation, thanks or praise. These people are diligent in their work and in the private side of their work precisely because they are committed first and foremost to good work.

THE MUNDANE AND THE ORDINARY VERSUS
THE GRAND OR HEROIC

In my early adult years I was part of a religious subculture that was taken with the idea that each of us was capable of extraordinary, heroic actions. We could change the world in our generation! Or so we thought. And the speakers at our inspirational gatherings would call us to leave behind simple and mundane expectations of our lives and through vision, passion and confidence in the sustaining power of God head out to the farthest reaches of our world to do "great things for God."

While we certainly must not underestimate the capacity of any one person to make a difference in their sphere of life or work, the unfortunate assumption that many of us carried away from such presentations was that ordinary, daily, routine, common work was not important. What really counted was the grand gesture, the dramatic stroke.

But the woman of Proverbs 31 reminds us that perhaps the most significant work we do is very ordinary and mundane. It is daily, routine work that in the end may be the most basic indicator of good work, particularly when it is done with joy and contentment. I think of the woman who taught kindergarten for thirty-one years with deep joy and a commitment to *each* child who came through her class-room. Her impact is felt not in a moment of greatness or in a brilliant response to a crisis, but rather in the wonder that for all those years she was a continuous learner, consistently present, not asking for or wanting a promotion (whatever that would be), but content, deeply so, to be present to each year's cohort of five-year-olds.

And I think of Chesley Burnett "Sully" Sullenberger III, who brilliantly maneuvered the US Airways flight that landed on the Hudson River west of Manhattan after hitting a flock of geese during take off from the La Guardia airport. Yes, it was a brilliant move, and, yes, he is to be praised for his heroic commitment to the passengers on that flight. But perhaps his real greatness is that he had been a consistent and excellent pilot year in and year out, carrying hundreds of passengers, some times two or three times a day, the vast majority of whom would never know his name or have opportunity to offer him thanks.

Good work requires of us an appreciation of the value of routine, ordinary, mundane rhythms of doing what needs to be done, each day and each week, thoroughly and with care. We cannot discount the significance of such work; rather, we need to appreciate that the impact of the woman of Proverbs 31, as it will be in our lives, comes precisely in the accumulation of work done in the quiet and daily practices that are inherent to the work given to us. Many people will find that their daily work is remarkable for its routine ordinariness, and, indeed, that work may have little direct meaning or fulfillment in and of itself. It just needs to be done; there is a family to feed and this is the job that has been provided. The meaning of the work is that it provides livelihood for a person or a family system. In this we never want to lose an appreciation that work in the end is a means of service, offered to God for the sake of others. And this is enough to make our work a religious act.

Much more could be said about the character of work from the reading of Proverbs 31. Many have noted, for example, that in her work the woman is attentive to both the poor and the arts, and they have wondered if attentiveness to the needs of the poor and the commitment to attend to beauty are inherent in all good work. Old Testament scholar Bruce Waltke observes that "pride of place is given to her ministry to the afflicted and destitute in the community."[2]

Others have noted her diligence—she worked hard, up early before dawn to attend to the responsibilities of the day. This observation is a reminder that all vocations, all good work, requires diligence. There is no easy road for anyone; regardless of our calling and the line or character of work we are called to, diligence will necessarily be a mark of fulfilling this vocation with integrity.

Two more things. We read that her husband trusted her (v. 11). This is quite remarkable, for, as Waltke points out, the Scriptures consistently condemn trust in anyone other than God—and yet here, without apology, the Scriptures highlight this trust given to another.[3] Indeed, this text celebrates that this person is trustworthy, dependable; her husband could trust her much like he would trust in God.

Finally, Waltke also points out that she is rejuvenated (vv. 17-18). She gains strength from her trading, or, more specifically, she finds spiritual vitality and renewal through her work.[4] Many assume that work is inherently exhausting; the more we do the more it will drain us. But this is a reminder that as our work is redeemed, while there will be a side of our work that will draw down on our physical and emotional strength, the work we carry may well be a source of spiritual renewal and vigor for us. And consider this as a passing observation: people often assume they have done good work if they are exhausted, and that they deserve time off because they are completely spent. But perhaps this exhaustion is a sign of overwork, which indicates that it may not be good work or that it is not the right work for us, the work to which we are truly called. If there is truth to this, perhaps we should stop trying to justify time off by explaining to people we are exhausted from our work and need some time away. Take the time, I say! But in our culture, where overwork is so highly valued, we assume that we can only take time away from the office and can only justify this time if we can demonstrate that we are tired, overextended and exhausted, and therefore "deserve" a break. This is truly not a Christian perspective on either work or rest, notably where rest is viewed as something that is earned or merited.

A THEOLOGY OF VOCATION

Closely related to the matter of work is the question of vocation and what it means to have a biblical theology of vocation. My assumption here is twofold: first, our work is done in response to the calling of God. God calls us to the work we do, and thus our work becomes something that we do as an offering to God. This suggests that everyone is invited to do good work that they are not craving to avoid.

As I write this my bank is on a marketing spree urging clients toward good retirement planning. They are suggesting that good planning could potentially lead to an early retirement. Of course, the assumption of the ads is that one should be released from work as soon as possible and be able to participate in any number of "retirement" activities, including sailing, golfing and sleeping in or enjoying an extended morning coffee while the rest of the human race is off to work. It is taken for granted that the ideal life is the work-free life. And if money is no object, then one does not work.

But the witness of the Scriptures and of the Christian spiritual heritage suggest that responsible human life includes stewardship of our capacities and opportunities. Being wealthy does not for a moment free us from the calling to do good work. To the contrary, a biblical theology of vocation provides us with a critical and essential lens through which to view our lives and what it means to be stewards of our lives. So, we can ask not only What is good work? but What is the good work I am called to?

It is important to recognize that some things are obvious: if we are parents, we are called to care for the children God has given us. If the downspout around my house is loose and water is pouring into the foundation of my home, I do not go on a prayer retreat to determine if fixing this is my calling! Rather, I put on rain gear and head out into the stormy weather to do what needs to be done!

Yet, we are so regularly caught up in the routines and the immediate demands of life that we do not stand back and ask, But what,
fundamentally, is the work I am called to? What is my vocation; what
is my life purpose?

For starters it is important to stress that we cannot respond to this
question unless and until we affirm the fundamental biblical principle that all vocations are inherently and potentially sacred. Whether
we are called into service in the church or in the world, whether we
are called to work with our hands, to religious work, to work in the
arts or to work in education and the sciences, each call has the potential for sacredness.

If a vocation represents a call of God—to serve God in the world—
that vocation is sacred for no more powerful reason than that it comes
from God. It therefore makes no sense to speak of a secular vocation;
such a phrase is a contradiction in terms. A vocation is *sacred* in that
it comes from God.

The Christian community throughout its history has wrestled
with this reality almost from the very beginning. For the early church,
deeply influenced by Hellenistic thought, any work that was "in the
world" or that engaged actively with society was viewed as not only
secular but probably evil. Thus the spiritual ideal was to leave the
world, be separate from it and live as much as possible a life of prayer
and study. The belief became deeply embedded in the psyche of the
church that if a person had a vocation, he or she was called to leave
so-called secular employment and accept service in and through the
church. For centuries it was assumed that a person with a vocation
was called to the life of ministry in the church, either as a priest or as
a nun. Protestant Christians have tended to use the language of "calling." If a person was called, it implicitly meant that he or she was
called to the gospel ministry as a pastor or missionary. But this notion is not consistent with the biblical witness, and at different points
in history the church has had prophets that called us back to a more
inclusive notion of both work and vocation.

Noteworthy in this regard is the contribution of the Reformers, particularly Martin Luther, though John Calvin's contribution is also very significant. Both called for a spirituality in the world that took seriously the home and the marketplace. On the one hand this meant that they affirmed the common and the ordinary; as Calvin put it, "In following your proper calling, no work will be so mean and sordid as not to have splendor and value in the eye of God."[5] He therefore insisted that each person should respect his or her own calling. Both Reformers refused to make the sharp distinction between sacred and secular that was so characteristic of the medieval world and still is evident in the language of contemporary Christians. But Calvin went further and affirmed that each person has been assigned a station or calling from the Lord; this vocation is not something accidental. Consequently, it is our *sacred* duty to accept and even embrace what God has called us to. The sacred is not distinct from the secular; rather the sacred is that which sanctifies the ordinary and thus makes it good and noble. For Luther, this was critical to his assumption that every Christian believer is a priest.

Luther and Calvin did not go far enough; they were still constrained by their social and cultural context, evident, in part, by Calvin's diatribe against ambition, and the assumption in both Reformers that we should accept our social station in life as itself of God. But when viewed through a wide-angle lens, we see that something revolutionary happened through their teaching that the homemaker, the shoemaker and the preacher all serve God, all respond to the call of God and thus all have a vocation.

Yet despite the power and influence of Luther and Calvin, the older, far-from-biblical notion that some vocations are more sacred than others is still locked in our psyches. As a young man I remember those occasions when it was suggested that if we really loved the Lord we would be missionaries, and if not missionaries, then pastors, and if not missionaries or pastors, then at least business people (in "secular work") who could support those with the "sacred" callings. Within my tradition this was captured in the words of A. B. Simpson, which would no doubt be typical of what many would have heard as young people and perhaps still hear today: "Your only excuse for staying home and not going to the mission field is if by staying home you can do more to further the cause of missions than by going."

While the motive behind such a statement is noble, I dare think what it has meant for so many who because of such a perspective have failed to affirm and celebrate the sacredness of their work. Though we have made major progress, this narrow understanding of vocation does not die easily. We need to thunder from our pulpits and celebrate at every turn in the life of the church that God is calling people into education, the arts, public office, business, engineering, medicine, the service professions—quite literally into every area and sector of human life. We need to proclaim this truth and celebrate it *often* because the older, unbiblical notion is so deeply embedded in our corporate consciousness. Further, we need to affirm that only those explicitly called to religious leadership should become pastors. Otherwise they fail to fulfill what they are *really* being called to do.

Implicit in this recovery of a biblical theology of vocation is a renewed appreciation of the full extent of God's kingdom. All vocations are sacred because the kingdom is not merely spiritual. God is establishing his kingdom on the earth as all creation comes under his divine authority. To that end, God calls and enables his children to be his kingdom agents within every sphere of life and society. Each vocation reflects but one means by which God, through word and deed, is accomplishing this.

It is important to stress that in all of this we must sustain a distinction between vocation and career. A vocation comes from God, and though it will encompass work in every sector of society, from the home to the marketplace to the church, it remains a fundamentally religious principle. Many people still confuse "vocational" with technical, as though one might attend a vocational school and train for a trade or profession rather than attend liberal arts school or institution. The irony of this is the assumption that if someone chose the academic route and not the "vocational" alternative, he or she was then not "trained" to do something useful! But again, this notion of vocation comes no where near approximating what I will be speaking of in these chapters.

Some have suggested that because the notion of vocation has been so denuded of its original meaning and force there is no reason to keep using the word *vocation*. But to do so would be to cave in to a false notion of vocation and thus lose use of a wonderful word. We must recover the original meaning; we must restore to our communities and to our language an understanding of vocation as "calling"— as something we recognize as both fundamentally religious and sacred, and as something that enables us, in response to the call of God, to embrace whatever it is that God would have us be and do in the church and the world.

Sustaining the language of vocation helps on two other points as well. First, we must distinguish between vocation and career. We may be called to particular work that is reflected in a career, an occupation done over an extended period of time in which we express a mastery or capacity for this particular kind of work. But we must not allow a singular career or occupation to eclipse our personal identity and sense of vocation. The two must be kept distinct.

Finally, the language of vocation is a reminder that our work is given to us by another, by the God who is our Creator. Thus our work is not our god; it is given to us as gift, as something for which we are stewards. In the end it does not define us, however important it is to us and to God. And in this regard, nothing so signals this as the observance of sabbath. In other words, we are called to work, but we are not called *only* to work. And we resist the deification of our work; we keep our work from becoming idolatrous by consistently, one day in seven, ceasing from it. A biblical theology of work, then, also includes the explicit call for regular sabbath rest—when we set our work aside and take time for leisure, recreation, worship and fellowship. We are not *workers*; we are, rather, children of God who are called *to* work. Our work is never the primary expression of our

identity, and through regular sabbath rest we reestablish our identity in God and in his love, acceptance and grace toward us (Ex
31:13-17). We violate the meaning of work when *all* we do is work,
when we lose a rhythm and routine of both work and play, work and
prayer, work and sabbath rest.

SEEKING CONGRUENCE

The Character of
Vocational Integrity

As noted, the word *calling* can be used in three different ways. We are called to be Christians. This is the most fundamental and basic sense in which we must consider the notion of vocation: we have been called to love God and our neighbors; we have been called to live by faith, to trust and obey God. We have been called to live in the salvation of our God and to participate in his purposes of hope and reconciliation in our world.

Then, as a third and in a sense the most immediate and daily sense of vocation, I spoke about the daily calling—to the tasks and responsibilities that require our immediate attention. And we must not disparage these duties that are given to us—whether it is to respond to the need of a family member or a neighbor, whether in response to a crisis or as the long-term care for a child from infancy to young adulthood. We can and must embrace these opportunities and not resent them or suggest that they keep us from our vocation. On any particular day I can with grace accept that this duty, task or responsibility is that to which God calls me.

But between these, as a middle or second definition, I spoke of something much more fundamental—something unique to each person. Each person has a fundamental calling or vocation. And this is, more than anything else, what each must discover. This second meaning is a critical means by which I fulfill my calling as a Christian. Yes, I am called to love God and neighbor, but how will this be expressed in my life? How am I specifically and uniquely being called to fulfill what it means to be Christian in this world?

Further, in the midst of all the daily demands and duties surely our hearts tell us something that is true: each of us has a unique calling and responsibility, something that in the long run is greater than the daily tasks that confront us—not in the sense that these tasks are not important but rather in the sense that there is a thread, an underlying purpose and work, that represents the way God has invited us to make a difference in the world.

Again I must stress that we should not confuse the word *vocation* with career. It is helpful, actually essential, to maintain a clear distinction between calling (or vocation)—in this second sense—and career or job or occupation. Though in some situations it makes sense for a calling to be expressed *through* an occupation; for many, the fundamental call of God—their vocation—is fulfilled outside of or alongside gainful employment, possibly as homemakers or as volunteer workers in a wide variety of roles. That is, many people may not have a formal or clearly defined career, but *everyone* has a vocation. We therefore need to distinguish between vocation and career, vocation and occupation and vocation and a job. I can lose my job; I might be released from a position. My career can come to an end when I retire from the organization I work in. But my vocation comes from God; it remains and is not in the end something that I choose or that someone else can give me or take away from me. It comes from God; it denotes my fundamental identity.

Further, even within the same occupation, different individuals might have different vocations. It is also important to appreciate that we are called to some roles only for a time—for a season—to accomplish something temporary. A person may be called to be a homemaker, but this is not likely to be for life but only until the children have become young adults. Another may be called to an administrative role for a time—perhaps only a few months or a few years—but it may be only temporary, a calling for *this* time but not the whole of a person's life. While these roles are important—God is calling us to them in the present—they do not represent our fundamental identity, our reason for being, our *vocation* (in the second sense).

Calling, or vocation, is much deeper and all-encompassing than career or occupation. Indeed, there are some who may not even begin to discover their vocation until after they have retired from a career.

It is sheer gift if we are able to fulfill our vocations *through* an occupation. But for many, a job is a means of supporting life and family; it is often a matter of getting whatever work might be available. As I hope to show, we must be both reasonable *and* idealistic. We need to discern our vocations and then also discern how God is calling us, within the complexities and demands of this world, to fulfill these vocations.

Then, with this understanding, we can face the most crucial question. That in discerning vocation, in responding to the call of God on our lives, nothing is so important, nothing is more central than coming to terms with our *selves*. The pivotal issue then is one of self-knowledge and of living out our lives in a way that is consistent with who we are, as individuals. Therefore, vocational discernment is in many respects a manner of nurturing a capacity for self-perception and self-understanding.

This means, among other things, that if we are going to thrive in this world—the social, economic and ministry context in which we live—our only hope will be that we have a life that is congruent with who we are: who God has made us to be and how God has gifted us, graced us and thus called us. If we are going to be all that we are meant to be, this is where we must begin. Ultimately, we are only true to God and faithful to our Creator when we seek this congruency.

I come to this conclusion in part through observation—by seeing those who thrive in their life and work, regardless of their vocation.

But it is also instructive to see that the Scriptures call us to this self-perception. A notable example, and one which can guide our thinking, is found in the words of the apostle Paul in Romans 12—instructions and commands that are very helpful.

In Romans 12:1-2, Paul calls for *moral* integrity; his appeal is for lives characterized by a renewed mind rather than a mind conformed to the world. He calls his readers to be *Godward*, to a godly orientation where their lives are lived congruent with the character and will of God.

Further, the last half of the chapter focuses our attention on others, the need for a posture and behavior of love toward them. That is, the apostle calls for *relational* integrity.

This is what makes the middle verses of the chapter particularly instructive. In verses 3-8 he calls for introspection; he urges his readers to look at themselves "with sober judgment." He urges us to live in faith and to examine ourselves carefully with the grace that has been given us. And then he calls us to live and work in a manner that is congruent with who we are and who we have been called to be. We are called to godliness, to the integrity of lives congruent with God's character, and we are called to relational integrity. But we are also called to live with vocational integrity, a pattern of living that is congruent with who we are. We have integrity when we are true to our own identity, true to ourselves.

Consider these verses carefully. When we ask the question What is God calling me to do—with my life, and specifically at this time of my life, we are wise to begin by responding intentionally to the two commands implicit in the words of the apostle Paul in Romans 12:3-8. These two commandments are liberating, and we come to them not once but repeatedly over the whole course of our lives. We are not speaking here of a single action or event or choice, but of two commandments—each part of seeking and discovering personal congruency—that have the capacity to enable us to respond with strength to each of the crises, or transitions or opportunities of our lives.

KNOW YOURSELF

The first command is simply "know yourself." This command is implicit in what we read in Romans 12:3:

> By the grace given to me I say to everyone among you not to think of yourself more highly than you ought to think, but to think with sober judgment, each according to the measure of faith that God has assigned.

The apostle Paul calls us to look at ourselves with "sober judgment." God has granted grace to each of us, so we can take an honest, critical and discerning look at ourselves. Indeed, it is not an overstatement to observe that when it comes to answering the question, What is God's vocation on my life, there are really two critical questions. The first: Who am I? And the second: Am I willing to live in humble acceptance of the call of God? We will soon look at the second, but for now consider that few things matter more that our capacity to know ourselves, to see ourselves *truthfully*. The reason for this is that God's purposes in the world are always consistent with the way that God has made the world. And, further, God's redemptive purposes will always be in deep congruity with how God has made the world. So, to ask how is God calling you or me to act in this world, we go back to an earlier question: How did God make us?

Make an appraisal of yourself—an honest assessment. Think of yourself in truth. Who are you? What makes you unique? How has God called *you*? We are not all the same. Rather, Paul compares the community of faith to a body (Rom 12:4-5), with different gifts, differing contributions, differing abilities. Vocational identity is found in discerning who we are within this mix. What is the ability, the talent and the enabling, and, perhaps most of all, the deep passion that God has given you? Where is it that God is calling you to make a difference for him in the church and in the world? Consider and think of yourself with honesty; make a *sober* judgment.

To live in truth, we must be true to who we are. But this is not possible unless we *know* who we are: how God has made us, how we are unique, how God has enabled us to serve him in the church and in the world.

Many of us hesitate to hear this word; something blocks us. Some of us have been taught all our lives to ignore ourselves—to focus on others and to live for others and to give generously. But we can neither serve with grace nor make a difference for God in the lives of others if we do not learn to live in this truth. The apostle Paul, in the same chapter, calls his readers to love and serve others. But he *begins* by first urging us to take a sober look at our own self. He calls for self-appraisal before he calls for genuine love; self-appraisal makes this genuine love for others possible.

If we seek to be anything other than who we are, we live a lie. To know ourselves and to be true to ourselves is actually nothing but being true to God. For to be true to ourselves is to be true to how God has *made* us, how God has crafted our personalities, how God has given us ability and talent and passion. God will call us to serve him in the church and in the world. But this calling will always be consistent with who we are, with who he has created us to be. Know yourself, for you cannot live in truth until you do.

A. W. Tozer somewhere speaks of the need to live with freedom from pretense; this captures it well, for in living truthfully we no longer live with a mask, a façade, but rather with a deep honesty about who we are and who God has created us to be.

Often, when it comes to calling or vocation, I hear people at all stages of life speak as though they are expecting some kind of heavenly or angelic voice, some "burning bush" experience to confirm whether they are called and to what they are called. They wait and hope for this dramatic intersection with the ordinary routines of their lives. But I am stressing here that while it is certainly possible that we might have such an experience, there is no substitute for the diligent and persistent work of seeking self-knowledge. It will take time, and it will require humility. Yet it is time well spent, and humility is truly an essential element of wisdom.

PRELIMINARY QUESTIONS: TALENT AND PERSONALITY

It is helpful to appreciate that self-knowledge requires that we attend to two preliminary questions. They are not fundamental questions, per se, but while not central, they both need to be considered sooner or later, perhaps even before we can get to the heart of the matter.

- What are my gifts and abilities?

- What is my unique personality or temperament?

Self-knowledge and the discernment of our vocation must include a recognition and affirmation of the *capacities* that we have, our gifts and abilities. The assumption, of course, is that everyone has talent or ability. We are not all equally talented; some are more gifted than others. Humility demands that we acknowledge this. But humility also demands that we accept the talent we *do* have. The parable of the talents (Mt 25:14-30) is a powerful reminder, not only of the reality of our talents and abilities, but also that we must invest these talents as good stewards. And we cannot be stewards unless we acknowledge the gifts and abilities we have. This is not arrogance or pride, but true humility—the humility of seeing, acknowledging and choosing to live in truth.

I grew up within a religious community that was hesitant to celebrate and acknowledge the abilities and strengths that God had given us. Ability, talent and excellence were downplayed. Commitment, generosity and faithfulness were valued. This orientation was captured in a phrase that I and many of my peers often heard: "God is not looking for ability, but availability."

This is an unfortunate message largely because it is partially correct and partially false. It has led many into occupations or careers they are not suited for. Their generosity and desire to serve has been genuine, but misguided. And they have often lived in frustrated failure, perplexed about God's faithfulness when they found they were no longer effective in their work.

It is more helpful to recognize that God is looking for people of ability who will make their ability *available* to God. He did this in the accounts recorded in Scripture; he does this today. We might like to think of King David as an instrument of miracles, but perhaps our primary reference for him would be his talent and ability. He was a gifted shepherd who could fling a rock with deadly accuracy. *This* ability made available to God, not a miracle per se, destroyed Goliath. And David went on to make all of his abilities available to God—as a poet, administrator, warrior strategist and more. The same could be said of each of those who responded to the call of God. Moses denied that he could speak well, but in so doing he was failing to acknowledge the way that God had gifted him. His was a form of denial and rebellion; it was false humility. Self-knowledge includes, and for some begins, when we acknowledge the ways we have been gifted. I am not questioning the possibility of miracles! Rather, God, as a rule, works through the ordinary and the routine; let's not see a miracle where in actual fact God worked or is working through the grace of talent and capacity that God has provided.

In this regard we can note that some are multitalented; they do two or three things well. Yet, overtime it becomes apparent that there is one strength, one capacity that is closer to the root of their being, closer to their heart, and something they *must* do if they are going to be who they were created to be. Parker Palmer calls this our "birth competency." It is something that is both discovered and developed, but we are born with it—it is inherent in who we are. Palmer says it is an "inclination or an instinct that can become a full-blown mastery."[1] We know freedom when we get to the root and discover this inherent capacity.

I need to make an additional comment about perceived "weaknesses." We often hear that we need to have a good sense of both our strengths and weaknesses. While I appreciate what lies behind this, it perplexes me that we speak of the things we do not do well as though they are weaknesses. Why are they called *weaknesses?* There are definitely weaknesses in every person—character traits that undermine our capacity to fulfill our potential. But these perspectives somehow imply that a weakness is something I do not do well.

Why is *this* a weakness? Just because I do not do something well does not mean that that is a *weakness* for me; rather, it is a limitation or perhaps a nonstrength. We might say that *incidentally* we do not do this particular task or that particular activity very well; it is not something that we would identify as a strength or a capacity. And then we can note that what is far more important is what we do well, where we have discovered ability and competency. What we do not do well is nothing more than a nonstrength. Nobody does everything well; what is imperative is that we each discover what we are able to do well.

Before we go on to the other factors that enable us to discern vocation, I need to make a critical point. When it comes to vocation or occupation, it is essential that we see that it is not merely a matter of aligning one's strengths and abilities to a particular job or employment opportunity. The issue of vocation is far more complex because as individuals we are far more complex. When it comes to vocation, we cannot think in a one-to-one correlation, in a kind of linear fashion, between our training and our occupation. We live and work now in multiple-career societies, so that what we were trained for perhaps many years ago may actually be incidental to what we believe will be the next chapter of our life.

Consequently, it is essential to see that the identification of gifts and abilities is but *one* element in this discernment process.

Another preliminary yet important question is to ask about personality or temperament. It is important to affirm that an essential element of self-knowledge is appreciating that we are each unique in terms of temperament or personality. There are different means that can enable a person to appreciate and accept his or her individuality. I have found the Myers-Briggs Type Indicator (MBTI) particularly helpful.[2] Like no other instrument, it has enabled me to accept who I am. This tool makes the assumption that we are each unique. There is no "right" personality. Our individual temperament is as unique to us as our fingerprint. And to live in the truth is to live congruent with who we are in terms of personality.

I will summarize the insights of the MBTI, but only as an example, recognizing that there are various ways that we might think about personality and temperament. The MBTI builds on a Jungian theoretical foundation in asking us to consider four questions as a means of discerning who we are. First, some are *extroverts* and some *introverts*, and we can usually get a sense of who we are by asking: Do we draw energy from being alone or from being with others? The answer is not a matter of what should be but a description of what is actually the case for us. Extroverts are energized by being with people and enjoy, as often as not, being the center of attention. Introverts tend to be more retiring and are quite content to be alone, or, when in a crowd, to avoid the center of attention. If you are honest with yourself, which is more true to who you are?

Second, the MBTI notes that there is another crucial distinction: some process information as *sensates;* some are more inclined to depend on *intuition.* Are you more inclined, as a sensate, to trust clear, certain and concrete facts, or are you more inclined, as an intuitive, to trust metaphors and think in terms of possibilities, to trust your intuition even more than you trust the "facts"? Sensates tend to be more in touch with reality; intuitives are more inclined to think in terms of possibilities.

Third, how do you make decisions? Some are inclined to decide on the basis of principle; they value logic, analysis and justice. Others, in contrast, are more inclined to consider the affective—the personal and relational implications of a choice. Some are what the MBTI calls *thinkers,* whereas others are *feelers.* It is important, as you think about yourself, not to ask what is right or correct, or how you should act or respond. Rather, simply consider how you are inclined to make decisions.

Finally, the fourth consideration has to do with whether we are more inclined to seek closure or to enjoy the spontaneous. Are you more inclined to live with order, structure and routine, or do you prefer going through life with more intense delight in the moment. The MBTI uses the descriptive *judgers* to identify those who are most at ease after a decision is made and who derive fulfillment from the completion of a task. *Perceivers* are those who find more joy in the process and find more satisfaction from starting a project.

These four questions can bring remarkable clarity to our lives and our personalities. Of course, it should be stressed that we are unique because (1) there are sixteen different possible combinations (types) of these four dimensions of personality, and (2) even if we have the same MBTI type, we are still different because of any number of other factors, such as gender, culture, upbringing and experience.

This is a very simple summary of the Myers-Briggs perspective, but it gives us an appreciation of the complexity of each person and each personality. Knowing ourselves includes how we are constructed psychologically and emotionally, not just how we are designed physically or otherwise. We are unique, and self-knowledge comes in understanding what makes us who we are and in accepting who we are. It was the appreciation of my unique temperament or personality that has as much as any other factor given me the freedom to accept who I am and to accept my vocation. Because I am not a sensate, for example, I am the kind of person who is not prone to be attentive to detail; it would make no sense for me to be an accountant. It would not be something I would do with joy and thus I could not do it with integrity in the service of others. It is not me.

While the MBTI and other such resources are potentially very helpful, remember the following: we cannot discern vocation and should not choose a career on the basis of either our talent or our Myers-Briggs type. While our calling will always in some way be consistent with our God-given gifts and personalities, we are going to dig even deeper to find the raw material for discerning who we are and what we are called to.

THE HEART OF THE MATTER

In the first edition of *Courage and Calling* I suggested that there were four compelling questions that we needed to raise in discerning our vocation: (1) talent or capacity, (2) desire and deep joy, (3) where we

feel the brokenness of the world, and (4) our personality or temperament. And then I said:

> No one of these questions takes priority or precedence over the
> others. Who we are and who we are called to be in the world is
> found at the intersection of all four. But it is likely that one of
> these questions will stand out for you or will be particularly
> illuminating as you seek to know yourself and to identify your
> vocation.

Since writing those words, I have been convinced from numerous
conversations and from a number of authors that each of these four
questions does *not* hold equal weight. Gifting matters, of course, and
having a good read on our temperament matters. God's calling will
not fly in the face of either our capacities or our fundamental way of
being in the world. And yet I am increasingly convinced that when it
comes to discerning vocation there is a deeper question that really
provides us with the insight we need to move forward. We need to
ask the truly fundamental question What is the passion, the desire,
that most reflects who I am?—reflecting more closely the intersection of questions 2 and 4 in the first edition of this book.

There might be different ways to get at this, or perhaps different
questions we might ask to get at the heart of the matter. And, indeed,
different authors do approach this differently. Brian J. Mahan asks:
What is it you really *want* to do? Peter Block puts it this way: What is
it that really *matters* to you? And David Whyte asks, Where are you
most "at home"? And then I will add a fourth question: Where do you
feel the brokenness of the world? But all four are seeking to get at the
same fundamental question: Who are you? Not merely on the sur-
face, but at the very heart of who you are.

In *Forgetting Ourselves on Purpose: Vocation and the Ethics of Ambition*, Brian Mahan uses ambition as a point of reference. He suggests
that what we *want* to do is not necessarily diametrically opposed to
the calling of God, as is so easily assumed. Mahan notes that so many
of us are part of a religious heritage that suggests that the affirmation

of self—who I am and what I am called to be—is not consistent with caring for others, that if we are caring for ourselves it must mean we are not caring for others.[3] To the contrary, he suggests that we need to be attentive to the longings of our heart, which he says are the "raw material of vocation," and that we often cannot get at this deep desire of our heart because we are too mindful, too concerned, indeed obsessed with what others might think of us.[4] Thus we need to be less self-absorbed to truly know what we want.

Desire matters; the psalmist assures us that God longs to give us our desires: "Take delight in the LORD, and he will give you the desires of your heart" (Ps 37:4). Our desires are twisted and self-destructive when they are shaped by greed, insecurity, a longing for comfort and ease, or an inclination to control or manipulate others (Eph 4:22-23). They can be rooted in pride rather than humility. But when we are right with God and genuinely long to respond fully to God, consistent with his call on our lives, then we must acknowledge the desires that God has placed in our hearts.

What do we long for more than anything else? What do we long for when our character aspires for that which is noble and honorable? When we set aside our longings for security, wealth, comfort, fame and even acceptance, what do we long for? Ultimately, what we long for will only be fulfilled in the kingdom, which is yet to come. But if God were to grant you a foretaste of that new kingdom, what would it look like for you?

One way to identify our desires is to appreciate what it is that gives us the greatest joy. It is worth noting that we will be effective in fulfilling our vocations only if we do what we are called to do out of joy (Heb 13:17). It is therefore important that we come to terms with what gives us joy, even if it means that we set aside the pursuit of comforts, wealth, fame or power.

Some time ago I heard of an exercise that I found particularly valuable as a means of assessing what gives us joy. The suggestion was made that we each list ten things that have brought us the greatest joy—either single events or activities we have opportunity to do regularly, or something that we did for a time.

I listed my ten things. Some of these related directly to my work—to a particularly successful group project I had participated in. Some of the ten items on my list related to the leisure side of my life, such as my enjoyment of the game of squash, something I had played regularly for over a decade. Others were events—such as the trip my family and I took on the trans-Siberian railway.

But then the exercise urged us to go further and examine what was *behind* each of these. One man mentioned his love of playing golf but then realized that he did not enjoy playing alone. He enjoyed golf because it gave him an extended time with two of his friends—together in the outdoors without interruption.

Identify what has brought you joy, but then look deeper and see if you can find the root cause of your joy. I recalled a project that I worked on and realized that the real joy behind the project was that we enabled many people to fulfill *their* aspirations, and it helped me appreciate my own deep desires—to enable others to be all that they are called to be.

This is but one way to identity and come to clarity about our desires. The important thing is that we grow in our capacity to be true to who we are by acknowledging the deepest desires of our hearts. What we long for is a key indicator of who we are and what we are called to be and do. It will assuredly be reflected in our vocation.

Another way is to ask this: If I were able to only do or be one thing, what would it be? I remember watching my preschool sons struggle with having visitors in our home, especially if the guests had small children the same age as themselves. The presence of other children meant that they were expected to share their toys. But it was sad to watch them hold all their precious toys in their little arms. They were not having fun, but at least no other children could enjoy the toys!

But we insisted that they had a choice to make. We asked them: Which of these toys do you want more than any other? You have first choice, but you must let go of and share all the other toys. And it was a good exercise for a little boy, an essential part of growing up. Because in time we need to hear the adult version of the question: If you could only be or do one thing with your life, what would you want it to be? and What do you long for more than anything? Part of the way to think about this is by asking, What brings me joy? Get to the root of the matter. It is not what you imagine might bring you joy; it is seeking what fundamentally and actually *brings* joy. We cannot buy into the lie that more money or more prestige would do it; we need to know our heart.

Peter Block comes at the fundamental matter of the heart through a different question. In his book *The Answer to How Is Yes: Acting on What Matters*, he provides a critique of the deep pragmatism of our culture, with its focus on the immediate, on what "works," on what brings measurable and tangible results quickly. But the result, he notes, is that this often means we do not attend to what really matters.[5] When we get at what really matters to us, we get to the passion of our hearts. But the "instrumentality of our culture . . . distracts us from the pursuit of what really matters."[6] We look at costs and cost savings prematurely; rather than first asking what is important, what really matters to us most. And many of the things that matter most "defy measurement," Block observes.[7] And he concludes that we have all too easily "yielded . . . to what is doable and practical and popular," and in so doing have "sacrificed the pursuit of what is in our hearts."[8]

What matters to us that reflects who we are and gives meaning to our lives? What matters to you is reflected in the life you live; it is reflected in the way you engage life, spend your money and your time. Block is blunt: "if we do not have time to do something, it is a sign that it does not matter," and he urges us to stop complaining about the economy, the limitations we are facing, the problems of our past and begin to take responsibility for our actions (to be the cause rather than the effect).[9] And then this leads him to ask: What courage is required of me right now?[10]

I wonder if another way to get to the "what matters to us" question is to consider what makes us angry. Anger is dangerous emotional terrain, of course; it has the capacity to singe our hearts, if we are not careful. And we are so easily angered by trivialities—when we are inconvenienced or hurt because we were not affirmed or thanked for something. But when our anger is consistent with God's view of our work, could it be that our anger reflects what matters to us? Could it be that by attending to what makes us angry we begin to get a read on what moves us?

Coincidentally, Mahan's and Block's books were suggested to me by two former colleagues: Bob Rose was president of Canadian Theological Seminary when I served there as the vice president and dean; he passed on the Mahan book. And Walt Wright was president of Regent College when I first went there as vice president and dean; later he directed me to Block's book. I need to thank my wife for the next contribution. David Whyte, in his *Crossing the Unknown Sea: Work as a Pilgrimage of Identity*, suggests that the antidote to exhaustion may not be rest but wholeheartedness, and that we are typically exhausted because we are not doing our *true* work, with our "true powers," to use his phrase.[11] And he asks us to consider the image of the swan, an awkward waddler on land but a thing of beauty in his "elemental waters." This leads to the inevitable question What are your elemental waters? And following this, What is your core, the core sense of who you are?[12] He concludes, "One of the distinguishing features of any courageous human being is the ability to remain unutterably themselves in the midst of conforming pressures."[13]

Whyte is on to something very helpful here: when in our work we are engaged with tasks, responsibilities, that are deeply congruent with our fundamental self: we are in our "elemental waters." When the young shepherd boy David refused the armor of the soldiers when he went to take on Goliath it was not so much that he wanted to trust in God and not in his own strength or capacities, though that was surely the disposition he brought to this encounter. Rather, he was not at home in that armor; he was at home in his shepherd gear and with the weapon he had mastered, not the sword but the sling. But the same would apply to those who simply do not feel at home in the office complexes of the downtown financial sector; it is not their world, the sphere or way of being they thrive in.

And then a fourth way to get at the heart of the matter. Consider this question: Where do you feel—and the operative word is *feel*—the deep fragmentation of our world? Another aspect of self-knowledge comes with the realization that we each see the world's needs differently. And our vocational identity is in some form or another aligned with how we each uniquely see the pain and brokenness of the world.

Often we miss our vocation because our sense of the needs of the world is informed and shaped by the expectations of others. Sometimes preachers or speakers outline the needs of the world in a way that is very compelling, and they describe these needs in such a way that they communicate that if we really care, then we will respond according to *their* expectations. They assume that we should see the world as they see it. But the needs of our world are complex, and we need to be alert to how others use the *should* word. If we are prepared to listen to our own hearts, we will recognize that we long to help and serve and make a difference. But it will be our own vision for a needy world—a vision informed by our own reading of the Scriptures, but also a vision sustained by the witness of the Spirit to our own hearts.

Where do you see the brokenness of the world; what impresses you to the core of your heart and calls you to be or do something? When you are able to set aside ego gratification and ask honestly what you long to do to make a difference because you see the need—quite apart from any monetary return or honor that might come your way—what comes to mind?

The apostle Paul in essence identifies *seven* different responses to the world in Romans 12:6-8; each of them is a response to a different way of seeing the world and its pain. But these need to be read openly and with discernment. Read them and ask, Which of these most fits who I am and how I see the needs of the world? This is no place for you to be burdened by how others think you should see the world; rather it is a time to turn from these expectations, especially from religious leaders, and ask yourself honestly, before God, how you perceive the brokenness of the world.

1. The *prophet* (v. 6) sees the profound need for people to live in the truth they already know, and responds to the world with a passion that people would live consistent with their own confession, convictions and values. Prophets call us to behavior congruent with our words. All of us believe this important, but prophets see this as the most critical need of all.

2. Some are *servants* (v. 7 NIV). It runs in their blood to be attentive to the practical needs around them. They tend to think that there is too much talk and not enough action. They are often good with their hands or particularly sensitive to what needs to be done, and are often at the task and even complete it before the rest even recognize that it needs to be cared for. All of us need to be attentive to the needs around us, but for those called as servants, it is their most fundamental passion.

3. Others are called to be *teachers* (v. 7). Some are found in classrooms, but not all. Some are scholars, but not all. A teacher has the conviction that the main problem in the world is that people lack understanding; if they could just understand, they would know and live the truth. Teachers may even be inclined to think that the world could be saved through education. The rest of us may find this naive. But that is the point; we see the world differently and have a different vocation. Teachers believe that transformation comes through learning.

4. Still others are inclined to think that the greatest problem in the world is the lack of hope, and their fundamental orientation is one of *encouragement* (v. 8 NIV). All of us are called to encourage one another. But the pattern of some reflects a deep-felt conviction that encouragement is fundamental to the world experiencing peace, justice and transformation. They see how discouragement is killing us. Some encouragers use words; they are masters of language and can speak in ways that inspire, renew the heart and give courage. Others recognize the significance of place and know that the spaces we live and

work in can undercut our courage and sense of well-being; they know how to design spaces of nurture, light and life.

5. *Givers* "contribute to the needs of others" (v. 8 NIV). These recognize that without funding much that is important does not happen. Sometimes these individuals are even inclined to think that finances make everything work! They are as often as not people who know how to make money, but who know how to give generously. The rest of us might think of them as a bit one-sided in their thinking, but it is not our call. And they are right; we need financial savvy and generosity to sustain the life and ministry of the church, nonprofit organizations that respond to human need, the educational institutions that provide centers of learning, and the community organizations that sustain our common life together in neighborhoods. Without the generosity of those who have the means to give, our lives would be significantly impoverished. All of us are called to give generously, but some have the unique ability and vision both to make money but also to give it away.

6. Then there are the *leaders* (v. 8). There is so much talk of leadership in our day that sometimes we miss the point of a text such as this, thinking that everyone is called to leadership. As with each of these orientations, we are indeed all called to lead as required and as the opportunity arises. But it is the unique passion of some to enable—through the contribution of administration and management—so that the organizations can flourish, so that everyone else is enabled to fulfill their giftedness. Those in leadership are servants of a different kind—bringing together and husbanding the gifts of others to enable us all to achieve something greater than the sum of the parts. They help us see the big picture and help us work together to fulfill our mission, our common vision, in a manner that reflects the fundamental values we hold together.

7. And finally Paul speaks of those who are called to demonstrate mercy (v. 8 NIV). While all of us are called to show mercy, these understand that the central need of those around them (and of this world) is for others to stand with them—to mourn with those who

mourn and weep with those who weep. While others may wonder how this solves problems and brings resolution to the issues before us, those who are called to show mercy recognize the transforming power of empathetic identification; they know that the demonstration of mercy is itself life and strength to another.

The point is that your vocation will in some fundamental way be aligned to how *you* see the brokenness of the world. It is then imperative that you respond accordingly. It is equally imperative that you not judge others who do not see or feel the brokenness of the world as you see it. They have a different set of lenses; they see the world differently; they have a different call.

So, four questions, each just another way to get at the heart of the matter: What do you want most of all? What matters to you? Where are you at home, in your elemental waters? And what breaks *your* heart because it breaks the heart of God?

SELF-DISCOVERY WITHIN COMMUNITY

We ask the questions of ourselves, and each of us needs to foster our own, individual capacity to respond to the question of self-knowledge and identity. But it is also important to stress that our self-knowledge and self-awareness happen in community. We come to know ourselves not in isolation from others but as part of the body of Christ. Paul's whole assumption in Romans 12:3-8 is that we would see who we are within the context of the community we belong to. Community is a vital dimension of vocational integrity.

Not only do we fulfill our vocation as a member of a community, the very *discovery* of our vocation happens in community. The community can be a threat to vocation. Often family, school, church and others can communicate expectations that undermine our capacity to know and respond to who God made us to be and what God is calling us to do. But, having said that, it is important to emphasize that we find ourselves in our communal associations with others.

In community we come to appreciate our gifts and abilities—by noting and having others note how we contribute to the well-being of the community. In community we see how we are unique and how the desires of our hearts are different than but also affirmed by others.

In community we grow in appreciation of the needs of others— within the church and in the world. And in community we see how we are different—in our actions, reactions and mental orientation, different in our personality or temperament.

Self-knowledge includes a mature sense of our talent and ability; further, we need to have a good read on our particular temperament or personality. Then, with these vital but secondary questions on the side, we must consider who we are at very core of our being. What do we want to do more than anything because it matters to us deeply and fits us perfectly? This represents our "elemental waters" and how we feel the brokenness of the world. And we understand best who we are when we are in community.

Coming at the end question of identity and calling from diverse perspectives is important for a number of reasons. One reason is that we often are distracted or led astray by good intentions. We mean well, but our sincerity might need to be challenged. Henri Nouwen writes forcefully about this in reflecting on his vocation.

My trips to Latin America had set in motion the thought that I might be called to spend the rest of my life among the poor of Bolivia or Peru. So I resigned from my teaching position at Yale [University] and went to Bolivia to learn Spanish and to Peru to experience the life of a priest among the poor. I sincerely tried to discern whether living among the poor in Latin America was the direction to go. Slowly and painfully, I discovered that my spiritual ambitions were different from God's will for me. I had to face the fact that I wasn't capable of doing the work of a missioner in a Spanish-speaking country, that I needed more emotional support than my fellow missioners could offer, that the hard struggle for justice often left me discouraged and dispirited, and that the great variety of tasks and obligations took away my inner composure. It was hard to hear my friends say that I could do more for the South in the North than in the South and that my ability to speak and write was more useful among university students than among the poor. It became quite clear to me that idealism, good intentions, and a desire to serve the poor do not make up a vocation.[14]

There is so much in what Nouwen says that I find instructive. First note that true humility accepts the fact that it does not make sense, it is not wise, to presume upon God's grace. Nouwen's personality and makeup were not suited to the work in South America. Notice also that he had the humility to listen to his friends, who enabled him to see that he needed to function in terms of his strengths and abilities—his speaking and writing. And, as he puts it so well, that he "could do more for the South in the North than in the South." And then it is worth highlighting his comment that idealism and good intentions do not constitute a vocation—even a desire, however noble that desire might be, to serve the poor.

Rather, our vocations are rooted in not who we wish we were and not in good intentions, but in how God has actually made us. But knowing ourselves and discerning our vocations is only half of the equation.

Turning back to Romans 12, we find implicit there a *second* commandment, which I have hinted at along the way.

BE TRUE TO YOURSELF

The first commandment is "Know yourself." The second, "Be true to yourself." Be true to who you are and who God has called you to be; fulfill the call of God—*your* call to be who you are called to be. That call will be consistent with who you are. Self-knowledge is indeed half the battle, but it is only half. The real challenge is to live congruent with who we are—with how God has made us, with the ability and talent God has given us, with the desire God has placed in our hearts, with how we see the brokenness of the world and with how God has crafted our personalities. To live in the truth is to live in agreement with this identity and the call implicit in this identity.

The New International Version of the New Testament captures well the energy of the text of Romans 12:6-8. Having called his readers to consider themselves with sober judgment, to do a self-analysis, Paul moves forward. The force of the text is evident in his call to live a life of service, but the apostle's call is to serve in a manner that is *congruent* with this identity. It could be paraphrased as follows:

If you have been called to be a *prophet*, then *be* a prophet; fulfill your call with faith.

If you have been called to *serve*, then serve, without apology, without hesitation, without comparing yourself to others, but with a joyful acceptance of who you are.

If you have been called to *teach* [v. 7], then teach. Not everyone has been called to teach. Not everyone has the ability that you have. Teach, for that is who God made you to be. You do not need to apologize or feel diminished by what you do not do. Rather, do what you are called to do.

If you have been called to *encourage,* if your unique contribution is to bring hope in dark and discouraging situations, if you have been given the ability to bring light and new perspectives, then do it, for we live in a discouraging world and every one of us needs people, at home and in the workplace and in the church, who have this ability.

If you have been called to make money so that you can *contribute to the needs of others*, then do it to the glory of God without any apology to the rest of us who can barely balance our checkbooks. You do not have to apologize for making money. Do it; it is a God-given ability! Only, be generous.

If you have been called to *leadership*, then again, do not apologize for the call of God. Accept this with grace and humility. Accept the opportunities for leadership that the Lord gives you. Let me also say this: if this is not your call, then beware of the burden of leadership. For it is not an easy yoke; you will do more harm than good. But if this is the call of God, then the Word of the Lord is, govern diligently.

If you have been called to *show mercy,* may your numbers increase. For in a difficult and broken world, a world of refugees, a world of economic recession and unemployment, a world of battered wives and broken homes, a world where there are homeless even in a land of plenty, in this world we urgently need men and women who have the unique capacity to *show* mercy and be the means by which we know the mercy and comfort of God. If this is your call, do it cheerfully.

Each of these seven, in some form or another, represents a basic vocational orientation. And each has the capacity to be reflected in many different occupations, careers, roles, volunteer ministries, responsibilities and ministries in the church, and in the home. And it is the roles and responsibilities that are given to us that enable us to accept and embrace our vocations.

If you have been called to government, then accept with obedience this responsibility. Politics is a noble calling. If you have been called into education—then thanks be to God for another person called to serve in the education system of our countries—whether in public or private institutions and whether to serve kindergarten children or university students. I will not soon forget an interview I heard on a public radio station of two men who taught kindergarten in a public school. And when it was noted that it is rare for men to be involved on that level of education, they responded by speaking of a call to be teachers but also to be surrogate fathers to so many who came from families with absent fathers. It was a memorable interview.

If you have been called into the arts—as an artist, a musician, an actor, a playwright, a poet—respond eagerly. Unfortunately, many do not know how to respond to and interact with artists. But ultimately you are fulfilling God's call on your life, not ours. There will be people to encourage you. Seek them out, receive their encouragement and keep to the task.

If you have been called into medicine or dentistry, or called to be carpenter or a plumber, you have a sacred calling from God. If you have been called to be a servant—meeting the practical needs of others as a caretaker, a secretary, a bank clerk, however your vocation is expressed, do it with joy, knowing that what you do you do as unto the Lord.

If you have been called into the gospel ministry, then embrace eagerly who it is that God has called you to be. But even here, it is wise to give focused attention to how your gifts, abilities and vision for the brokenness of the world affect the way that you serve. Some are called to be church planters; some are not. Some are called to be pioneer missionaries; some are not. Some are called to be teachers and translators; some are not. Some are called to be pastors and preachers; some are not. In other words, even within the gospel ministry, there are all manner of roles and responsibilities. The essential and mature act is simple: come to a full realization of who you are and what you have been gifted to do, and embrace it eagerly. Do it. Be true to who you are. Be true to your call, true to how God has made you. Your call is not a superior call or a more sacred call; it is merely *your* call.

There are many things that could derail you, and we will examine these in some detail in the chapters that follow. But we must affirm that foundational to vocational integrity is not only self-knowledge but the commitment to be who we are called to be, which is consistent with who we are: our strengths, our desires, how we see the needs of the world and our personalities. But when we are true to ourselves, we are true to God and to others, for we are living congruent with who God made us to be.

Some might wonder if over the course of our lives our vocations might not change. In other words, is it possible that people's sense of identity and calling could change in light of changes in their own heart, perhaps through conversion, or changes in the environment, the circumstances around them? While I am hesitant to say that it is not possible for a vocation to change, what I have been suggesting all along is that vocation is rooted in our fundamental identity—the essence of who we are. Our vocation is, then, congruent with how God has made us. Conversion, or a change of heart and heart orientation, becomes the means by which we discover this identity; it does not change our call but rather transforms it. We might say that prior to conversion we lived falsely; with conversion we find ourselves and our vocations.

Further, while it is true that we will be called to respond in different ways to different circumstances, is it not the case that we are merely finding diverse expressions of the same fundamental vocation? And, ideally, over the course of our lives we will come to clarity about who we are and what we are called to be, responding to the changes and opportunities in our lives. But along the way our fundamental identity does not change; we merely grow in our capacity to live in a manner congruent with that identity.

It is also important to stress that when we are married we of necessity find our vocations and fulfill them as married persons. The apostle Paul takes it for granted, in 1 Corinthians 7, that a married man lives with a fundamental orientation toward his wife, and that a married woman is "anxious about the affairs of the world, how to please her husband" (v. 34). That is, if we are married, we respond to our vocations as married people. This requires a fundamental commitment to the vocation of our spouse—to appreciate, encourage and work along side that vocation. Husbands and wives are clearly called in complementary fashion. And while there may be stress and tensions along the way as they each negotiate their understanding of vocation with the other, there is no inherent reason why this should not be possible. Both are called; both have a vocation. Neither is more essential in the kingdom work of God than the other.

Deep within the corporate consciousness of our culture is the idea that women are called to stand by and help their husbands fulfill their vocations. But all of us, particularly husbands, need to come back to the extraordinary words of the apostle Paul where he reminds us that a husband is called to love his wife as Christ loved the church, which means that he is to give himself for her so that *she* can flourish (Eph 5). Clearly, as a married man, a clear priority that I have before God is to enable my wife to discover, embrace and fulfill her vocation, a vocation that will certainly be a complement to mine but which will have an internal and inherent integrity and focus of its own.

THE NEED DOES NOT DETERMINE THE CALL

There is something basic that is implied in all of this: the need does not determine the call. On the one hand, it is simply not possible. Most of us live in circumstances that force us to recognize more needs than we could possibly fill. I am an administrator of an academic institution; I cannot possibly respond to all the needs around me—everything that I think needs to be done. It is not possible. And this is true of every one of us—regardless of our vocations and our life circumstances. Those who suggest that need determines the call are doing nothing but creating an artificial burden for their hearers.

This does not mean that we become oblivious to the needs around us. Not at all. Any caring person will respond with compassion and generosity to need. But the difference is that people of vocational integrity do not let the myriad needs around them derail them from fulfilling their vocation. Neither do they let the perspective of others derail them from how God is calling them to serve him in this world.

Consider the account of Jesus himself in Mark 1. There we read that Jesus had a full day of ministry in Capernaum, teaching in the synagogue, healing the sick, enabling the blind to see and casting out evil spirits from those who were possessed. Then, in verse 35, we read that early in the morning he went to a solitary place to pray.

Simon Peter and the other disciples came looking for him. They urged him to return to Capernaum, because the whole town was looking for Jesus. Jesus was in demand; there were expectations from the townspeople and from his disciples that he would meet their needs. But then we read the stunning words where Jesus says that he would be proceeding to other villages to preach, "for therefore came I forth" (v. 38 KJV).

Such a sense of purpose! Such an intentionality to his day and his work. He knew what he was called to do, and the needs around him did not determine the call for that day. And, if the Messiah himself is limited in this way, how much more are we.

We might be tempted to see in this scenario a cold-hearted Jesus. But in the verses that follow we read that in compassion Jesus reached out his hand and touched a leprous man. No, Jesus did not ignore the needs around him. He was filled with compassion and responded generously as he was able. But he was not derailed from his vocation.

In John 17:4 we have the remarkable words where Jesus says to the Father: "I glorified you on earth by finishing the work that you gave me to do." I long for the same: that I would be able to come to the end of my life and know before God that I had fulfilled my vocation.

But we will not be able to do this unless we learn to say no. We will not have this privilege unless we come to clarity about who we are and what we are called to do. This requires focus, discipline and courage. But the result is freedom—freedom from ambition, freedom from the pressures and expectations of others, freedom to be who we are before God. It is a freedom to embrace the call of God upon our lives with joy and hope.

Jesus reminds us that his yoke is easy, his burden is light. If a yoke is easy, it means that it *fits* us. It is designed around the contours of who we are; it is congruent with the character, strengths, potential and personality that we are before God.

On some simple but fundamental level, then, I am suggesting that our only hope for vocational clarity is that we come to terms with our own hearts—with what we individually believe is happening in the very core of our being. Each of us has something that we feel is the very reason for which we have been designed, created and redeemed. In the end we embrace this call, this purpose, because this, so help us God, is who we are. In the end there is something to which we say: "This I must do." And we will do it, regardless of whether we have parental approval, regardless of whether we get praise or financial return. At this point we understand that we must give up our lives for the sake of others, for only then will we find our lives (Mt 16:25). We do it because we must. And we accept this as of God—as that which God has placed in our hearts. What drives us is the very conviction that God has placed it there. This is vocational integrity and personal congruence.

CHAPTERS IN OUR LIVES

Vocation and the

Stages of an Adult Life

Older notions of vocation and vocational development assumed that people wrestled with matters of vocation as a young adult. It has been commonly assumed that vocational counseling was provided in high schools for those seeking to choose a career. But in a true understanding of vocation, we discover that vocational questions follow us throughout the course of our lives—and that perhaps vocational counsel needs to be present to us at each transition. The questions remain the same: Who am I, and who has God called me to be? And yet it is essential we recognize that we consider these questions in very different ways through the various transitions of our adult lives.

Students of adult psychological development generally agree that there are three distinct phases in an adult's life. Though we move through these phases in our own time and at our own pace, there is a remarkable similarity, regardless of culture, gender, personality or vocation. What follows is a simple outline of the phases of adult development—not a sophisticated analysis but adequate for the purpose of thinking in general categories about the phases of vocational development.

Keep in mind also that vocational identity is a critical dimension of our faith development. For most people, vocational questions are fundamental to their faith and growth in faith. Even though as a reader you are perhaps at one stage—perhaps in midlife—and thus may be inclined to skip over the other two sections that speak to those at another stage of life, there are two things worth remembering. First, life is relatively short and we are wise to address vocational questions in one chapter of our lives in light of what has already happened in our vocational journey. Second, we are often in conversation with others who are working through different issues, perhaps reflecting their own stage of life. And a meaningful conversation with them necessarily takes account of where they are on the adult journey of faith and vocational development.

FROM ADOLESCENCE INTO EARLY ADULTHOOD

The first transition, and probably the most critical, is the move into adulthood from adolescence. This transition occurs at or around age twenty. For many it happens in their late teens. For others it does not come until they are well into their twenties. Regardless of when it happens, the critical issue is this: it *must* happen. Personal congruency and vocational integrity require that we take adult responsibility for ourselves, and as adults, we must ask and then courageously answer the question What is God calling me to be and do?

This inevitably means some kind of separation from parents. The idea is surely included in the thought behind the words of Genesis 2:24, where we are told to leave our father and mother and cling to our spouse. We cannot become an adult without leaving our parents—leaving them in the sense that we take personal responsibility for our life.

Vocational integrity and vitality are only possible if there is a break from parents, from home, from adolescence. The problem is that often this break is delayed or denied. Parents sometimes prevent their children from moving into full maturity. In a superb biography of the composer and musician Mozart, Solomon Maynard contends that Mozart's father insisted on keeping his son in a state of dependency. Leopold "infantilized" his son, and Maynard goes on to show that many of the problems of Mozart's short life were due to his failure to move into full adulthood.[1] This pattern is repeated often—whenever parents, for whatever reason, intentionally or unwittingly, prevent their sons or daughters from leaving them, from becoming full adults.

Often, though, parents are not alone in this game. Young people may play along because they fear the independence and responsibility of adulthood. They remain dependent—emotionally, financially and otherwise—because they find security in the parent-child relationship. They are afraid of growing up, afraid of being on their own, afraid of being an *adult*.

Moving into full adulthood is not just an ideal. It is essential for personal and vocational maturity. If we never leave our parents, we tend to remain dependent. But the problem is more subtle, for what tends to happen is that we inadvertently treat the organizations we work for as though they have a parental function. We expect the one who supplies our pay check to be our "parent," caring for us. And we move into a level of emotional dependency that undermines our capacity to make necessary choices—to leave when we need to leave, to find emotional support outside the structures of the organization, to be true to God's call on us. Organizations will always let us down. And we will continually be disappointed and feel betrayed by organizations if we do not move out of a parent-child relationship of dependence.

Fundamentally, what happens in the break from parents is that God becomes our Father, our parent. We move from dependence on human parental structures to a mature, adult dependence on our Father in heaven. This is what I long for for my sons—that they would no longer call me father but brother, for we are each, then, children together of God our Father. Sure, I am still Dad in one sense. But I need to affirm to them that they are accountable to God and not me.

What this means, of course, is that there is a very close connection between faith and vocation. Each of us must, in the end, choose for ourselves what we will believe and by what faith we will live. While we certainly may have faith as children, maturity comes when we embrace an adult faith that is our own, a faith that gives meaning and focus and purpose to our lives. But it can only be this to us if it is something more than our parents' faith; it must be our own.

Parents have a whole range of expectations for their children, expectations that are often communicated in subtle ways. And the desire to please parents runs deep in the human psyche, so deep that many adults are in some ways still in an adolescent mode; they continue to function in terms of what their parents would expect and want, sometimes even after their parents have died. They have not become their own selves; they have not become adults.

There are many reasons why parents hesitate to free their children to accept, before God, who they are and who they are called to be. In some cases it is their own pride—their desire for the affirmation that comes when their children have a particular role. In other cases it arises from their disappointment with themselves, with their own failures and thus the hope that their children could become or accomplish what they were not able to be and do. I recently read of a man who has had a very successful and satisfying career in broadcasting. He spoke of how in his twenties he was pursuing a Ph.D. in English literature but that early on in his studies, he recognized that he had no heart for it, no passion for an academic career. And then at one point it dawned on him: his father, who had never had an opportunity for an advanced degree, was passionate that his son achieve what he had not had the opportunity to do. And thus the son found freedom, realizing that he needed to follow his own heart, his own sense of call, and not presume to bear the emotional load or expectations of his father.

Some parents long for their children to follow along in the same line of work as themselves, such as medical doctors who long for their children to enter medicine, or those in business who assume that their sons or daughters will take over the family business. In many families the pressure from parents is not so much that the chil-

dren would follow their parents but that they would enter into the
gospel ministry. We typically admire a family where all or the majority of the children become missionaries or pastors or doctors. And
yet, perhaps when we hear of such situations we should be suspi-
cious. It is surely possible that each one is called to this specific ministry or occupation. This is possible. But they *each* need to know,
personally, before God and no one else—including their parents—
that this is what they are called to be and do. They must each know,
to the depth and core of their beings, that they are doing this not to
gain the pleasure or blessing of their earthly father but in response to
who they are and who God has crafted them to be and how God has
animated them.

And if it should happen in such a family situation that after a time
one of them says, humbly and with courage, that he or she is called to
be a carpenter or an artist, then the Christian community must rally
around and encourage, support and sustain this person, whether or
not it includes parental blessing and especially if this blessing is
given reluctantly.

Through reading in the fascinating field of family theory or family systems, I have been introduced to the principle of *differentiation*. This concept has enabled me to see that if we are to mature
emotionally, vocationally and spiritually—so we are not shaped un-
duly by the criticism or praise of others, able to live by our own
convictions and conscience, and able to relate intimately with others and to differ graciously with others—we must come to a distinct
differentiation. And at root, or at least where this begins, is with a
mature separation from our parents. People who are well-differenti-
ated are not easily susceptible to flattery or to emotional manipula-
tion. Mostly this is the case because they are themselves; they are
individuals. As such they are capable of generous service while also
knowing when to say no. Further, they are able to hold their convictions firmly without losing the capacity to learn more or to change
their minds. This does not mean that they are gullible; to the contrary, they are able to learn with discernment, a critical apprecia-

tion of what they are hearing or reading.

Much more could be said, but what strikes me here is the critical need for a clear break from parents. We do not become differentiated individuals or adults unless we in some significant and discernible measure, *leave* father and mother.

In passing it can be noted that many expressions of adolescent turmoil—what in many cases might be thought of as teen rebellion—is often nothing more than a young person seeking to establish personal identity. Often, the more defined or strong the parent or parents, the stronger the resistance to the parental expectations or ideals. In these times a young person is merely trying to find differentiation—his or her own identity. And what is needed from parents, more than anything else, is patience, understanding and acceptance.

Those same qualities are needed in many school systems. Many times the rules and regulations of a school are designed to establish a particular pattern of behavior, and the system cannot tolerate any form of eccentricity. And many times what is viewed as rebellion is merely a young person insisting that they will not conform to a prescribed pattern of behavior that is contrived and artificial. Schools certainly need rules; every community needs guidelines to govern their common life. But in many school systems the regulations are rooted in a desire to instill conformity rather than to guard genuine community. And many young people will instinctively resist. Rightly so. Some will do it quietly in ways that are less disruptive. While some will resist in ways that harm themselves and perhaps others, their motive must be recognized as not in itself wrong.

Everything I have said about separation from parents is offered fully conscious that in Asian and Hispanic cultures—and I offer this as one who has grown up in Latin America and lived for much of my adult life in Asia—people tend to stay with their parents longer and on the whole, are more amenable or at least susceptible to parental pressure. At least this is what is assumed. But my observation is that nothing I have said is less applicable in these settings; it is merely that the pressure for conformity and compliance to parental expectations may be greater. If anything, this cultural reality only reinforces the need for intentionality when it comes to parental separation.

Early adulthood includes the break from parents. But there is more to the transition from youth to adult responsibility than independence. These years form a period of learning and self-discovery. Ideally, it should be a time to learn—to get a formal education that is foundational to life. One common mistake is that of assuming too early that we know our vocation, and thus we pursue an education that later seems irrelevant. The best advice is simple: keep your options open. Your twenties are a time to learn, to grow, to establish friendships, to make an initial exploration into an occupation, but most of all to get to know yourself.

This does not mean that we do not engage in an occupation. It is merely that it is wise to keep our options open. Do not specialize too early. Do not make assumptions prematurely about what you want to be and do. Do not fret if in your late twenties you still lack clarity about your vocational identity. That is fine. See this as a time for learning and self-discovery, and possibly, for some, a time to get married and start a family. And when you marry, see this as your further opportunity for self-discovery and development, not as another form of dependency, little different that what you had with your parents.

And yet the bottom line remains the same: the central question for young and emerging adults is whether they will grow into the capacity to take personal and adult responsibility for their lives.

FROM EARLY TO MIDADULTHOOD

If we have made a good and healthy break from parents and adolescence, then it is likely we will be able to process the next transition of our adult lives. It will not be any easier; it is merely that we can wrestle with midlife questions on their own terms rather than carrying the baggage of adolescence through the process.[2]

Students of adult psychological development recognize that there is a critical transition from early to midadulthood. It happens at different times for different people, though for most it begins in their midthirties. Regardless of when this transition comes, it needs to happen. It is a point where we move directly and intentionally into our vocation, both understanding what our vocation is, and accepting, indeed *embracing*, the call of God.

It was Carl Jung who, at least in terms of modern psychological studies and insights, recognized the significance of midlife choices. At around the age of thirty-eight he initiated a major split with his mentor, Sigmund Freud, a divergence that was necessary if Jung was to come out from under the shadow of Freud. And there is little doubt that if Jung had not made the break, he would not have been the great psychiatrist that he was. Eventually he laid the basis for intentional reflection on the middle years of our lives. He noted that our early years—childhood, adolescence and young adulthood—are times in which we get established in the world. For most it is a time to select a career and establish a family. But in the midst of it, inevitably we will begin to ask the fundamental question of *our* identity. Who, in the midst of all of this, am I?

It is probably fair to say that we do not really know ourselves until our midthirties, which is why we cannot make the transition to midadulthood—full adulthood—until this time. Clarity for vocational purposes can only come after we have lived with ourselves long enough to be able to ask, for example, what matters to me more than anything else?

Then we have an inevitable choice to make: will we respond to our vocation with focus, direction, purpose and courage. By our midthirties we should know ourselves well enough to have a good sense of who we are—our strengths, our desires and our temperament. We should have a good read on what it is that we do that is the fullest expression of who we are.

The choices involved may be difficult. For many, they involve saying no as much as saying yes. If we are gifted in more than one way, then we need to discern and affirm what it is that is most significant for us, and what brings the fullest expression of our identity.

I am a capable teacher and preacher, and enjoy both thoroughly. I enjoy the classroom and the opportunity to lecture, lead discussions and interact with students. And preaching is a love of my life: the exposition of Scripture within the context of worship. But in my mid-thirties I began to see that there was a third strength that was increasingly significant for me. I realized that I enjoy administration. I saw that I was intrigued by the challenge of enabling institutions to fulfill their identity or mission. And friends and colleagues were increasingly looking to me to play that kind of role. Over the course of a few years I came to the conclusion that administration and leadership are probably the *primary* contributions I have to make.

But this involved making a choice. We cannot be all things to all people. We need to choose, and our choice will mean saying no to some alternatives and eagerly embracing others. This may sound easy, but I know from my own journey through midlife that it can be characterized by much inner turmoil. Yet there are words from Ralph Waldo Emerson which have always remained with me, words to which I often return, words which for me capture the essence of what it means to mature vocationally through midlife. They come from his essay "Self-Reliance":

> There is a time in every man's education when he arrives at the conviction that envy is ignorance; that imitation is suicide; that he must take himself for better or worse as his portion; that though the wide universe is full of good, no kernel of nourishing corn can come to him but through his toil bestowed on that plot of ground which is given to him to till.[3]

This captures it! And the crux of the matter for so many of us is whether we turn from envy, refuse to compare ourselves with others, reject any idea that we are diminished by the giftedness of others, and appreciate that we will not be all that we would have *liked* to have been, but that we can, with God's grace, be all that we are *called* to be. Inevitably this means that we must make a choice—to accept for better or worse who God has called us to be and embrace that calling. Now in midlife, we have the possibility and the potential to become ourselves, our true selves. And this means that we choose to accept who we are. My own sense is that we do not become completely ourselves until we work through, in midlife, the fundamental question of our identity and calling, which is but another indication of the close connection between vocational development and faith development. It is not until I really know myself and accept and embrace who I am that I am able to, in some significant measure, give myself completely to God.

To embrace our vocations in midlife means that we accept two distinct but inseparable realities. First, we accept with grace our *limitations* and move as quickly as we can beyond illusion about who we are. Second, it means, positively, that we accept responsibility for our gifts and abilities, and acknowledge with grace what we *can* do. Some will struggle more with the first—accepting their limits; others with the second—taking responsibility for their abilities and capacities. But either way this is the heart of the matter—to accept my limitations and take responsibility for my abilities. If we do not make this choice, the failure to do so will eventually catch up to us. We will either get caught up in a pattern of busy, hectic lives, harried by work that consumes seven days a week and leaves us exhausted, or we will find that we are increasingly withdrawn, going through the motions of work, perhaps, but lacking passion, focus and the capacity for doing diligent and meaningful work.

There is a third way: effective, meaningful work, done at a leisured pace, with passion, focus, energy and, no less significant, joy. And the difference is typically fairly straightforward. In the third way, people know themselves and are at peace with their strengths and their limitations.

One of the critical questions of these years of our lives will be the simple but profound question of whether we will be our own person, true to our own conscience and identity, or whether we will buy into the "company." For some this will be a simple question: Are you a "company person" or your own person? Are you willing to live by your own convictions and your own conscience, regardless of the implications, or will you believe what the company believes? Will

you be *you*, or will you live by pretense, by an identity, a conscience
and a belief structure that is not your own, but which you think will
gain the acceptance of those in power? What made Florence Nightin-
gale, Nelson Mandela, Rosa Parks, Dorothy Day extraordinary people? They were gifted people, certainly. But the critical factor that
shaped their lives was their courage to go their own way and challenge the system, if necessary, even if it meant they were jailed, mar-
ginalized or discounted. They had courage; they refused to compromise conscience.

It is worth noting that many times the expectations of the company are more imagined than real. They are in actual fact self-
imposed rather than imposed by the organization. Many individuals
like to live by the rules and expectations of the organization because
they like the security of the bureaucratic structures. They speak of
the regulations and requirements of the organization in ways that
should be challenged, because no one is in fact insisting on a particular policy or pattern of behavior.

Jackson Bate, in his superb biography of Samuel Johnson, makes
some poignant comments about the middle years of an adult life. He
notes that the middle years are the first major shake-up of our sense
of self and identity since adolescence, as we face the prospect of old
age. And he notes that while some may avoid asking the hard questions and facing up to their true identity, the encounter with our true
selves can be deferred, but not avoided. Eventually we will be forced
to face up to who we are and what we fear. Samuel Johnson, he notes,
managed, as many do, to put it off—to postpone the inevitable by
sheer bustle of activity and accomplishment. But eventually it caught
up to him, as it will for everyone, and it "exacted a fearful psychological toll."[4] And the unfortunate truth is simply this: if we fail to
make some tough vocational choices in our thirties and forties, our
indecision will catch up with us; we will pay for it in our fifties.

The ideal, of course, is that we would embrace this time of change
and accept it as a time to make some tough choices, which will take
honesty, discernment and courage.

This is fundamentally a spiritual crisis, but particularly a crisis of identity. In terms of our faith development we are well enough along in life to know what matters to us most and what our faith represents—a complete adult trust in God as reflected in our resolve to love God and others. There is no doubt that if we face ourselves honestly, we will know that no matter how accomplished we are or how talented, capable or connected we might be, we are not really in control. Facing this and accepting it is fundamental to both our spiritual maturity and our capacity to embrace our vocation.

Now, it is important to make the following observation: knowing our strengths and limits, and recognizing and affirming our deep passion does not immediately mean that we will quit the job and become a freelance writer, if that is our passion! Rather, vocation is fulfilled within the limitations of family needs, the economy and, for some, personal health. And yet . . . and yet . . . we can start to nurture the dream and allow whatever time or opportunity that comes to begin to act on and nurture that dream.

I found noteworthy something I read about Jacques Ellul. He was a French professor and sociologist whose published work had a profound impact on the way philosophers and others think about the use of technology and technique. And yet he was inclined to think of his theological work as his most important contribution. And while he maintained his other scholarly publications, he began early to write on theology even though he did not initially view this as his primary area of expertise, finding as often as not just an hour a day to write in this area. And in the end he died having contributed a remarkable number of publications to discussions about biblical interpretation (his studies on 1 Kings and the book of Revelation, for example), ethics, and a Christian perspective on politics and urban life. Note that this was a seemingly "secondary" stream of his life for much of his career, but in the end it was perhaps the most important work that he accomplished.

Three other principles that are crucial to our midadult years will be stressed more in the following chapters. One is our capacity to be continuous learners; the second is our capacity to bounce back from and learn from failure and setbacks; and the third is a healthy routine of rest and sabbath renewal. In all of these ways, our midadult years are very important in our vocational development.

In this connection it would be appropriate to make particular mention of continuous learning. More will be said in this regard in chapter nine; I will be stressing the fact that our capacity to be continuous learners is fundamental to vocational fulfilment. But as we move into midlife this is particularly crucial: as we resolve to accept whatever we have learned for what it is, but also to see that we must either put it behind us or, better, build on it, as we embrace new opportunities, new challenges and new circumstances that we could not possibly have anticipated when we chose an area of study in our early adult years.

Particular reference should be made to the primary home caregiver (usually, though not necessarily, the woman in a marriage). In the case of the one who gives the most care to children, there is a necessary transition when the children grow up and leave home. Such people cannot say that their vocation is "raising children" unless they are called to work in an orphanage. We are responsible for raising our children with care. And it is a noble task to stay at home and care for home and family. But eventually the children grow up, and the primary caregiver will go through a crisis of identity if she or he does not anticipate this transition.

What often happens is that women do not know any other role than that of mother and they keep trying to mother—their children and others—long after they should stop mothering. Rather, when the children grow up and leave home, the primary caregiver can respond to a vocation and move into a role that corresponds with her or his strengths, vision and calling. This does not need to be a waged position. This person does not need to be gainfully employed. Everyone does not need to "work outside of the house" to have a sense of worth. But each person has a call—a vocation. It may be to provide hospitality, expressed primarily in receiving guests and travelers into the home. The point is that from the midthirties till the midforties, though it will vary for each family situation, a transition needs to come as the children grow up and eventually take adult responsibility for their lives. Even before the children move on as adults, a mother who is a primary caregiver can come to clarity about her own identity, calling and potential.

The midadult years are also critical to a married couple as they come to terms with the way God is calling them *together*. Some hard choices will need to be made, as a couple decides who will be the primary wage earner and whose vocation will be fulfilled more flexibly. Many men are choosing to step aside in their career development, if only for a few years, to enable their wives to get the study, training or experience they need to both discover and express their vocation. It is important to stress again that vocation is not the same as career or role. We do not need to be gainfully employed in order to have a vocation. A vocation can be fulfilled in a wide variety of ways, and in principle, every vocation should be capable of being fulfilled without requiring a position, an office or a career. But it is important to stress that for a married couple this sense of vocation is negotiated as they work out in complementary fashion what it means for each of them to have a reason for being, a purpose for their existence.

All of this would probably correspond to what Erik Erikson calls *generativity*—that transition in life when we move into emotional, vocational and spiritual integration, something that we likely do not experience fully until we are into our fifties but which can only come if we move intentionally into being true to who we are, if we accept who we are and live with integrity in light of who we are. I am suggesting that we are wise to recognize that by our midthirties the challenge of being true to ourselves represents unique choices we cannot afford to ignore. For only as we accept and become completely ourselves—without pretense, envy or illusion—are we able to give ourselves fully to God and to others in generous service.

For many people the midlife years will include a significant crisis or setback. And how we respond to whatever has happened to us is crucial to our vocational development. Maxine Hancock observes that three seventeenth-century figures—George Herbert, John Milton and John Donne—had their career hopes dashed and, ironically, their power and influence as writers and preachers came out of this disappointment. John Donne, for example, wanted to be a civil servant, but rather became one of the finest preachers of the seventeenth century.[5] Maxine Hancock observes that they each started out in one career direction and were redirected, by deeply disappointing circumstances, into places of life and work that were very fruitful.

Transitions are a part of life, and we no doubt feel these very keenly in our midadult years. We may come to one, if not several, crossroads: a crisis of employment as the company where we work is restructured, or a crisis of our own hearts, as we become increasingly aware of what we are called to do. Or perhaps our children have now grown up and we can begin to embark more intentionally on the journey of our own vocation. Whatever it is, against the backdrop of whatever setback or disappointment, we had better get on with it. We are not getting any younger.

FROM MIDADULTHOOD TO OUR SENIOR YEARS

Western societies use the word *retirement* to speak of a transition that occurs in our careers or occupations. For most, the assumption is that at age sixty-five we will retire from our work. This notion of retirement developed in the 1930s, when life expectancy was lower and when it was appropriate for individuals to be released from hard physical work for the last few years of their lives.

And yet, though many seniors can expect to have healthy, active lives for twenty years or longer after retirement, the old notion has remained, and for many it has come to be associated with a life of leisure. Others, however, recognize that there is something flawed in the idea that in our senior years, we make a transition from responsibility to leisure, from daily work in the office to a daily stroll on the golf course. What has happened, of course, is that we have confused calling or vocation with career. Christians may retire from their jobs or careers, but we do not lose our vocations. We can and must continue to discern the call of God and continue to ask how he is calling us to make a difference—within the options and limitations we inevitably will face.

But there is also an element of truth in the concept of retirement in our midsixties. For there is a necessary transition from our mid-adult years to our senior years. For most the transition begins at or around sixty. Retirement from our occupation may signal this transition or be a significant part of the move into our senior years, but it is only one aspect, and for many it will not be the most significant aspect of becoming a senior member of the society.

And this is also, as much as the earlier two transitions, a necessary move—for we *are* older, we do not have the same physical capacities. Our role within the church and the world *does* change. And I am increasingly struck by this: we do not live well unless we retire well, meaning, unless we effectively embrace our senior years. These are the capstone years, the crucial and vital years, and for many, potentially the most fruitful years of their lives.

I am going to speak of the need for letting go. But first we must affirm the capacity that we each have to make a difference in our senior years. Perhaps because I am soon going to move into this chapter of my own life, I am more aware than before of those who in their senior years are making extraordinary contributions; rather than "checking out" they are embracing opportunities in their seventies and beyond that reflect a deep maturity in their vocations.

P. D. James, when an octogenarian, comes out with yet another of her fascinating crime mysteries. Christopher Plummer, doing some of his best work as an actor, is in his seventies. Toronto-based Jane Jacobs, master of the way that cities work (or do not work), is publishing yet another vital analysis of urban life just before she turned ninety! And then also I think of George Mitchell who at age seventy-six was appointed United States special envoy to the Middle East to seek a diplomatic resolution to one of the most intractable political circumstances we can imagine. He had demonstrated remarkable skill, persistence and patience in other conflicted situations, and now, when others were off to the golf courses of Arizona, he is in the midst of seeking to make a difference, drawing on a lifetime of experience, including the work he had done to help bring about the peace accord in Northern Ireland.

For many seniors this transition represents a great opportunity. Frequently, they now have the time, the leisure and the financial independence to finally embrace, fully and eagerly, their vocations. Some discover their identity and calling as they have never seen it before. As I heard one person refer to his work, he spoke of everything before his retirement as but *prelude* to what he finally and with enthusiasm was able to speak of as his very reason for being. That is, for many seniors this chapter of their life is the time when they can finally do what they most love doing. And thus, as I heard one broadcaster explain why he was retiring at age sixty-five, he was now going to keep promises that he had made to himself rather than just those made to his public. It meant that he was going to write a novel, and he needed to get away from public life so that he could devote himself to the task that lay before him.

But regardless of whether we are just discovering our vocations or just finding that we are able to engage that vocation in a meaningful way, the point is that even in our senior years, indeed particularly in our senior years, we still have a calling and we do not lose or even really change vocation just because we are over sixty years old. But the expression or focus of that vocation, the way in which is it fulfilled, *will* change.

The most obvious external feature of this transition is that we let go of the roles, titles, offices and occupations that previously gave expression to our vocation. We let go of the formal structures of power and influence. We retire from these responsibilities. The reasons may be simple: we do not have the physical strength or emotional patience or even the desire to continue to hold on to the formal structures or roles that once meant so much to us. What we begin to see as seniors is that our vocations are fulfilled in more subtle but, in the long run, more influential forms. Now we really learn how to make a difference.

For some, as I noted, this chapter of their lives becomes nothing but an opportunity for leisure. And this is unfortunate. Others, in contrast, insist they do not want to retire, that they want to continue working and resent any suggestion that they must let go of their position or responsibility. It is important to stress that in fact no one can force us to retire from our vocation. Perhaps the company might insist that we step down from our position; perhaps we have to retire from our career. But our vocation? That is another matter. In other words, rightly or wrongly we might be asked to retire. Perhaps the organization we work for wants to invest in younger people. Whatever the reason, we must ask: If this door is closed for me, what way is open for me to make a difference in a manner that is congruent with my capabilities and passions? In this sense, retirement is always our choice.

Regardless, our senior years do represent a change. Ideally, our senior years should bring more flexibility and less organizational pressure; we are less bound to artificial and rigid work schedules that may be imposed on us by others. It is not that we are less engaged but rather that there is a significant difference in the rhythms of life and work. It may be that we spend less time doing more, meaning that though we invest less time, we have a greater sense of what really matters. And I am not suggesting that there is no leisure. Indeed, we may finally get to the golf course with some regularity, travel at a slow pace through southern France, spend time with our grandchildren and get to what we always insisted we would do, read Tolstoy's *War and Peace*! It is rather that in our senior years, with less physical and perhaps emotional strength, we have a greater sense that God actually carries the day and that even if we invest fewer hours in our working lives, those hours are more carefully invested, so that increasingly our work reflects opportunities that matter to us more than anything else.

I should also add that we are no longer talking about fixed retirement dates. For many, retirement will not come on the first day of the first month following their sixty-fifth birthday; rather, they will move into their senior years gradually, perhaps over a ten-year span. And yet, retirement will come, in the sense that we let go of the roles, the titles, the offices that gave expression to our vocation. And while we fear that if we let go of these our influence will diminish, we find that, to the contrary, it might actually increase.

But what is the character of this influence? This is the crucial question when it comes to understanding the nature of our calling in our senior years. One helpful way of thinking about vocation in our senior years is to consider vocation as marked by two essential characteristics. From the Scriptures it would seem that those who are seniors have two primary responsibilities—two fundamental ways they make a difference: sharing *wisdom* and giving *blessing.* First, it is assumed in Scripture that the elders are the wise women and men of their communities. They contribute through words of counsel, admonition and encouragement.

Senior adults long to be heard and appreciated. They long to be recognized. But all our lives we have assumed that we are heard and recognized when we have an office—a platform, title, position or role that provides a forum when people need to listen to us. Now the structures are gone. The platform is removed. And we are only heard if we are *actually* wise—if we actually have something to say that is helpful, insightful and illuminating. This is frightening. Will we be heard? Do we have anything to offer the next generation, those who might be willing to grow in wisdom and learn from us? If we are not confident that we have anything to offer, we might be tempted to resist letting go. But nothing is gained by clinging to the formal structures of power of influence. We need to let go and allow our influence to flow from who we are as persons and what we have learned along the way, rather than seeking an influence based on position or office.

The role of the senior is also that of granting a blessing. Indeed, in reading about Isaac, the patriarch of Israel, we get the idea that his *only* job description is that of granting a blessing to the next generation. We tend to undermine the significance of this. We are inclined to think that the powerful and influential people in a society and the church are those with the positions, the titles, the visible and obvious signs of decision making. But real power comes in the capacity to bless.

As I watched my sons mature and grow through their teen years, I have asked along the way, who do my sons listen to and respond to? Who, of all the people they have contact with, can I say really influences their behavior? There is no doubt that the answer is found in the idea of blessing. It is *not* those who use the word *should* when speaking with them or those who have expectations. Rather, it is those who enjoy them, are generous with time and energy, and listen to them. It is those who *bless* them.

It was my privilege some years ago to be associated with an annual family camp—a group of Christian doctors and dentists who meet together each summer for a week of rest and recreation. I was their devotional speaker on a couple of occasions. It has impressed me that my sons loved being part of that camp. When we were there, other men spent time with my sons—on the water, teaching them how to water ski or wind surf, but also in quiet times of conversation. These men seemed to have no other agenda than to enjoy the teens at the camp. And they had an immeasurable influence on my two sons. It seemed like they never used the word *should*, which all teens hate, and had no other plan than to bless my sons and the other teens at the camp.

Those seniors who bless have the greatest influence on the generation that follows. The temptation is to assume that those who follow us are not as committed, not as dedicated, not as good as we are. We so easily bemoan the next generation, which seems not to maintain our values. But those who bemoan the next generation grow more bitter, angry, disappointed and cynical. Those who bless not only grow old with grace and joy but also have a disproportionate influence on the generation that comes. There is a time to judge, a time to assess and a time to critique. But the power of blessing is so great that I wonder if we lose the right to judge the older we get. And part of why I wonder this is that I am so convinced of the power of blessing.

A window into this reality is found in the role of the grandparent. We often note, sometimes jokingly, that grandparents get all the joy of parenting without any of the grief! They can dote on their grandchildren, bless them, enjoy them, delight in them, encourage them and then not bother being around when there is need for discipline.

But while we chuckle about this, there is an element of truth in it: *parents* have that role. Grandparents have another. In the same way the senior members of the community fulfill their vocations in different ways, and the capacity to bless is central for each of us.

The role of grandparenting itself is for many a vocation. Tim Stafford, in his fine study *As Our Years Increase*, notes that the average woman is in her midforties when her first grandchild is born. This means, then, that 80 percent of all women have a grandchild by their midfifties and that grandparents over sixty-five have grandchildren who are either adolescents or young adults. Stafford notes that this means that increasing numbers of grandparents are available to have a profound and influential role in enabling young people to move into adulthood and maturity.[6] Many can speak of the powerful and formative influence of grandparents in their lives, and this potential is obviously something that could be a very significant part of this chapter of our lives.

No grandchildren? Then merely ask whom you could be grandmother or a grandfather to? We lived for many years in the Philippines when our children were younger, and I often gave thanks to God for the senior colleagues who chose to act as surrogate grandparents to our children, and who as such had a formative influence on them—largely through their capacity to bless and enjoy my sons.

To bless is simply to affirm the other, to take particular delight and joy in the other in a nonjudgmental or prescriptive manner. It is often evident in the joy that someone takes in being in the company of the other or in the gifts that are given—the gift of time, of opportunities and of skills passed on (e.g., when an older person takes a young person to the zoo, or an older man teaches a younger man how to repair an engine). But the time spent with the other and the skill passed on is grounded in joy in the one who is blessed, in giving freely without prescription. We must learn how to do this and resolve to be people who will bless others. We will not be a source of wisdom, heard and appreciated for our counsel, if we do not bless; for of the two roles of our senior years—sharing wisdom and blessing—wisdom follows blessing.

But I need to return to something I mentioned earlier in this chapter. I am convinced that part of the essence of vocational identity during this period of our lives is that we let go of power and control: people listen to us because we are wise and because we bless, not because of our office or any formal structure of power. This is why it is essential that we learn how to let go of power and resist the temptation to hang on to power as long as we can—however easy it is to justify the notion that we are needed. Winston Churchill was a great statesman of the twentieth century; unfortunately, he clung to power much longer than he should have or needed to for the sake of his country and the causes he had given his life for. He hung on to power when he should have risen above it, and there is little doubt that he would have had more positive influence on the events of his time if he had stayed out of office (ironically). He stands, then, as an enduring reminder to all of us of the critical need to let go of the formal structures of position, office and control, and allow our senior years to be those of blessing and wisdom—remembering that in a very particular sense we are not able to have lasting influence *unless* we let go.

Ironically, Mikhail Gorbachev might well represent the opposite of Winston Churchill. Richard Nixon said of Gorbachev: "He has decided that he would risk his power in order to save his reforms, rather than risk his reforms to save his power." As such he opened the floodgates of democratic freedoms in the Soviet block that eventually led to the end of the Cold War. Nixon's words remind me that many individuals lose their positive influence and their ability to make a difference *because* they hold on to the formal structures of power.

We can only let go of the traditional symbols of power if we have learned, through the course of our lives, that our worth and ultimately our influence come from the inside, from the quality of our inner lives rather than from the positions we hold or the symbols of power we have—such as a large desk, a corner office, the right kind of suit and the right kind of car. The difference we make is rooted in the quality of our lives and in our ability to grant wisdom and blessing rather than in any particular role or responsibility we might have—whether it is that of a pioneer missionary or a business executive.

I am not saying that if we have turned sixty-five we should no longer be in office. Not for a moment. Nelson Mandela assumed the presidency well after he was sixty-five, and it was an eminently appropriate thing for him to do. But I am saying that if we continue in roles of formal position or power, we hold these differently and we function differently. Nelson Mandela was the president, but his deputy actually ran the office of the president, and Mr. Mandela's role was in many respects that of father or grandfather to the new South Africa. Pope John XXIII assumed the office of leader of the Roman Catholic Church when he was an elderly man. He viewed his role as one of blessing the movements of renewal and change that were opening the gates of reform within that church. Yet for all of us the time will come to graciously let go, to allow others to exercise formal authority. And I am increasingly convinced that we will likely do this best when we practice along the way: letting go of control and formal authority over our children—let it go. I have been the senior pastor of two congregations; when I am invited back on a return visit, I do not come as critic but as one who must bless my successor. This applies to each of the positions I have held; we let go and move on. Again and again I see organizations struggle largely because of poor leadership transitions, when a former senior pastor muddies the water for a successor, or when the president of a not-for-profit sticks around in an "emeritus" role, that so frequently complicates the capacity of the successor to lead effectively. It is often the case that the best legacy we leave is to make a clean break, insist that we are not indispensable and in every respect bless the one who succeeds us (meaning, that we refuse to be a critic or judge of those who follow us.)

One more point before we wrap up this section on vocation and our senior years. Our health is more vulnerable as we get older, and we are not likely to be able to serve with generosity in our senior years unless we manage to sustain some measure of good health. This suggests that the older we get, the more crucial it is that we invest time in sustaining our physical well-being. We must be intentional and remain physically active: keep walking, keep limber, keep a diet, which is likely a matter of not only eating *better* but also eating *less* than when we were younger. (The point needs to be made to those who are younger as well: many seniors are not able to embrace generous work and fulfill their vocations because when they were younger, they did not sustain a pattern of fitness and good health.)

In summary, the essence of vocation and vocational transition for each of these phases is as follows:

- Young adults: take responsibility for your own life
- Midlife adults: accept yourself for who you are, for better or worse
- Senior adults: let go so that you can bless and offer wisdom

In each case the issue is fundamentally a spiritual one. As a young adult, will I choose to take responsibility for my life before God, to live as one who responds intentionally to the call of God? The crisis and choices of midlife are just as much a matter of the spiritual life. We will only come to a clear sense of vocation if we develop a deeper spiritual life, from which we can, with grace, accept our limitations but also embrace how God has gifted us. And the transition of the senior years, the transition of letting go, will only be possible if our identity is ultimately tied to God and not to our work and our position in the world.

VOCATION AS SOMETHING DYNAMIC

The main point of this chapter is that a vocation matures and develops. It evolves to a fuller level of maturity and expression; it changes focus in response to changes in our life circumstances as we mature, grow older and see ourselves and our world differently.

In the following chapters we explore the different factors that contribute to vocational integrity and vitality. It is helpful to realize that though these factors are important for all, we each wrestle with vocation differently, depending on where we are in our adult development. Further, as we consider the mix of strengths and abilities that we have, we will find that at different points in our lives the way we work may involve different combinations of strengths for different situations at times and in ways that only come to make sense in retrospect, ways that could never have been planned or even anticipated.

Here is where the realities of the new economy are actually something profoundly positive. For many if not most people, their full self-discovery will come when they are forced to let go of one role or place of work and respond to a new challenge or opportunity. The fact that change is unavoidable confirms again that we cannot be reduced to a particular role and that we will have to reinvent ourselves for new situations and a new challenges.

It is also helpful to see that we wrestle with fundamental matters of faith at each transition—whether as a young adult when we choose a faith of our own, to give purpose and direction to our lives; or in midlife when we are not all that we hoped we would be and can learn to trust God in the midst of the limitations we encounter in midlife; or in our senior years, when the only way we can let go is through a fundamental faith in God, who is bigger than our work, our careers and our ministries.

Moreover, we need to also stress that vocational discernment and development is not just about occupational choice, but about the whole of our lives and in the context of *each* dimension of our lives. We consider and reflect on occupational choices, possibilities or problems in the context of everything that we are—as fathers, mothers, church members, community residents and volunteers. This means that as I think about work or ministry or opportunities, I think about them in light of everything I am called to be and do as a

Christian believer, and I think about this call, this vocation, in the light of the immediate priorities and circumstances of my life. This means that regardless of what I might be in the long haul, for this chapter of my life I may need to embrace the opportunity to be a father or a mother, or respond to a current need because God is clearly putting it before me. Then I must trust God, with patience and humility, for the opportunities and responsibilities that might come down the road and that reflect more fundamentally who I am being called to be and what I am being called to do.

At each phase of our lives we need to ask two questions. First, what is the one thing that I must do *now?* What are my vocational priorities for this chapter of my life? We answer this in the light of our current life situation. It makes a profound difference, for example, if I am the father of four children, or if I recognize that I need to make a college education a priority, or if I need to go back to school as a midlife transition. That then becomes my vocational priority for this chapter of my life. For another person, the vocational priority might be a fifth-grade boys' Sunday school class, where that particular responsibility reflects a central part of who that person is and what he or she is called to be and do. In other words, the most important things we do may not be waged, whether it is service in our local church, in our community or in the service of some environmental cause.

It would be appropriate to make reference to volunteerism. For seniors but also for many in midlife who either do not need to be waged because a spouse provides adequate income or who are unwaged because they cannot find work, the challenge is to volunteer in a way that is both meaningful and makes a difference. There is, increasingly, a revived appreciation of the critical roles and contributions played by volunteers. Many essential social agencies depend on competent, committed volunteers to fulfill their agendas. And in fact all of us volunteer or at least should volunteer to do work that is meaningful and makes a difference. But even then we need to see this work as something we are called to do, not merely as busyness or activity for activity's sake.

Coming back to the dynamic character of vocation, it seems fair to say that for many if not most of us, a sense of call will come at *three* times in our lives. First, typically there is some sense of call that comes either before or during the transition into adulthood—and it will reflect faith commitments. It will probably be conceived fairly broadly—a call into business or medicine or engineering or the pastorate. For some it will be very precise—a definite sense of call to a particular avenue of work or a career or perhaps to the gospel ministry. The call is there for all, but not all recognize it.

Then as likely as not, another call will come in midlife that will represent a narrowing of perspective—a focus within the context of the bigger picture. For some, midlife may represent a completely new direction, but most of us come to know ourselves, our abilities and our desires well enough to know that we cannot do everything; now we have to choose in response to who we see God calling us to be. This in no way minimizes the first call, especially for those who had a very definite and specific sense of call in the first instance. Rather, this second call enables the first to be fulfilled and possibly gives it more focus. Naturally, it also reflects a more mature self-awareness.

Then there is the call that comes as we make the transition into our senior years—a call that is no less significant or momentous in our lives than the first two. This moment in our lives is significant in part because we are able to hear the voice of God without concern for the expectations of peers or of organizations, or the pressure of career or employment. We can genuinely step back and see how our lives thus far have been but a prelude.

But though there will be different chapters and three different calls, it is also important to see that there will be some theme or undercurrent that brings unity to who we are and who we are called to be. We may not see what unifies our lives until later in life as we begin to look where we have been and what we have done. But it is there, nonetheless, and each chapter will be but one expression of that underlying theme of our lives. Yet vocational development should not be construed as a single rising curve, as so much misconceived careerism is viewed. We are not climbing ladders; we are not doing things in order to make our resumé more impressive. Rather, we are working out the story of our lives, and this will include both setbacks and failure as well as surprises and opportunities we could never have foreseen. We will embrace the opportunities that come today, often with little idea of the implications down the road. We are not building careers; we are responding, at this time and in this place, to a call—to a sense of vocation that is congruent with who we are and that ultimately comes from God. And so a homemaker may become the president of the Philippine Islands, as was the case for Cory Aquino, but just as easily, the president of a university may choose to step aside and become a writer. When we think in terms of vocation and reject careerism, we can accept with grace that God will call us in ways that would confound those who only think in terms of "getting ahead."

I need to make an important point here. Very frequently the whole question of vocation is an inordinate and inappropriate burden. We often face young people with the question What are you going to do with your life, with the expectation that they should know and should get on with that life. But it is oppressive and an unnecessary burden.

Young adults are only responsible for the present, not for the *whole* of their lives. Further, they are wise if they keep their options open and do not make assumptions prematurely about their future, about what they are likely to do as the focus of their lives. We can embrace the present with a full awareness that in the future we will probably be surprised by what comes our way.

Further, as is implicit in my previous comments, we must live and work within the context of both the limitations and opportunities that are current and real in our lives. I am convinced that in principle we should be able to fulfill our vocations anywhere: even if we are confined to a concentration camp. We simply need to ask, What needs to be done here? What are the strengths and passions that I could bring to *this* situation and *this* opportunity, in the light of what needs to happen and in terms of the opportunities before me.

Many people bemoan that they do not have the opportunities they think they either deserve or that they view as essential to fulfill their vocations. But humility and thankfulness require that we ask what needs to be done. Perhaps there is a spouse who needs my attention; perhaps I am mother to a child sick at home this week; or even if a child is handicapped for life, I may conclude that my call is to care for that child, for a day or perhaps much longer. I may be confined to a hospital bed, perhaps for weeks. But I can still ask, within this limitation, what are my opportunities? More specifically, what is God calling me to do here, at this time, in this place, in a way that I can be a means of life and grace to others?

Further, this means that I must be open to surprises as well as opportunities. We fulfill our vocations in community, and we will have different contributions to make in different communities and perhaps in different ways at different times. In one setting I may well draw on my gifts as an administrator, but elsewhere it may be clear that others are doing the administration ably and my calling in that instance is both to encourage them and to perform another role. This is why it is important and critical that we *not* allow ourselves or others to be reductionistic in the perception of our calling—reducing us to or defining us by a particular role or responsibility.

Perhaps you are an Old Testament professor now, and it is very possible that that is what you will be for the whole of your active career. But who knows? God is calling you to teach Old Testament now, but there is no need to make undue assumptions about the future. I grieve at the number of missionaries convinced that their call to be a missionary was "for life" and find that they are incapable, it seems, of rethinking their identity and their call. They have been reduced to a particular role or career. But the same could be said of anyone who defines her or his identity solely in terms of a particular role. It was a wise old academic dean who at his retirement gave a talk to younger deans and concluded his counsel by saying they should never let others define them solely in terms of their role as a dean. They are, said the older dean, always more than a dean. This is so crucial, of course, when it came time to let go of my role as a dean.

This is why I hesitate when confronted with tests or questionnaires that seek to enable individuals to determine their gifts, in a vacuum, in isolation from a particular situation or set of circumstances. We should always respond by saying, "Well, it depends." A good case could be made that the so-called gifts of the Spirit are given to the church, to the community of faith, not to individuals, per se. Then we can work with the assumption that each community has the gifts it needs to flourish. The question then is, What gift or strength am I being called of God to do in this place at this time?

Second, we need to ask what we are required to do to keep alive, especially through learning but also through friendships, leisure and recreation that both prepare us for what the next chapter in our lives might be and enable us to grow in both wisdom and joy.

Third, remember this: each transition will involve some kind of loss. Growth will always be costly; a new venture will always involve some form of letting go. It may be a matter of separation—from parents or from those who are part of an old way or an old world. It may involve leaving behind the comfortable and the secure. Each transition will be a small death, and the new life, the new opportunity and the new challenge will only come as we let go.

In all of this I must stress something repeatedly: vocation and career are not the same. It *may* be that they coincide. But for many that will not be the case. Remember then that at each phase of our lives we need to ask, Who am I and what, fundamentally, am I called to be and do. What is my purpose, my reason for being? Second, we must ask what we are being called to do *now*—in the immediate. What is the current duty, responsibility or job that God is placing before us? And how can we fulfill that current responsibility in the light of who we are? The current responsibility or job may be quite mundane—caring for children or getting a job to pay the rent. Or it may be that for now we are called to study. But it is God's call for the moment, for the time being. And we accept this as from the hand of God. But we

see it in light of the complete picture of who we are and who we are
called to be.

THE HEART OF THE MATTER

The heart of the matter, in the end, is found in the answer to a simple
question: How is God calling me to serve him at this time and in this
place? In chapter two I identified questions that might enable us to
think critically about ourselves—to know ourselves better and have
a more nuanced appreciation of how God is likely calling us. But in
the end it is something that arises from our hearts. A vocation cannot, in the end, be discerned by answering questionnaires or filling
out forms. Somewhere, mysteriously in the depths of our heart, God
is calling each one to make a difference. And these questions are only
meant as pointers along the way.

But the questions I raised can only help us make sense of our own
stories; for in some sense what I am called to do next flows out of my
personal narrative thus far. As I consider the next chapter of my life,
I do so in light of my story thus far. And I answer these kinds of questions in light of that story and use those same questions to make
sense of the narrative of my life—to know more fully who I am and
who God is calling me to be.

Further, in discerning vocation, we always do so in light of the
actual life circumstances that are before us. It is not likely that a rural
peasant girl from Ecuador is being called to become a NASA astro-
naut. It is possible, certainly, but not likely. This is not to underestimate the possibilities of God's grace but merely affirms that God
works in a real world and enables us to make a difference in the midst
of our actual life circumstances. In light of my story thus far and the
actual circumstances of my life, how I am being called to bring glory
to the Creator and serve the world in love for Christ and for others.

AS UNTO THE LORD

The Pursuit of Excellence, Truth,
Diligence and Generosity

We long for work that is meaningful, joyful and significant. We long to know that the work of our hands and the work we do with our minds and through speaking is good, that in word and deed we are doing something that is fundamentally positive and worthwhile. Thomas Merton ably describes the lack of true and good work, when work loses its vitality:

> Unnatural, frantic, anxious work, work done under pressure of greed or fear or any other inordinate passion, cannot properly speaking be dedicated to God, because God never wills such work directly. He may permit that, through no fault of our own, we may have to work madly and distractedly, due to our sins, and to the sins of the society in which we live. In that case we must tolerate it and make the best of what we cannot avoid. But let us not be blind to the distinction between sound, healthy work and unnatural toil.[1]

Merton's statement reminds us that we long for two things: (1) work that is meaningful and rewarding, work that we enjoy and where we feel we are doing something significant and valuable. We long to know that we are making a difference.

But further, we long to know (2) that our work brings pleasure to God and has his blessing. That is, there is within us the desire for our own sake to have work that is meaningful and rewarding, but we also want that work to be something that is done for God.

Two texts of Holy Scripture capture this in phrases that are worth keeping in mind. The first comes from Ecclesiastes 2:24, which speaks of finding enjoyment or satisfaction in our work, for this work "is from the hand of God." God gives us work, as a gift, and we find joy and satisfaction in that work.

The second reference is in Colossians: "Whatever your task, put yourselves into it, as done for the Lord and not for your masters" (Col 3:23; see also Eph 6:5-8). While St. Paul is speaking of those who were slaves, the principle would be applicable to all regardless of the work they are called to.

The fundamental features of vocational integrity are simple. They are captured in the two principles outlined in chapter two: *know yourself,* and *be true to who you are.* But there is more that fleshes out what it means to have integrity in our activity in the world—our work, our career and our vocation. And this "more" enables us to work with joy and satisfaction.

For this, we first need to know that what we are doing comes from God; we take joy and pleasure in our work or responsibilities because they are given to us by God. Whether it is the task of raising children, running a business, providing pastoral leadership for a church or teaching a class, it is from the hand of God, a gift to us. Second, we need to have a sense that what we are doing is "done for the Lord." It is something we do with a Godward orientation, something we offer back to God. In other words, our work is both given to us by God and is offered back to God.

It has been my impression for some time that three of Paul's epistles essentially are calls for vocational integrity: 1 Timothy, 2 Timothy and Titus. This is particularly the case with 2 Timothy. We can easily read this letter and imagine the elder apostle who writes to Timothy and issues a call for this man to fulfill his call and to do so with diligence, focus and courage. While Timothy's was a specifically religious vocation, it is not difficult to extrapolate from Paul's words and identify the qualities and characteristics that have immediate application to all, regardless of call or vocation. We find described here what it means to do our work with joy and satisfaction, because we do it as something we have *from* the hand of God and that we do as *unto* the Lord.

Four qualities are stressed and emphasized—each of which is clearly something that the apostle Paul views as essential if Timothy and others are to have vocational integrity. These are captured effectively in four words: *excellence, truth, diligence* and *generosity*. Each of these is an antidote to what Merton calls "unnatural toil." I will identify these and then add a fifth, which stands alone, provides the context and enables us to do work with these qualities: the practice of sabbath.

Sabbath represents a crucial way of being, critical for a simple reason: each of four first listed—excellence, truth, diligence and generosity—can be embraced and pursued "to a fault." The pursuit of excellence can become perfectionism, the pursuit of truth bigotry, diligence nothing more than hectic activity and even generosity can be misguided. What we must call one another to is the pursuit of these qualities in a life-giving manner rather than "to a fault," which is deadly and not good work at all. This fifth element, sabbath rest, makes the other four ways of doing our work truly grace-filled.

EXCELLENCE

First, the apostle says to Timothy: "Do your best to present yourself to God as one approved by him, a worker who has no need to be ashamed, rightly explaining the word of truth" (2 Tim 2:15). Paul here is reaffirming a vital principle of the spiritual life: we are given gifts and capacities, and to be true to ourselves we must exercise them to the *best* of our ability.

The Bible assumes a fundamental commitment to excellence. But there is an important element to this biblical assumption that must not be overlooked: excellence is ultimately judged by whether we did *our* best. If we have ten talents, we are judged differently than a person with four. We are judged according to our distinctive circumstances, opportunities, education and ability.

Excellence is found in fulfilling our vocation in the service of truth to the very best of *our* ability, with a continued commitment to serve God as well as *you* are able.

Implicit in this call to excellence is the assumption, of course, that we owe it to ourselves and to God to do our best. But there is surely the assumption as well that if a job is worth doing, it is worth doing well, and that if we really care for others and desire to serve them, we will do our best.

But the point of reference for what is excellent continues to be and must be *our* best. We are not judged by some arbitrary or contrived standard; we are judged simply by whether we did our best. Having said this, within each discipline or craft or occupation, there is a distinct sense of what is good and what is minimally adequate. When my teeth are being repaired, I relax in the dental chair because I know that a master is hovering over me and is diligently at work on my molars. And I will accept nothing less than the very best work; they are my teeth, after all. And if my dentist calmly informs me that she has bungled things, but that she has been sincere while doing it, sincerity would count for nothing if she was liable for malpractice.

But within minimal standards of what is good within each craft or occupation, we are each ultimately accountable for doing our work to the very best of our abilities, and we should not be satisfied with anything less than our best.

Our only hope for excellence, over the long haul, is that we capture something that the apostle Paul speaks of in 2 Timothy 2, that we do our work "as unto the Lord," rather than for human masters or employers. In other words, our criteria for excellence is whether we can confidently tell God that we have done our best. Because in the end it is only God who knows if it was. Some people have a remarkable ability to "wing it," whether in academic work, in selling a product or in public speaking. And because of their facility they are not pressed to prepare carefully or do background research. Inevitably, though, it all catches up with them; the quality of their work begins to fade, and the initial aura of excellence is lost.

In the end only you and God know if you did your best. And if we do our work "as unto the Lord," then we will do our best regardless of what others say or think. I do not know what good dental work looks like. I just want pain-free chewing! But I delight in knowing that my dentist takes pride in her work quite apart from whether I ever appreciate the care she has taken in the craft.

There is something that needs affirmation in the quest for excellence. It is the essential principle that excellence comes slowly and incrementally; it is learned through rehearsal and practice and more practice. Great singers were not born great singers; gifted hockey players did not come out of the womb stick and puck in hand. Rather, they practiced and practiced and practiced. Sidney Crosby's journey to become captain of the Pittsburgh Penguins hockey team has become legendary: the thousands of pucks he fired at the dryer in his parents' basement. Talent without practice is worth little.

You can always keep this principle in mind: if excellence comes slowly and incrementally, through practice, then resolve that you will get better, each time around, at what you do moderately well. If you are a moderately gifted preacher or administrator or writer, resolve not that you will be a great preacher, administrator or writer tomorrow, but rather that tomorrow you will be better at your craft, if only marginally so, than you are today. Over time you will become a master of the craft.

What is implied in all of this is that talent means nothing in and of itself. A capacity or ability must be honed, disciplined and nurtured. Our skills need to be honed. And this takes time, commitment and discipline. Practice. This is the same for all, whether they are good writers, surgeons, counselors or public speakers.

But each of the four qualities can be embraced "to a fault." We must distinguish between the love and pursuit of excellence and perfectionism. Perfectionism is a misguided pursuit of excellence. A genuine love of excellence is rooted in a conviction that God deserves our best and that other people deserve nothing less. But the perfectionist is self-centered: excellence has become an end in itself. Perfectionists are always dissatisfied—with themselves and with others. Their work is never a joy because it is never good enough. *They* are never good enough. Rather than delighting in work well done for the sake of others, they are consumed with themselves and their own performance. Rather than working joyfully with others, they are demanding and uncompromising, incapable of accepting the miscues of others.

The genuine love of excellence is rooted in a desire to serve well. Further, because it comes from the hand of God, we therefore offer it back to God as our act of thankful worship.

TRUTH

Good and rewarding work, work that is done "as unto the Lord," is offered in the service of truth.

When the apostle Paul writes to Timothy, he calls him to a ministry of truth—in word and deed—that for him particularly comes through in his call to preach and teach. In the same verse where Paul urges Timothy to "do his best," he adds another qualifier—it is his best in the service of truth; he is to do his best at the noble task of "explaining the word of truth" (2 Tim 2:15).

Timothy was called to be a teacher and preacher of truth. The apostle Paul speaks to this when speaking of his own calling. He insisted that he was not a "peddler" of God's Word (2 Cor 2:17). He notes that "we refuse to practice cunning or to falsify God's word; but with an open statement of truth we commend ourselves to the conscience of everyone in the sight of God" (2 Cor 4:2).

The same principle applies to all who make their living through speaking, whether they are teachers, politicians or counselors. If we are nothing more than peddlers, speaking in a manner that is self-serving rather than truth-serving, we clearly violate something at the heart of who we are called to be.

But this is not unique to those who are called to speak. All authentic vocations are focused on truth. My wife is an artist: she has vocational integrity only if she is truth-full. The same applies to a novelist, a businessperson, an individual in advertising, law or medicine. That is, we can be true to ourselves perhaps, but then use our vocation for selfish ends or at the service of that which is false. For a lawyer to violate the trust of her profession and to seek or defend that which is patently false, or for a businessperson to sell a product he knows is faulty, is to violate what it means to do our work with integrity. Further, it turns work on its head and makes it self-serving rather than in the service of others. Integrity requires a fundamental honesty with our customers or clients, our employees and our stockholders.

A carpenter who works with wood and a landscaper who designs the spaces around our buildings are both working with God-given materials, and they have the opportunity to work with integrity, in the service of the truth, or to do shoddy, artificial and contrived work.

Vocational integrity is only found with a focus on and service to truth, and this arises, of course, from a fundamental loyalty *to* truth. But here also we must raise a warning. It might be hard to conceive of someone serving truth in an excessive way—that is, "to a fault." But consider this: Is there not something wrong with the fundamentalist whose supposed commitment to truth negates all other perspectives or points of view? And when I speak of a fundamentalist, I have the religious bigot in mind as much as the politician or the nationalist. Something is askew when our passion for truth blinds us to other perspectives and to the grace to be able to differ graciously with others and learn from others who may see things very differently than we do.

Someone gets locked on a principle or a conviction which represents one dimension of the truth, and they become crusaders for that perspective and for that conviction which may in itself be true, but which becomes deadly in the hand of a zealot. Genuine love of truth is always complemented by humility evident in a gracious, teachable spirit. Beware particularly of those who, as the apostle Paul puts it, get caught up in argumentation and debate, consumed with "wrangling over words, which does no good" (2 Tim 2:14). Paul calls Timothy to the service of truth, but he also urges him to avoid the quarrelsome, and to do his work with gentleness, kindness and patience (2 Tim 2:23-25).

There is yet another way in which truth intersects vocation. We are only truthful in our vocations if we are true to our word. People of integrity do what they say they will do and live in a manner consistent with their professed values. This includes not only the preacher who calls us to walk in the light, it includes the teacher, whose life and actions speak more loudly than the content of the lecture, the politician whose commitment to fundamental values ultimately determine the quality of the leadership provided, and the engineer who understands and works with the integrity of a material and its capacity to do what it has been designed to do.

DILIGENCE

The theme of diligence comes through often in the apostle Paul's letters to Timothy and Titus, but especially at the high point of his second letter to Timothy, where he urges Timothy to proclaim the message and to be *persistent* in this task (2 Tim 4:2).

Diligence involves persistence. Timothy is urged to persevere in his work "whether the time is favorable or unfavorable . . . with the utmost patience" (2 Tim 4:2). In other words it involves doing our work with a care and commitment that does not waver depending on the level of affirmation we are getting on that particular day. We do what we do because it needs to be done.

But more, diligence also involves what Paul speaks of later in that same chapter when he calls Timothy to "carry out your ministry fully" (v. 5). Diligence includes *thoroughness*. Which means there is no substitute for hard work. There is no easy task—easy in itself. For an athlete to compete well, hard work is involved, regardless of how gifted or talented that athlete happens to be. And much of that hard work happens behind the scenes, in rigorous fitness programs that continue day in and day out, far from the eyes of sports fans.

Musicians can only become accomplished at their task if they practice with thoroughness and persistence, which provides little reward or affirmation. But the same principle applies to all of us. Those in administration know that a great deal of the work that needs to be done just has to be done—whether anyone notices or particularly cares. Attention to detail must be a personal commitment or it is not a commitment at all. Learn to enjoy the satisfaction of a job done well. Learn to enjoy your work so that there is a sense of satisfaction in the quality of the work itself rather than in the gratitude or approval of others.

In this there is no easy way. Watch for the patterns of corner cutting. I am not suggesting that we love details for the sake of details, rather we need commitment to persist and to do our work completely—with care and *diligence*.

But do not confuse diligence and hard work with hectic activity or overwork. Many people are consumed by work and by all the things they think need to be done. Like the perfectionist, they are never satisfied; as Thomas Merton puts it, their work is "frantic, anxious work." The antidote to laziness is not hectic activity. The irony is that when we are consumed by hectic activity, we are essentially doing our work and that of others, which means that we are not doing our work well, with care, diligence and grace.

In saying this I fully acknowledge that there will be seasons of our life and work when we feel and live under the tyranny of the moment—an athlete preparing for a big event, a professor at the end of term pressing to complete all of the grading or a businessperson who stays late in order to have the shop ready for a special promotion the next day. When we come to live habitually in this way we know something is skewed; our lives and work reflect empty busyness, not true diligence.

GENEROSITY

Our work and the fulfillment of our vocation has integrity when we do what we do with *generosity*. In 2 Corinthians Paul reminds his readers that by virtue of the work of Christ we no longer consider others in purely human categories; rather, we see them as new creations (5:17). We see them with hope and potential; we see each other and every human being as having incomparable worth and significance.

This, for St. Paul, lies behind his insistence that we live for others, in generous service.

It is helpful to distinguish between *generous* service and *calculated* service. Calculated service "counts" the cost and considers the return. Generous service is given freely—as one for the sake of another. It is not given even for the thanks that we might receive; it is given freely and with generosity. Simone Weil says of *true* service that it "is as instinctive and immediate as it is for oneself to eat when one is hungry," and, she adds, "it is forgotten almost at once, just as one forgets yesterday's meals."[2]

The reason for this lies in the basic assumption that in actual fact our service is *for another*. We serve Christ in response to his love, and we serve in his name. We can give freely within our families, to our friends, within the context of congregational life and in the world. Indeed, it is probably critical that we see our work, whatever form it takes, as something that we do for God and not for others. And though we may be paid for our work, in payment that is necessary for us to meet our financial needs, our service does not need to be calculated. I may get paid to teach in the public school, but why should I not see myself as being there in the name of Christ to serve the children in my classroom and to serve with generosity with my colleagues? Beware the subtle temptations to calculate service given. Generous service is not rendered in order to procure a secondary or indirect result, to win a following or to gain the cooperation or loyalty of another.

Further, it is also important to stress that generous service empowers those we serve. False forms of service create dependency; true service, given in love, enables another to grow, mature, stand alone and eventually give, as we serve one another in mutual interdependence. Which means that in true service there is always giving and receiving. A hospital nurse may recognize that he or she is also the recipient when serving a patient, and remains open to the subtle and joyous ways in which patients can give in return. And by this I do not mean that we serve for the thanks and recognition we will receive, but rather that we also need the other, the very one we serve. Pastors can consciously live in the recognition that they are served by their parishioners, again, not as contributors to their projects but rather as those who both give and receive in mutual interdependence.

An important and necessary qualifier needs to be added here. Just as God has not gifted us to do everything, even so we are not called to be or do everything for everyone who comes our way. It is Parker Palmer, I believe, who once noted that though God loves everyone, I am not called to be the means by which everyone knows and experiences this.

We do not have supernatural strength or stamina; we are limited beings. And moreover, we have priorities. There are times when generosity toward others undercuts my capacity to be genuinely present and generous with my wife, my sons and my grandchildren. It is simply not possible to be generous at all times and in all places with all people; we have limited time and energy.

Those who try to be all things to all people, those who sacrifice fundamental relationships, such as with spouse and children, because they are consumed with their work in the world, are perhaps generous, but this is a misguided generosity. It is so easy for some to fall into the trap where they are very solicitous toward others but neglect their own family. What is usually the case is that someone is seeking to be more than God is calling him or her to be, and doing more than God is calling him or her to do. Often what drives such individuals is a longing to be affirmed and appreciated. Their work, in other words, is not tied directly to their call. For God would not call us to do more than could be done within the whole context of our lives and our relationships.

Whenever we are consumed with work, busy with hectic activity, it is imperative that we back away and prayerfully discern our calling—to clarify what God is calling us to be and do—with generosity—in this place and at this time. We cannot fulfill our vocations well if we are physically and emotionally drained, or if we are impatient, tired and frustrated with people. Part of true service is learning the simple art of saying no, of recognizing our priorities and our limitations.

SABBATH

Excellence, truth, diligence and generosity. These are the qualities that make our work enjoyable and satisfying, as something that we have received from the hand of God. They are also the indicators that we are resolved to do our work "as unto the Lord."

But each can be life and each can be death. When any of these qualities is pursued as an end in itself, it has a shadow side that makes work hell. The pursuit of excellence becomes the burden of perfectionism, a burden to you and to those with whom you work. The pursuit of truth becomes bigotry—a misguided zeal for one dimension of truth. The pursuit of diligence can become nothing more than hectic activity which leaves a person overworked and exhausted, not a servant to others but a burden to self and others. And a misguided generosity leaves us overcommitted, eager to give but without a sense of purpose and focus to that giving, without reasonable constraints.

Consequently we must ask what can enable us to pursue each of these qualities as life-giving objectives? What can keep us from the shadow side of each?

Our only hope is to keep a balance, which comes with sustaining whole, integrated lives. To be people of work and leisure, persons of prayer and work, men and women who are called to both worship and service.

Remember that our work is never the whole of who we are; it comes with the assumption that we can never be defined purely as a "worker." We are persons who have work to do, but we are always more than workers. Our work is never the sum total of who we are, and even though our work is important to us, it may often be the case that it is not the most important thing about us.

And we must sustain a clear sense of the relational dimension of our lives—that we are spouses, parents, friends, who live and love as members of communities.

All of this is only possible with a clearly defined pattern of *sabbath* renewal in our lives. For the ancient Hebrew people the sabbath was observed with great care as a day of rest. This day gave perspective to the whole of their lives, particularly to their work. It was a weekly reminder that their ultimate identity was not wrapped up in their work, but that they belonged to God.

Through sabbath observance the Hebrew people affirmed that their livelihood was the *means* by which the Lord provided for basic human needs, yet it sustained the perspective that ultimately the Lord provides. The sabbath also provided them with a necessary rest—a re-creation, an enjoyment of God's creation and of one another.

By regular sabbath rest I am freed from seeing my work as a burden; it is ultimately God's work that is entrusted to me for six days a week, but I am not responsible nor need I feel the burden of carrying this work seven days a week.

The sabbath gives perspective.

In our urbanized world, where medical staff, pastors, police officers and many others need to work on Sunday, it is imperative to recognize that the principle of sabbath rest applies to all whether or not the same day of the week is observed. Further, sabbath rest is not so much a "day off" as a day when we rest from our work and re-create—in worship, leisure, prayer and fellowship—all with a view toward delighting in God, his creation and others, particularly family and friends. We should not even call it a "day off," for this does nothing more than define our sabbath rest negatively in terms of the absence of work. But the sabbath rest is meaningful in its own right, as something we are called to along side of work and which we enjoy because we love God and others.

I would also note that *each* day can and perhaps should include *sabbath*, times of quiet, perhaps in the early morning, or for others at midday when they step out of the office and find a quiet church sanctuary for a few minutes of silence and meditation.

But each of these acts—whether one day in seven, or a few minutes of silence in the day—are ways by which we step back from and find perspective for our work.

FOUR PRACTICES THAT GIVE INTEGRITY TO OUR VOCATIONS

We do our work with excellence and a commitment to truth, diligence and generosity, and we do so with a resolve to set our work aside one day in seven for sabbath rest. In all of this we are sustaining a commitment, of course: that it is not merely *our* work but work that is given to us by God and which we offer back to God, as stewards of our lives. And yet there is always a tension: so easily our work becomes our work and no more, without a sense that this is truly from God and offered to God. And here is where I have found it helpful to consider four practices that the church has always affirmed as somehow a necessary complement to the work we are called to:

- generous hospitality

- advocacy and care for the poor

- generous giving of our means

- intercessory prayer

These are spiritual practices or disciplines, means of grace to us that foster our capacity to be aligned, in word and deed, with Christ's purposes in the world. We want our work to be aligned with what Christ is doing, and could it be that in these four practices we are forced to attend to Christ himself and be present to how Christ has specifically said that he is present in the world? We do this not merely by spiritual practices of disengagement but also by practices that engage us with the world that is, as God grants us grace, aligned with what Christ is doing in the world.

By hospitality I mean hospitality to children, as Jesus welcome children, to the foreigner, alien and immigrant—hospitality as an act of welcoming Christ into our lives, our homes and our communities. The author of the letter to the Hebrews puts it this way: "Do not neglect to show hospitality to strangers, for by doing that some have entertained angels without knowing it" (Heb 13:2). And the text continues with a call to visit those in prison, suggesting that we take hospitality to those who cannot come to us.

Care for the poor is a commitment we share in recognition that when we feed the hungry, clothe the naked and visit those who are in prison we are, in some sense, visiting Christ.

In our giving, the generous sharing of our material possessions and our financial resources, we are, in a sense, giving to Christ himself and to the work of Christ in the world.

Finally, in our intercessory prayers we are affirming yet again that Christ is the one who brings about the fulfillment of his reign, in his timing.

The point I am trying to make is that regardless of our callings, the specific work to which we are called, we can never say that we do not have time, that our work is too important or that our callings are so all-consuming, that we have no time to offer hospitality along the way, care for the poor, generously share our material resources and, finally, give time to intercessory prayer

It is important to stress that with all four we might be distracted from our callings because of a misguided generosity. We read, for example, that in the early church those called to the ministry of the Word and prayer were enjoined not to neglect this calling by waiting on tables (see Acts 6:1-4). I have often wondered whether God is sometimes calling those who are devoted to intercessory prayer to get off their knees and start being the very means by which God is fulfilling the prayer of their hearts.

We also note that though Jesus is so clear about his own calling to teach (Mk 1:35-38), as he heads off to other villages to fulfill his calling he stops along the way and responds with compassion to someone who asks to be healed. God gives us work to do that is other than the work represented by these practices. Yet, could it indeed be the case that all of us are called, along the way, to be people of hospitality, service, generosity and prayer—that my work, for example, as father, academic administrator and teacher only has authenticity, is only truly "as unto the Lord," when the work as father is complemented by prayer for my sons and their children, if my work as an administrator is complemented by regular prayers for those whom I serve, and if my work as a teacher includes intercessory prayer for my students. Could it then also be that if I do not have time for these four spiritual practices (or at least feel that I do not have the time) it is likely because I am doing more than what I am called to?

Consider each of these four with me. Hospitality is only genuine if it is offered with no strings attached. In other words, it is not to be confused with the salesperson who is making a commission or the fundraiser who makes "friends" so that a contribution follows, or even the church that is in the midst of a membership drive. We must be alert to self-serving forms of hospitality. When we show hospitality it is about being alert to how we can listen to the other—listening precedes speaking—and where we are being called to share a meal with the other.

It is also clear from the words of Jesus that we can never say we do not have time for the poor. The profound call of Matthew 25:35-36 and the following verses rings across the centuries to the church in every generation: I was hungry, I was naked, I was sick, I was in prison, and you fed me, clothed me, took care of me and visited me. Could we say the same here: that our vocations, regardless of their focus, only have integrity if along the way we are advocates for and servants to the poor.

We also need to speak to the spiritual practice of giving—the intentional sharing of material resources—in much the same vein: a practice that gives integrity to our vocations regardless of the focus of our work. We see the example of the early church (Acts 2:44-45) that clearly viewed the sharing of resources, notably with those who were in need, as an essential part of their corporate vocation as the church. But this theme comes through most strongly in the writings of the apostle Paul, who emphasizes the importance of sharing our material resources and any wealth we have been given. He gives this particular prominence in 2 Corinthians. At the conclusion of 1 Corinthians he suggests that on the first day of the week (Sunday) we make it a regular practice to contribute from the "extra" that we have earned. But in 2 Corinthians 8–9 he provides the spiritual rationale and focus for giving, and speaks of it as a vital practice of the Christian life, a source of blessing but also of alignment with the purposes of God in the world, suggesting that a key benefit of our giving will be that no one will have too much and no one will have too little (2 Cor 8:15).

In the next chapter, chapter six, I will make the observation that money can be a threat to our vocations and distract us from our calling, regardless of our vocation. And thus the practice of giving can keep us from viewing our vocations as a means of accumulating wealth. Perhaps, when we earn more, the real benefit is that we have more to give away.

Finally, a similar principle applies when it comes to our intercessory prayers. The church is a community of intercession for the world; a congregation is a praying community; it prays for the needs of the community, local and global, not merely for that particular church's involvement in the world, but for the world. We pray as a vital means of service, both as a faith community and as individuals. Intercession is the necessary element of and complement to the more public work we are called to. And many—whether a quilt maker, an office worker or a ticket agent—pray for others and for the world as we work.

It is best that hospitality, works of mercy, giving and intercessory prayer are done quietly, if not in secret; consider the wisdom of anonymous giving, prayers quietly offered and works of mercy that do not draw attention to the giver. Indeed, Jesus suggests in Matthew 6:4-6 that our prayers and our giving should be done in secret.

Each of these four might also be a vocation for someone, a central, defining way by which they are called to be in the world: the innkeeper or the orphanage director who is called to show hospitality to children with no homes, the relief and development worker who daily is caring for refugees, the foundation director whose work is to give away inherited wealth, or the person called to quiet isolation and a day filled with intercessory prayer. But for most of us, one of these will be not so much our vocation as a vital way by which we foster our capacity to be in but not of the world, to be in the world and fulfill our vocations with grace, integrity and generosity.

CONCLUSION

In light of the challenges and opportunities that Timothy faced, the apostle Paul was not asking him to be a hero, a miracle worker, but merely that he remain true to his vocation.

The same applies to us. We may see the tremendous needs of our world and be tempted to be heroes, charging off to save the world. But we are called back to vocational clarity and commitment, to fulfilling what we have been called to do in the service of truth.

At times our vocation is undermined because of pride. We are unwilling to accept what God has given us because we are not prepared to accept some aspect of our calling—it may appear to lack the prestige, the status or perhaps the remuneration we believe we deserve or want. We are always looking ahead—doing what we do so that we are noticed, so that we will be promoted, so that we obtain another job, perhaps. And the consequence is that we are consumed with ourselves. Whatever the reason, if we are not true to ourselves, we are living a lie. The longer we live the lie, the sooner it will be that we are nothing more than hollow men and women.

Our only hope is to intentionally embrace the call of God. This is joy, and it will sustain us and give life to those with whom we live and work. There is great joy in knowing what God has called us to be and do, and to act with courage and humility in response to a needy world. Joy is found in giving ourselves fully—eagerly and passionately—to this call.

For this to happen, though, we must learn to *think* vocationally, to which we will now turn.

THINKING

VOCATIONALLY

Wisdom for the Road

We tend to easily get caught between two extremes; we see these extremes in ourselves, and we are aware of it when we converse with others.

Rather than living full lives, some have lives filled with daily routines of busyness and hectic activity. Their days are consumed with running from one thing to another, and they have lost the capacity to live with serenity. They are exhausted and, as often as not, confused. They are sincere in their desire to serve and to do good work, but their generosity has left them overextended. The danger is that they are little more than busybodies.

For many, hectic activity provides a kind of perpetual adrenalin rush. Often those consumed by busyness feel as though this pattern of life and work legitimizes them. They feel important; they feel needed; they feel alive. However, they have a false sense of life and importance, and eventually it leaves them feeling hollow.

It is evident to them that their active lives have no meaningful boundary. They have lost a sense of when it is right to say no to an invitation or expectation. So they live on a superficial plane, making the best of life but doing things with mediocrity, never getting to the bottom of the pile on their desk.

Then, often in dramatic contrast, others basically putter around. They are not busy and their lives are certainly not hectic; rather, they just go through the motions with little if any sense of purpose and focus. They are no longer genuinely engaged with life and work. In some cases they are overwhelmed by the needs around them and do not know where to begin. In other cases either sloth or loss of passion have overtaken them; they are apathetic and have lost a desire for work; there is little joy in their work. Some have moved into retirement and because of a pension or inheritance they do not need to work. Others are part of a company with secure employment, so they show up and do the minimum required of them. I have seen this in major industries and in local churches; no one is going to push for their release, and their minimalism gets them by.

In both cases the effects are contagious. Hectic people on the one side and putterers or minimalists on the other. When the other person is either overly engaged or disengaged, it affects our own personal capacity to be truly engaged with the work we are called to.

It seems to me that for all of us, the best response to our circumstances is to ask vocational questions: What is my calling? What is the work I need to take up? What is my divine necessity? But when we ask these kinds of questions, we do so because of a unique way of viewing our lives and the world. We might speak of it as a disposition, a set of lenses, a way of thinking. In this chapter I will speak to this way of thinking—of our need to cultivate a theological vision of life and work, and to then approach our lives and our days with this vision.

THE BENEFITS OF THINKING VOCATIONALLY

The advantages of thinking vocationally are many. But each is really just another way of saying that we are freed from the burden of pretense, freed to be who we are truly called to be. This freedom is ultimately expressed in joy. It is helpful to enumerate the benefits and show how they lead to freedom and joy—the freedom and joy of people who know who they are called to be and have the courage and capacity to embrace that vocation.

Freed from comparing ourselves to others. To think vocationally means that we make a self-appraisal. We look at ourselves; we identity, accept and embrace who we are called to be. This focus on ourselves frees us from comparing ourselves to others. And this liberates. When we refuse to compare ourselves to others, when we reject envy and jealousy of others' gifts and abilities and opportunities, we are freed to be who *we* are. This means, of course, that the giftedness of another person is not a threat to us. As James Fowler writes, "In vocation we are augmented by others' talents rather than being diminished or threatened by them."[1]

Comparing ourselves to others is a real problem in this era of massive television exposure. The television elevates the gifts of some, making them "stars" whose influence, glamour and style can easily discourage we who will never be stars. *Why should I teach an adult Bible study class,* someone might wonder, *when everyone has the option of watching and listening to a famous teacher on video?* The pressure makes some think that since they cannot be stars they might as well not be anything.

But a true sense of vocation is rooted in the reality that there is something we must do. Think of your vocation as something you *must* do—even if it means you will never be famous. You are faithful to *your* vocation, ultimately, because you resolve to be true to *yourself,* for only then can you be true to your God.

If we are freed from comparisons, we are also freed from competition. We can reject the notion that to fulfill our vocation we must get ahead of others or fear that their development or success will limit us. We can genuinely celebrate the accomplishments of others without fear that this somehow diminishes us. We can actively seek the grace of not being threatened by the gifts, talents and abilities of others, or resent the opportunities or openings that are given to them.

Freed from artificial standards of excellence. When we approach our lives and work through the lens of vocation, we are called to excellence based not on competition but rather on being true to ourselves and our own potential.

The challenge of doing our work with excellence is not a burden, then, but something that frees us to exercise the gifts and talents we have, without fear of failure. Failure is just part of the learning process; it does not need to diminish us.

Because there is no artificial or burdensome notion of excellence, it also means that we are free to accept our limitations as much as we do our potential. Our limitations—those limits to our abilities or even those areas of nonstrength, the things we do not do well—can be accepted with grace and humility. We do not need to feel diminished by them.

Only as we embrace a standard of excellence that fits who we are, not something artificial, can we move into emotional maturity in our capacity to think vocationally. I will come to the whole matter of emotional maturity in part two. But for now it is worth noting something attributed to Martin Luther King Jr., who, it is said, sought a particular freedom—an emotional freedom from an inflated head when praised and a crushed spirit when criticized. Both affirmation and criticism will come our way; our work will be praised and it will be judged inadequate by someone at some point in time. Indeed both praise and criticism will come more than once! We need both; affirmation and criticism are essential to our development and to the discernment process. We need the encouragement of affirmation; we need the discipline, the accountability and the checking of our aspirations that comes with criticism. But both affirmation and criticism can derail us emotionally. Our sense of vocational identity and our commitment to excellence, understood in terms of our vocation and in light of our own capabilities, free us so that we can hear *both* affirmation and criticism with grace. We are not flattered by praise; our spirits are not crushed by criticism. This is an essential posture from which we are able to live and work with freedom and joy.

Freed from the burden of pleasing everyone. With this understanding of vocation, we are freed from the burden of being liked by or trying to please everyone.

For one thing, it is simply not possible. It is a burden that we cannot possibly bear. Those who are trapped in this dilemma are soon caught by critical matters of integrity. A leader simply cannot satisfy every constituent or member of an organization, and a parent simply cannot provide everything that his or her child asks for. When a politician thinks he or she must always please others and has an underlying passion to be liked, then this person cannot have a consistent policy platform. It is not possible.

But, what is worse, not only is it a burden, it always leads to a lie; we end up living by the expectations of others and what they want us to be and do. Some manage to do this for a remarkably long period of time. Such people are chameleons. They make whoever they are with believe that they have their best interests in mind; they parrot what the person they are speaking to wants to hear. But inevitably this is a lie. When it comes to tough decisions, whether in the home or in the office, they end up trying to cut it both ways. We cannot live with integrity unless we are true to ourselves; we cannot live with integrity and please everyone.

Beware of the passion to be praised by everyone. It is an impossible burden.

Freed from the urgency and tyranny of time. Further, when we think vocationally, we are freed from the oppressive burden of trying to get as much done as possible. We are freed from trying to do too much or from doing work merely to try to legitimize ourselves or to show our worth. We are freed of hectic work for work's sake and can freely spend our time and energy knowing that there is plenty of time in each day to do what we are called to do. As James Fowler notes, when we are freed from the burden of trying to do as much as possible—the tyranny of time—"time is our friend rather than our enemy."[2]

When we think vocationally, we are freed to enjoy times of worship, play and leisure, without the worry that we should be working, that we should be accomplishing something or getting something done before a pressing deadline. God never calls us to be or do so much that we have to sacrifice the fundamental relationships of our lives or violate our need for sleep, rest, friendship, worship and recreation. Thinking vocationally frees us from the burden of a perpetual sense of urgency. What God is calling us to do now, at this point in our lives, can be done within the limitations of our current life situation.

Freed to love others. In Romans 12:3 the apostle calls us to look at ourselves with sober judgment—to think truthfully and honestly about who we are. Then, in verse nine, he calls us to love one another with the specific call to "let love be genuine." I am convinced that there is an underlying logic to the progression of Paul's thought at this point: that we can only truly love another without hypocrisy when we think vocationally, when we truly and graciously identify, accept and embrace who we are.

Any other posture is a burden; it is not genuine love. Sometimes our generosity is misguided and our love for others is offered out of a busy and hectic spirit rather than out of serenity and joy. Sometimes we are caught up in the desire to be loved and the hope that everyone will like us, and this inevitably undermines our capacity to love genuinely.

When we think vocationally we are freed from what A. W. Tozer calls the burden of pretense, and we enter into the freedom of humility. He reminds us of the joy that comes when we are freed of artificiality, of the burden of trying to impress others.[3] In other words, by a recovery of the principle of vocation, we are able to embrace authenticity, genuineness and truthfulness. This is freedom.

THE OBSTACLES TO VOCATION

Having identified the benefits of thinking vocationally, we should consider what might undermine our capacity to think vocationally. The obstacles are different for different people, but what follows is a discussion of the kinds of things that most of us will encounter—those things that will impede or undermine our capacity to discern and embrace our call. In most cases they are burdens that weigh us down.

A sacred-secular distinction in the understanding of vocation. The first obstacle is essentially theological—the failure to appreciate the sacredness of all vocations. This sacred-secular split reflects a particular notion of how God operates in the world. By denying the sacredness of *all* vocations we become caught in one of two traps. The first is that we accept a vocation that is not fundamentally our own. We go into the pastorate or become missionaries because we think this is a more noble way. But it is a burden because it is not our personal call. We accept a role because we think we should, but we cannot experience the joyful abandon of those who know they are doing what God is calling them to do. Inevitably, when this happens, we are a burden to those around us. Our lack of joy with our actual vocation can only mean that we are not living and working in harmony with others, for we are not in harmony with ourselves.

Others may not have become missionaries or pastors, but they feel as though they *should* have done so. If this is not their calling, it means that they have not eagerly embraced what God is truly calling them to. Rather than celebrating and embracing his or her call, the farmer or the businessperson is apologetic about the work he or she does, and believes it as far from the ideal of what a Christian should be doing. People like this often pressure their children into religious work as a way of compensating for their own failure to be "all that God wanted them to be."

But this subtle pattern of defining what is truly "sacred" happens in much more subtle ways in many different work settings. It was amazing to me to discover that among missionaries in the Philippines there was an implied hierarchy, and that the "real" missionaries were doing evangelism and church planting; the "quasi" missionaries were doing administration or relief and development. In the academic world there is a remarkable inclination to celebrate the research scholar and not recognize the sacredness of every role that is critical to what makes a college or university effective.

When we fail to affirm the sacredness of all vocations, we create burdens for people—the burden of assuming a role or responsibility that is not truly their own, and the burden of not embracing the work

God has indeed called them to. In both of these cases people not only carry a false burden but become a burden to others.

Failure to distinguish between vocation and career or occupation. For others, a major obstacle to vocational fulfillment is the failure to distinguish between role, career and vocation. These people understand their vocation to relate to a very particular situation—perhaps a particular role or occupation. I remember hearing a young missionary say that he was called to the Philippines for life. And I was amazed at both the audacity of such a suggestion (since maybe the Filipino people would not want him there for life!) but also at the limitation that this imposed. God is not capricious, but if we are going to think vocationally, we must be more flexible. And we cannot tie our sense of vocation to a particular place or role.

We could be dismissed from the company or the organization we work for. But that does not mean that we would lose our vocation. I know of women who cannot think of themselves in any role other than as a kind of auxiliary to their husbands. In such a case, for example, a pastor's wife will have a crisis of identity and call if her husband chooses to leave pastoral ministry. But quite apart from that kind of development, these women have so linked their sense of call to a particular kind of role or responsibility that they undermine their own capacity to truly think vocationally. That is, whether we have identified our sense of vocation with a particular company or organization, or whether we have overidentified ourselves with the vocation or occupation of a spouse, we undercut our capacity to take responsibility for our own lives and vocations. This is not to question the value of commitment to a company, a church, an organization or school, or to our spouses. I value highly those who work with me who demonstrate a deep commitment to the organization we are a part of, and who are prepared to live out their days in eager service within the organization. But something is askew when we cannot imagine being anywhere else and when our whole lives are consequently wrapped up in a particular organization. We set ourselves up for vocational crisis when we identify ourselves too closely with either an organization or a person, such that we are lost and at sea when inevitable changes come.

Organizations change. They must, not merely to survive, but to respond effectively to new opportunities and circumstances. But those who are overly identified with an organization find they are consistently on the defensive, doing all they can to resist the changes that are necessary for the well-being of the organization. They are not really committed to the organization but to what the organization used to be or what they wish it continued to be.

THE THREE CLASSIC TEMPTATIONS

The greatest threats to vocational thinking are three classic temptations, which essentially manifest themselves in some form of the temptations Jesus faced in the desert at the beginning of his public life and ministry (Lk 4:1-13): the desire for *power*, the desire for *material security* and comfort, and the desire for fame or *prestige*. It is all too easy for us to make vocational choices rooted in or motivated by these powerful and subtle temptations; it is easy to rationalize our choices around each of them. But they have an insidious effect on a vocation.

Many have rationalized ignoring God's call because they could not bear the thought of a drop in their standard of living or the threat of financial insecurity. Many have chosen a line of work for the simple reason that it seemed to guarantee a healthy pension and thus a comfortable retirement. Many have fallen into debt or bear financial obligations that undermine their capacity to embrace what God is calling them to be. Money is not evil, but the desire for material well-being and security has driven many to adopt a life inconsistent with their vocation. I ache for people who absolutely hate their jobs, yet they continue to carry that stress, not because they lack financial means but they hope to stick with it long enough, meaning twenty or more years, to have a comfortable retirement.

Wolfgang Amadeus Mozart is now known best as a composer. But he faced huge pressures from his family to be a performer rather than a composer because performing was more lucrative. Yet Maynard

Solomon notes that though a brilliant performer and a widely acclaimed pianist, Mozart believed he was called to be a composer.[4] And it goes without saying that his impact as a composer was exponentially greater.

Others are driven by different agendas. For many in my religious community, the focus of praise and prestige is on religious vocation. One cannot help but wonder how many become missionaries because this is what is affirmed; there is a great deal of praise and uncritical affirmation for those who choose to serve in this capacity. I remember a student in a course I taught on vocation who spoke of a missionary convention where at age thirteen he was praised and brought up to the front of the church to be "prayed for" when he indicated that he was willing to be a missionary. And this young man, now later in life thinking back on this event, suggested that it was too much praise and affirmation for a thirteen-year-old. Not only did it feed his ego at the time; worse, it profoundly undermined his capacity as he grew older to really think critically and with discernment about his call.

While some may respond to the above by suggesting that this young man needs to be faithful to the call he received at age thirteen, a better response might be to affirm that as Christian communities we need to trust the call of God on each one, and affirm and encourage individuals to accept *whatever* it is that God is calling them to do.

This praise of which I speak can so easily be a distraction, for young people and just as easily for those of us who are older. It is simply all too easy to accept an assignment or choose a responsibility because we crave praise, affirmation and prestige.

There are others whose vocations are set aside and sometimes even suppressed because of the temptation to power. It is sad to see people accept positions of supposed influence because they are drawn to the apparent power that accompanies certain roles (e.g., moving into administration or management when called to something else). I had to repeatedly ask and confirm whether I am indeed called to academic administration. But even when I was a missionary I was impressed with the temptation, especially for men, reflected in a desire to be elected to the governing executive committee or to be elected field director. As young men we longed for this quite apart from whether it truly reflected our fundamental call and identity, and without reference, it would have seemed, to whether such an election would keep us from that call.

I will be speaking about emotional well-being in chapter ten. But it is worth noting here that when we accept or pursue positions, roles or occupations out of a longing for material plenty, prestige or power, it is because we hope that in so doing we will fill some emotional vacuum, some deep and perhaps legitimate longing that has not been fulfilled, which we hope will be met through money, power or fame.

Often I hear, for example, of men who, because they never received the approval they needed from their fathers, hope to find it through some other avenue, often their occupational career. Therefore one of the most fruitful exercises in vocational thinking is to challenge motives and probe what is leading us to do what we think we must do.

MISGUIDED SENSE OF DUTY

A misguided sense of duty is also an obstacle to vocational fulfillment. This manifests itself in a variety of ways.

Parker Palmer speaks, for example, of those who feel obligated to the time and money invested in an educational degree or a training program.[5] The pressure may come from their own sense of duty or from those who helped pay for the program and expect that a specific career will reflect that training and help to pay off the bills!

The problem is twofold. First, many enter into costly educational programs before they are able to discern their true identity and calling. Second, there is the unfortunate idea that when people spend an inordinate amount of money to study in a particular field (e.g., medicine), this money is somehow wasted if they do not specialize in that field (e.g., become doctors).

But what we consider wasted is relative. How much greater is a wasted vocation—a person who out of a sense of duty to a medical degree does not leave medicine when she knows, deep in her gut, that this is not her calling! But this also reflects a narrow conception of how God works in our lives. With God there is no wasted time; we should and will be surprised by how our lives are patched together and how they unfold in the tapestry that God is creating in and through us. We cannot always see how things are working themselves out. All we can do is choose, for now, for *this* day, to be true to who we are and who we are called to be. No education, however wonderful or expensive, should undermine our capacity to think clearly about that call.

A misguided sense of duty is exposed in another way when individuals confuse compliance with the important and legitimate discipline of spiritual submission. We are called to live in submission within Christian community. We cannot function effectively within an organization if we do not acknowledge and live out of the reality that someone has to have authority and will probably make decisions we will not always agree with.

But *compliance* is another matter. When those in authority call for compliance they are calling for unthinking, undiscerning obedience. And many religious leaders are happy to fuel this idea, suggesting that anyone who differs with them is disloyal, to them or to the church. They assume that compliance and submission are one and the same.

We are called to accountability and submission; we are called to live in gracious harmony within the Christian community; and this means that we need to let leaders lead. But we must never equate the voice of leadership with the voice of God. We must always distinguish between the prompting of the Spirit on the one hand and the voice of human authorities on the other. Our fundamental posture must be one of submission and honor, but we must live and work with the assumption that the voice of God and the voice of those in authority over us are not necessarily the same.

Another and related way a misguided sense of duty undercuts our capacity to fulfill our vocations is when we act on the fear that someone will be threatened by us. We hesitate to act and embrace an opportunity and perhaps even our calling because we do not want to do anything that might make some other person feel diminished. It is really *their* problem, but we take it on as *our* burden: wives that do not want to threaten their husbands or friends who do not want to outshine their peers, or employees who do not want to threaten their supervisors.

While it is imperative that we live with sensitivity to the emotional well-being of others, we cannot afford to be straightjacketed by their emotional immaturity. We owe it to them, but ultimately we owe it to God and to ourselves to "fan into flame" the gift and opportunities God has given us. We are accountable for our stewardship of those gifts. And ultimately, we are not really doing others a favor when we protect them from their own emotional insecurities. All we are doing is hurting ourselves.

Though this will be discussed at length in chapter eleven, we also have a misguided sense of duty when we stay with an organization or a job long after we should have resigned. We have made duty the highest value. Some individuals have so equated their identity with a company or an organization that they sustain a level of duty that is inappropriate; the consequence is a disconnection from their vocation. Rarely is an individual called to make a commitment to a company, a school, a religious organization or a movement that would qualify as a lifelong covenant commitment. Rarely. In most cases God calls us to hold lightly to our institutional commitments—to serve eagerly with others but also to recognize that God will sometimes call us to leave. We should not be capricious in our commitments. But neither should we overstay when God calls us to move on. This relationship with organizations is so important to our vocation that it merits an entire chapter (chap. 11).

Maturity is found when we resolve that we will be true to who we are called to be and resolve that we will not live by imitation of others, or by compliance or conformity to others' ideals for us. If we have a sense of duty, it will be reflected in a resolve that we will be faithful to who we are and who we have been called to be.

FAILING TO APPRECIATE OUR LIMITS

Finally, two more major obstacles or blocks to vocational thinking, which on first reading may not seem very similar but have one common feature—the failure to understand the meaning of limits to our lives and work.

It seems that all some people can think about are their limits, and they tend to overstate the boundaries or limitations of their lives and work. Others, at the opposite end of the pole, fail to see any limits at all!

The first group are usually those inclined, for whatever reason, to feel victimized, to blame others for the limitations they are feeling. They may blame their parents, their previous employers, their colleagues or their current employers. Rather than taking responsibility for their own sphere of life and responsibility along with their own actions and reactions, they blame others. Their feeling of victimization is a straightjacket. And they speak of themselves as though they are martyrs.

At the other end of the spectrum are those who see no limits. They are the heroes who with messianic idealism see themselves as doing great and noble things for God, often for religious causes. And they are inclined to call others to be great heroes in their work for God. Deep within the notion of American culture, a viewpoint that has affected so many in the West, is the idea that anyone who has the will and determination can be and do anything. It is suggested that this is merely a matter of hard work and determination. But this is a false perspective; it is simply not true, not because there is *no* truth in this notion but rather because it is *partly* true. Its truthfulness lies in the value of hard work, but its falsehood arises in the notion that we are all called to be heroes, doing great and grand things for God.

The problem is simple: God often calls people to the obscure, the ordinary and the mundane. Some of the most important work that God accomplishes in the world is fulfilled by ordinary people doing ordinary work. This is not and cannot be merely tolerated, but rather is something we must embrace and even celebrate. And some people miss their vocations because they are looking for the heroic. This in some measure is a failure to accept the limitations of life—that God's work through us is often in the small and the ordinary. But on the other hand, it is also a failure to realize that the work we are called to do will often be very difficult, and anything we accomplish will be incremental and slow, in part because we are not heroes but merely people who in our day-to-day work are doing our best.

The genius of truth and freedom is found in accepting our limitations without overstating their significance. It is found in accepting with grace that we live with limits, but also keeping an eye to the possibilities of grace without being heroic, grandiose or naive.

I have identified several potential obstacles to vocational discernment—the theological obstacle of a sacred-secular distinction, a failure to distinguish between vocation and career, the three classic temptations, a misguided sense of duty, and finally the failure to appreciate the significance of limits. This is not meant to be exhaustive, but I have listed the kind of things that could undercut our capacity to be all we are called to be. Further, it is helpful in a review of any list to honestly consider what is the greatest threat to our own vocational identity and fulfillment. We all wrestle with these matters in different ways, and thus it is helpful to consider what might undercut capacity to embrace our calling. The more honest we are, the greater the likelihood that we will be able to confront this threat and over time "fan into flame the gift of God" (2 Tim 1:6 NIV).

In the end, though, the greatest threat to our vocations is fear (see chap. 8).

TWO ESSENTIAL CAPABILITIES

Our capacity to break past the impasse of our vocational development comes in learning to *think* vocationally. This includes two distinctive capabilities, two capacities that by themselves are of little value but which together enable us to think in truth and to think and act well: the capacity of *retrospection* and the capacity of being *fully present*.

Retrospection. One of the most significant capacities of those who think vocationally—accepting the benefits but also confronting the obstacles, accepting with grace our limits but also our potential—is retrospection, the ability to see and appreciate our own stories and the footprints of the Spirit throughout those stories.

Self-knowledge comes through looking back at the work of God in our lives, our actions and responses to events and opportunities, to the accidents of history and the wonder in how they have led to this point in our life story. If we know ourselves, it is because we know our history—our personal history.

Retrospection includes appreciating the nature and character of our family of origin. What did it mean to grow up in this particular family at this particular time? How have we been shaped by the character and patterns of behavior of our parents, and what is the meaning of our birth order? How did the dynamics of family life make us who we are?

We discover our vocations through retrospection, seeing how our identity and our call have unfolded in our experience. When I speak of the factors that shape our sense of vocation, these are elements of our identity that only make sense to us through our own story—the events and circumstances of our lives. And it is often in the telling of this story that we come to clarity about what is important to us and what, more than anything else, we know we are called to do. This is so because vocation is never discerned in a vacuum; there will always be a story, a continuity with our past, something that brought us this far and that now suggests where we might be headed.

But let me also quickly add the following: the past is not an obligation; God is always capable of surprises and of leading us in directions or ways of engagement that we could not have seen coming. And yet I suspect that the seeds of that new chapter in our lives were always there and only now are being watered. Years in an office complex with numbers, and now, out of the blue, a person wants to be a novelist? Well, it might not be out of the blue; there may be a series of journal entries, over the years, that spoke of the day when the opportunity would be there to write.

Sometimes through retrospection we come to the recognition that what we are already doing may well be what we are called to do. That is, in the very doing of a task or a role, we see a reflection of something fundamental about our identity and calling. I became the academic dean of a seminary in Manila, Philippines, for no more noble a reason than there was no one else available to fill the post! But then, in the doing, it became clear to me that this was probably what I was called to do. And many similar stories could be told—of writers who discovered that they were called to write when they had the opportunity to write and took advantage of it, and one writing opportunity led to another. This is why I urge young adults to give themselves in generous service that may include a variety of activities and responsibilities. For we discover ourselves in action, but then, of course, in action that becomes the fodder for reflection.

Retrospection also includes coming to terms with the difficult moments in our journey. Difficulty itself will be the subject of chapter ten, since we must make sense of the setbacks and in some cases the suffering that shapes our lives. But to see how difficulty informs our present, we must reflect critically and discern how difficult events in our lives have made us who we are. What does it mean when we have been released or turned down for an employment opportunity? How has a closed door led to opportunities we might not have had otherwise? How has a death or a major loss in the past shaped us, informed our actions and influenced our responses? Who we are is known by a reflection on the past—knowing and interpreting the story of our lives.

Fully present. Stressing the importance of retrospection is a not a call for a sentimental view of the past. There is nothing gained through nostalgic sentimentalism, living in regret or living in the past, wishing that things had been different or turned out differently. We must look back, but we look back so that we can be fully present to this situation, this moment, to the real circumstances of our *current* life situation.

In other words, everything in our lives is a prelude for *this* moment, *this* event and the opportunities that lie before us *now*. We are called to be fully present to this moment, to turn from regrets or nostalgia, to turn from anger at those who may have limited us in the past, to ask how we can be fully present to a set of current needs, potential acts of generous service, now, in this moment and at this time.

What enables us to be fully present is the capacity to see our present in the light of our past, our story and the set of circumstances and events, including our actions and reactions, that have brought us to the present. Retrospection is the capacity to think about the past in a manner that can enable us to be fully present now.

Remember also a simple rule of thumb. God only leads us one step at a time. And we should never overstate how significant one step or phase in God's providential guidance might be. I left seminary in the late 1970s convinced that my calling was fundamentally that of preaching. Eventually, though my sense of vocation *included* preaching, it was only one part of who I was called to be. In retrospect, it is also clear to me that preaching was a very good place for me to begin my public ministry. But I am very glad that wise counsel freed me from remaining locked on one track when God was leading me to build on that and go another way.

The purpose of retrospection is to enable us to be fully present. This is evident and ably illustrated for those in professional sports. One of my favorite athletes was the Spanish tennis professional Arantxa Sanchez Vicario. She did not immediately impress me as a formidable athlete. She is only 5'6" tall, and nobody would have thought of her as one of the stronger women on the professional tennis tour. But what made her remarkable is her capacity to focus.

After she won the semifinal game that placed her in the Wimbledon championship match, the July 7, 1995, London *Times* commented on her extraordinary performance. It was noted that Sanchez Vicario was not dispirited by a bad sequence of points, was not vulnerable to gamesmanship and contrived interruptions by her opponent, and refused to let poor calls by the umpires throw her off her game. Most of all, she kept her short legs going tirelessly. And she did all this in the face of the seeming athletic superiority of her opponent.

She remains, for me, a testimony to all of us. Many gifted people fail to achieve their potential for the simple reason that they are too easily distracted. They are not focused. Many are complaining or nostalgic about the past. Either they are bitter because something was "taken" from them or done to them that they view as having hurt or limited them, or they are nostalgic about some previous chapter of their lives.

Others are "ladder climbers." They are never fully present to a situation because their focus is on where they hope to be; this occasion, this opportunity and these people are merely a means to an end.

While I would be the first to tell people that this is but one chapter to your life and it may be that in the future God will take you elsewhere, there is something perverse—vocationally perverse—in the work of someone whose tasks are only done to be noticed or so that they can get the experience they need to get the job they really want. And, naturally, the people with whom they work feel used.

I have no problem with the person who recognizes that she is not really called to the pastorate and needs to explore all the options to see what God is really calling her to do. But in the meantime, this individual has a parish with *real* people and *real* problems, and she needs to be fully present to them, awaiting the time that God calls to close the door on this chapter of life.

I have no problem with a young college professor acknowledging that he will not likely be at this college for the rest of his life. Fine. But in the meantime, be fully present to *these* people, *these* colleagues, *these* students, the mission of *this* college.

A mother naturally assumes that she will not always be a mother, and that another chapter will come in which her focus will be elsewhere. But for now she is a mother, and her child and her family will be the focus of her attention—without regrets, or with longings to be freed from this burden but fully present, knowing that the children will grow up soon enough. (Indeed, it will surprise her how quickly.)

If we are fully present to this moment, to this time of our lives, it is through our capacity to be present *in light of* the past. Sanchez

Vicario was never so present to a rally that she forgot the score. She was not ahistorical. She knew the score, and, if anything, this heightened her capacity to be present to the moment. In other words, people who are informed by their stories, through retrospection, have a greater capacity to be fully present to the events, circumstances and opportunities of the moment. Thinking vocationally means both—fully present to this moment *and* retrospection. The one enables the other.

INTENTIONALITY AND MINDFULNESS

The bottom line in all of this is that to think and act vocationally we must think and act *intentionally*. We are not merely acted upon, and thus not merely reacting to our circumstances and to what is forced on us. Rather, we respond thoughtfully and our actions are focused and purposeful. It means that we refuse to be victimized by our circumstances or by other people. It means that we have resolved that our actions will not be determined by our fears or by the unreasonable expectations of others, but rather by who *we* are and who we have been called to be.

The bottom line is simple: Will we choose to act and react in an *intentional* way? Will we be acted on or will we take responsibility for our lives, for our future? Will we live in disappointment and bitterness because we were not treated as we think we deserve, or will we let the past go—forgive and without recrimination embrace the possibilities represented in our today and our tomorrow?

Will we resolve to act intentionally rather than automatically? Will our actions and our responses be measured, thoughtful and focused?

Often it is noted that if we are going to live with sanity and grace in the midst of hectic noise and competing demands and expectations, we have to learn to say no. But the problem for many people is that they fear saying no because they do not know if they are shutting down the very thing they are being called to be and do!

In other words, we can only learn to say no to the invitations, demands and expectations that come to us when we have clarity—and this is something that must come from the core of our beings—about what we *are* called to do, about what we know we must say yes to. Our no frees us to say yes.

FOUR CALLINGS

Business, the Arts, Education
and Religious Leadership

As we come to the midway point in this book, I will now step back and consider four distinct occupations as a way to illustrate these reflections on vocation thus far:

- the calling to business and commerce
- the calling into the arts—visual as well as musical and dramatic
- the calling to education, teaching and scholarship
- the calling to religious leadership or pastoral office

In looking at these four callings, please be aware that I am of course not prioritizing these or suggesting that they represent higher or more important callings. Rather, they are merely illustrative ways of entering into the idea of vocation so that we can speak concretely. Here, in other words, is what it looks like on the ground. Some readers will without a doubt identify with one of these callings. And others, I trust, will see these as examples, case studies, that more fully open up an appreciation of the inner soul and contours of their own vocations.

Additionally, though I will be speaking of occupations, I am not equating occupation with vocation. By using occupations to illustrate vocation, I could easily be accused of doing precisely what I said we should not do. These are, potentially, occupations; for some these could very well be ways in which they are waged, and how they therefore make a living. Yet, what I hope to show is that they are not so much occupations as ways of being in the world, ways of seeing the world, feeling the deepest need of the world and responding with passion.

As I look at these four, there are two words that will shape this exploration of calling. First, consider that a vocation is a *charism*, a gift of God to the church and to the world. Each vocation, including these four being considered here, is God's gift. God graces the world through the talents, commitments and energies of each one, and this grace in and to the world is the grace of God manifested through the extraordinary diversity of callings—of the multiple ways people are called to make a difference with and for God in the world. Each is a gift; from God's perspective, each is a charism.

As an aside I should perhaps add this: there is a less than subtle agenda in profiling these four. What I hope to demonstrate is that each is very much a gift of God that we all need. We live *daily* in dependence on those called into each of these "occupations." Yes, daily. Life is not conceivable without each of these four, and in profiling these we can perhaps grow in our appreciation of our deep interdependence as we each fulfill our vocations.

From our perspective, from the human side of the tapestry that God is weaving, this charism is expressed as a *necessity*, the second word that informs our understanding of vocation. I am borrowing this word from two authors, Henri Nouwen and Annie Dillard.

Henri Nouwen speaks of the priority of solitude for the life of prayer, and our need for what he calls "receptive solitude." He makes the observation that solitude is so very essential, for only there, in quiet and with distance from others, in silence before God, can we come to terms with ourselves and begin to build our lives in response to God and to God's call, "according to this necessity."[1]

Dillard uses the powerful image of the weasel, specifically one she

met while walking an overgrown path. In reflecting about this encounter and the way of being a weasel, she was struck by the wonder
that the weasel lives by necessity, with, as she puts it, "a fierce and
pointed will," living as one is meant to live, "yielding at every moment to the perfect freedom of single necessity."[2]

Consider the following from both sides: each of these four—business, the arts, education and religious leadership—is a gift from God,
a *charism*, and each is for someone, for many, a profound *necessity*,
something they *must* do if they are to be consistent with the call of
God on their lives.

CALLED TO DO BUSINESS

In the Scriptures, we have a noteworthy example of someone called
into business and commerce in the depiction of the wise woman of
Proverbs 31, with its recurring reference to the "merchant":

> She is like the ships of the merchant,
>   she brings her food from far away. (v. 14)

> She considers a field and buys it;
>   with the fruit of her hands she plants a vineyard. (v. 16)

> She perceives that her merchandise is profitable. (v. 18)

> She makes linen garments and sells them;
>   she supplies the merchant with sashes. (v. 24)

This woman is celebrated as a merchant because of her capacity to
produce wealth, to provide a solid economic foundation for her
household and community, and for her generosity toward those in
need. Her "genius" is an *economic* intelligence.

This profile of the merchant as a model of embodied wisdom is a
reminder to us of two things. First, that business, the production of
goods and services, is indispensable for human life. We live daily in
dependence on those whose goods and services make our lives possible and enrich our lives in countless ways. When my wife and I
were having our house built, I happened to drop by the worksite after

our affable plumber had roughed in the plumbing. I was in awe; I had no idea what lay behind the walls and in the floors of houses I had been living in all my life. There was so much that I had taken for granted: I just turned the tap, and water poured out! And, of course, foul water was mysteriously taken away. Well, there is no mystery, just as there is no mystery to how a city works and is kept supplied with food, clothing and countless other services without which a city would not survive. It is business, the production of goods and services, that makes this happen.

Second, the profile of the woman in Proverbs 31 is also a reminder that when business is done well, it is worthy of our praise; it is a thing of beauty and wonder: a product well made, a service delivered with excellence and attention to detail. And this is, of course, a gift from God, a means by which God fulfills God's purposes in the world.

Yet, throughout history the church has generally been quite ambivalent about the calling to business. Perhaps it is the economic component that makes us feel uneasy: the money! Whatever the reason for the ambivalence, it has been a recurring problem, so much so that the typical businessperson does not feel legitimized by the faith community they are a part of. Often, no doubt, they feel valued because they help pay the church bills. But do we value them for the work they do; do we view them as gifts of God to the world, and thus that God is fulfilling his purposes in the world specifically through their work in business and commerce?

One test of whether we really believe in business is whether we recognize that an entrepreneur engaged in a new start up will need to devote countless hours to getting that small business going, and that will mean less time devoted to church affairs and other religious activities. Is this OK? Indeed, will this person feel the support and encouragement of the faith community as he or she gets this new endeavor going?

Or consider the growing propensity to speak of "kingdom business" or "business as mission" for those who view their work in business as a key way to engage the world for Christ. But, while good, is their involvement in business only a means to an end, either to create wealth to support religious work or, in some cases, to gain access to countries that would not grant a visa to a religious worker but will grant visas to those who will do business? In the second case, how frequently does it seem that business is not legitimate in its own right but only as a means of doing what supposedly really counts, religious work.

As I am speaking of it here, I am insisting that the work of business, of producing goods and services, is good work, necessary work and, indeed, work that reflects the calling of God on some, as a means by which God fulfills his purposes in the world. This work has value in its own right; it needs no other justification than that it is done in response to the calling of God.

As will be the case with each of the four callings I am profiling here, not all business is good business. Of course not. But this could just as easily be said for each of these four. Some may respond, "Sure, business is a calling, but then it must be done in a godly way!" And the response, of course, is to say that this is certainly the case, but it is no less true of the artist, the teacher and, and this must be stressed, the pastor. All four can be done in a way that undermines the purposes of God, and all four, including the call to business, can be done in a way that is deeply congruent with the ways of God in the world.

The work of those called into business will be consistent with God's purposes if their business is characterized by, at the very least, four marks. And, as will be evident, there will be echoes of these marks in each of the four callings to which I will speak.

The pursuit of excellence. I spoke of excellence in an earlier chapter, when I addressed how excellence is a mark of all who respond to God; we do our best for the simple reason that our work is an act of worship to the one who called us to this work. This finds expression in business in the quality and integrity of the product or service offered.

As in all matters, excellence is pursued not as an end in itself, and not merely because a quality product brings with it customer loyalty; rather, for the Christian, excellence is a matter of vocational integrity: we do our best, attending to details on everything from the toys produced for children to the mechanical trustworthiness of an aircraft to the beauty of the design for an office complex. We shun mediocrity and decry shoddy craftsmanship. We take delight in work done well, knowing that our standards exceed those of the most demanding customer because our ultimate accountability is to ourselves and to God. We view our work "as unto the Lord."

Respect for money (rather than a love of money). There is no avoiding the economic component of business, and there is no need to want to avoid it. Money is not evil; economics is fundamental to life. And the financial component is merely a means to an end: to be assured that quality goods and services are available to those they are produced for.

What those called into business know so well, perhaps better than the rest of us, is that the Bible is so true when it speaks of the insidious effects of the *love* of money. When a business is profit driven rather than value driven, when what propels someone forward is greed and the love of money, the net result is always the same: it ultimately destroys and corrodes the soul and the fabric of a society. Thus we must speak of the foolishness of building an economy around the so-called gaming industry—gambling as entertainment. The Christian community needs to call it what it is: whether it is casinos or video lottery terminals, these forms of industry have *no* redeeming value and their presence in a community corrodes the economic fabric and thus undermines the social network. The reason is simple: the industry is based on the love of money, the desire for the quick buck rather than for fair wages for honest labor.

Those called into business know that there is no good business without a profound *respect* for money, for the economic component. They aspire for well-crafted business plans that give careful attention to the bottom line. They realize that they cannot give away anything free. If you are a friend and hope that your auto dealer friend will give you a below-market-value deal on a car, with no profit for the seller, all you are doing is forcing him to charge others an even higher price so that he can break even. But they also know that the love of money and greed will destroy their business, for they destroy the soul and purpose of business.

Commitment to economic justice. We cannot speak of business without speaking of justice—meaning that we need to speak specifically of economic justice, the justice of the marketplace, of buying and selling at fair prices. The great and passionate longing of the Old Testament prophets is that justice would flow like a mighty river, and their witness is a clear reminder that there is no righteousness without justice; indeed righteousness and justice are virtually synonymous and, further, there is no justice without economic justice.

Thus Isaiah, for example, speaks of the emptiness of worship that is not matched by justice in the marketplace (Is 58; see also Mic 6:8), and the justice of the marketplace that is profiled here is that workers are paid a fair wage.

What this means is that we do not enrich ourselves at the expense of others; we are committed to fair wages; we are resolved to always pay a fair price for a product or service. We are not asking to buy things at the lowest possible price so that we can resell them at the highest possible price. On both ends of the spectrum we are seeking justice, fairness and ultimately what is good for each person involved in a transaction.[3]

On a personal level, then, we are not asking which coffee in the supermarket is the cheapest but rather which brand of coffee represents a fair and just wage for the growers, the shippers, the suppliers and those who staff the registers in the grocery store. Something is amiss, profoundly so, when we only shop at megastores that cut corners at each link in the economic chain, forcing only the producer to take the economic risks and through sheer size forcing down the wages of those who move the product all along the way to the customer, who goes home satisfied with having gotten a deal without any awareness of the real cost of the item purchased.

The same principle applies on a macro or environmental scale: good business means that we do not enrich ourselves at the expense of the generations that follow us, and thus we do business with a respect for the land, the water and the air.

Making a difference through our giving. If you are called to do business, you will surely have an aptitude for it, and if you have this capacity, the odds are that you will make more money than you need. As we sometimes like to suggest: if you are not making a good living in business, perhaps this is not your calling! While it is possible for a gifted businessperson to struggle financially, as a rule, those in business earn well and, more to the point, earn more than they need.

So the business community typically provides funds to support the arts, hospitals, relief and development agencies, educational institutions, and churches. Colleges and universities, orphanages and hospitals, art galleries and community centers are all deeply dependent on those in business and commerce. Those called into business have the potential to establish a twofold legacy. First, there is the benefit created directly through their business: if they are selling shoes, they think both of all the people who are well shod and of those employees who in the production of the shoes are able to earn a fair wage that supports and provides their children with an education. But there is also a second legacy: that most who are called to business have the capacity to leave a legacy in the arts or the care of the poor or in education, in the medical field, or in a dimension of Christian mission or witness.

As a businessperson, then, consider how God may be calling you to make a difference. Consider this question on two levels. First, locally, in your own city or community: where is there a need, an opportunity, something tugging at your heart that represents an investment in that community—whether scholarships for underprivileged youth, or the opportunity to fund the redesign of a park with tree plantings and a safe apparatus for children to play on, or the half-way house for those leaving prison and needing to be transitioned effectively back into society?

Then, think also on an international stage. Read the paper; listen to reports from those who are involved in the global South—Africa, Asia and Latin America—and ask: Where can I partner with others and invest in a nonprofit that is making a difference in a way that reflects some of my own core values and commitments? Make a difference in your own village; make a difference in the global village. There is wisdom in doing this quietly. Sure, there is a thrill to establishing a "Carnegie" or equivalent library in central Iraq, but perhaps we should shy away from leaving our mark, our name, on those investments. Leaving a legacy means that we just happened to have the opportunity to be there at the right time with the financial resources to make something happen. But in the end this is not about us and our wealth and our largess; it is about what God is doing. In the end our contribution is small, regardless of the size of the gift. It is just one part of what God is doing, but it is all *ad majorem dei Gloria*—to the greater glory of God.

All of this is offered with deep gratitude to those who ply their craft in the world of business and commerce: whether it is the airline company, a huge corporation or the self-employed plumber. I celebrate the firm that has the infrastructure to employ hundreds in producing quality automobiles and equally the bookseller just down the street from where I live. Our prayer is that each thrives in their work, that God would bless them and that their work would prosper and be a source of blessing to many.

CALLED INTO THE ARTS

While our culture and religious traditions might be ambivalent about business, this is likely even more pronounced when it comes to the arts. While the testimony of Christianized Europe suggests that at the very least there were chapters in the history of the church when the arts were valued, the deep pragmatism of Western culture has infiltrated the church and left many wondering about the value of the arts.

The exception to this, perhaps, is that our culture tends to like artists when they make us feel good: thus the propensity to proliferate sentimental music and visual kitsch, which a true artist disdains and is a form of false comfort.

Here too, as with the calling to business, we must speak of the *charism* of God: the grace of the Spirit to the church and the world through the lives and work of those who are called to music, to writing fiction, to the dramatic arts, to the visual arts and to the work of design.

If the vocation of the businessperson finds expression in the description of the woman of Proverbs 31, the vocation of the artist is cogently portrayed in the description of Bezalel in Exodus 31:2-5:

> See, I have called by name Bezalel son of Uri son of Hur, of the tribe of Judah: and I have filled him with divine spirit, with ability, intelligence, and knowledge in every kind of craft, to devise artistic designs, to work in gold, silver, and bronze, in cutting stones for setting, and in carving wood, in every kind of craft.

The work of the artist comes in response to a call. This description of Bezalel highlights that his vocation is a charism; it is the fruit of the "divine spirit" he was filled with. And within these few verses the essence of this call, its heart and soul, comes to light. The gift of the artist, at least as it is expressed in the calling of Bezalel, is threefold:

- He is given talent and ability, clearly the capacity for working with the materials from which he will do this craft.

- He is also given intelligence, specifically the intelligence or understanding that is particular to his calling, which in this case surely means an aesthetic sense.

- He has been given knowledge of his craft.

The filling of the Spirit was to this end, and this anointing was not arbitrary. Bezalel and his fellow artists are anointed to bring ability, intelligence and knowledge to their craft.

To what end? What is the essence of the gift of God through the artist? What is the "necessity" from which the artist does his or her work and without which they are not true to themselves and thus to the call of God. Surely it is, at the very least, to enrich our lives from the inside out, to foster a depth of appreciation of the beauty of God and of God's creation. The arts assure that we are not one-dimensional people but alert and attentive to the beauty of God because we are attentive to the response of our own hearts to beauty—in worship and in our lives in the world.

Christian worship. This text in the book of Exodus is a reminder that Christian worship depends heavily on the work of the artist. Whether it is the writer who crafts the songs or those who accompany our worship, we cannot conceive of worship except as designed, led and accompanied by those gifted as musicians and singers. But we are also deeply indebted to the visual artists, those who design our spaces of worship and who then in turn design and foster beauty in our worship. Indeed, beauty in our worship (and our world) is the sign of and the vehicle by which the Spirit is present in our midst. We are embodied souls, and in ways that enliven the human soul, when we see and experience beauty, we are drawn to God and come into a knowledge of God.

This does not occur merely when we see the wonder of a valley, the ocean, the mountain or the spread of the prairies. Rather, our response to God is heightened by the artist who fosters our capacity to appreciate the beauty of God in the created order. Whether it is the string quartets of Mozart, the sculpture of Michelangelo, the paintings of Goya, the landscape designs of the Japanese, the photographs of Ansel Adams, or calligraphers whose deft pen strokes reveal the beauty of words, all are offered, potentially, as a prayer to the Creator.

Each art form lifts our spirit and draws us to God.

In daily life. We depend on the work of the artist in our worship, but in the comings and goings of our lives we need the work of artists to remind us of the transcendent, of the beauty and glory of our God, whether in the design of our buildings, the art on our walls, the music we attend to or the layout of our gardens and parks.

It is precisely through the arts that our joy is made full because the arts, in worship and in life, lift our spirits and expand our hearts and souls so that we can know more of the breadth and depth of the glory of God. Thus, as Hans Rookmaaker says, "Art needs no justification."[4] It fosters worship; it fosters our *capacity* for worship; it cultivates within us a Godward orientation in daily life, increasing within us a capacity for an attentiveness to the presence and beauty of God at home, at work, in the neighbourhood, in the airport or the train station, the school or the hospital.

We will never appreciate the work of the businessperson until we recognize how indispensable their work is—the goods and services without which we cannot live. The same with artists: we will not recognize their place in the purposes of God unless we appreciate that beauty is utterly indispensable to life. That through the arts we find our deepest and fullest sense of identity, purpose and meaning. Those of us who have been raised in Protestant evangelical circles likely assume that beauty is marginal to life. To our loss. We urgently need the deep corrective on this score that comes from other Christian theological and spiritual traditions.[5]

But not just any art will do. By this I do not mean that a Christian artist must produce religious art, as though this is more consistent with a Christian's vocation. Unfortunately, much religious art is poor art, whether in music, the visual arts or the design of church buildings. And as such it is not a witness to the glory and goodness of the Creator.

Rather, what makes art authentic—evidence that the artist is faithful to the call of God—is surely, at the very least, the following:

Commitment to excellence. Mediocrity is an anathema to the artist, and no one knows better than the artist that excellence is the fruit of practice and more practice, incrementally finding our stroke or feel so that we get it right. Poets and novelists know that their best work only comes as they revise and revise and revise again, attending to the details. Artists by their art call all of us to excellence in our work. The artists in our midst inspire all of us to do our work well.

This is why our places of work need art. If you own a business and you want excellence from your employees, display first-class art on the walls and in the interior design. Let artists serve you and your company by fostering through their work a disdain for mediocrity and a desire for quality in all that we set our hands to.

But remember: we are not born geniuses, and excellence does not come in a swish of inspiration. It is, rather, the fruit of practice, working and reworking to get it right. Also remember this: bad art may well be worse than no art at all, for bad art tells a lie. When it comes to the arts, excellence is critical.

Commitment to intellectual honesty. Artists, at their best, hate kitsch and despise sentimentality. This suggests that artists faithful to the call of God are honest about the pain of this world, its fragmentation and the violence of a creation gone askew. Their genius is not to deny the pain but to witness to the glory of God and the possibilities of grace in the very midst of the fragmentation. Art sustains our hope not by sentimentality but with a rigorous honesty.

The advertising industry urgently needs true artists, those who are faithful to their craft: women and men who can design ads that are not manipulative, that are not condescending and do not trivialize our sexuality.

This also suggests that artists take their materials seriously. They value honest materials, not pseudo wood or brick. For example, I always find it ironic and not a little troubling when I am a guest preacher at a church and next to me or on the Communion table in front of me I find a vase of dusty plastic flowers. The irony can hardly be missed: I declare the truth next to pieces of plastic that are pretending to be something they are not.

Commitment to their calling rather than to acclaim or the commercial potential of their calling. Artists need to make a living, of course, and artists need to be heard and seen—at least the art needs to be heard or seen or read. And yet the grave danger for artists is that they might be commercialized or commodified, driven more by their financial potential rather than their calling.

As with those called to do business, we must respect the economic side of our work; there is a cost, and we cannot expect artists to do good work while we pay them on the cheap. Artists need to make a living and need to receive a fair wage for their craft. If we are willing to pay $60 for a sports ticket, then surely we should be willing to invest some money in original art.

But artists compromise their art when they design or create something because it will sell, pandering to our tastes rather than cultivating our capacity for good, honest art that may trouble us as much as it comforts us, that stretches our imaginations and infuses us with hope. There is a certain vocational integrity in artists who refuse to sell signed prints of their work.

In *The Gift*, a classic on the vocation of the artist, Lewis Hyde comments on the inevitable tension for the artist between the market and the gift exchange—the gift of art as gift and not as something commodified for commercial purposes.[6] There is the idealism, of course, of the artist who defends him- or herself against all temptations to commercialize their vocation. But as Hyde points out, while that must remain the primary orientation or propensity, since the marketplace can so easily destroy the gift of the artist, these two worlds do need to be reconciled; artists can live in a market society. Some artists step completely outside the market economy; perhaps these artists have a benefactor or inherited wealth that shields them from the market. But others have managed by having secondary jobs by which they pay the bills; thus their art itself is freed from financial pressure. They become, you might say, their own patrons; they have paying jobs all day and write poetry late into the night, knowing full well that the poetry will never be the source of their livelihood.

This suggests that the artist will often live around the edges of the economy, managing a living but barely, living with limited means because what matters most is their art. Accepting this is inherent to accepting the call of God to be an artist. I offer this observation, not to, as Hyde puts it, "romanticize the poverty of the artist," but rather to testify to the common experience of artists, those who have plied their work in obscurity as well as those who are well known.

No place for self-indulgence. When the artist becomes bigger than the art, when the film actor is a star and then more important than the film, when the artist becomes a celebrity whose ego fills the room, the vocation of the artist is compromised. This is so with all vocations. Few things are more insidious than when the ego of the corporate executive is bigger than the mission of the organization. Yet it is perhaps most obvious for the artist: they simply have to give the priority to their art and not view their work as a means of their own glorification. The true artist defers to the art itself and to the God the art witnesses to.

I wonder if the Toronto International Film Festival should have a policy: none of the actors in the films shown may come to Toronto. This is about the film, not the actors, directors or producers. Stay home so that the art can be appreciated. We are so easily distracted by the cult of the celebrity that we lose a sense of the integrity of the art.

I think, for example, of the humility of Johann Sebastian Bach, who was never taken with himself but only with the God and the Christ to whom he witnessed in the grandeur of his music. This is so in all art, but it is most obvious when it comes to the role of the arts in worship. Here is where the interplay between our egos and the glory of God is most at play. Here is where we must be most insistent that in worship there is no stage and there are no "performers," except, of course, the people of God who offer their worship to the living and ascended Christ. And here too I wonder: should the artists, who are so essential to our worship, intentionally take a back seat? Is there ancient wisdom in having the organist, in older building designs, literally out of view? Is something amiss when the artist is visually front and center?

But this same principle applies in the world; we need artists who know the power of self-effacement. Many of the greatest artists have no need for fans, no desire to be a celebrity, to be interviewed or to be on the front cover of *Time* magazine. They just want to be faithful to their craft, and, for the Christian, to be faithful to the One who has called and gifted them. German poet Rainer Maria Rilke, in correspondence with a younger poet, says that most of all the poet needs to ask, "Must I write?" and to inquire this of his or her deepest self, and if therein the answer is "I must," that the young poet should then "build your life in accordance with this necessity; your whole life, even into its humblest and most indifferent hour, must be a sign and witness to this impulse."[7]

To these women and men we raise a glass and offer a toast. May God indeed bless your work and anoint you with the Spirit for the grace-filled task of expanding the horizons of our souls, fostering our capacity for beauty and thus for God, fueling our imaginations and thus inspiring us and giving us hope for the work to which we in turn are called.

CALLED TO TEACH: THE VOCATION OF THE SCHOLAR AND THE EDUCATOR

I wonder if as we look back over our lives we will increasingly recognize that the greatest gifts that are given to us are our teachers. Perhaps this is a very slight overstatement; perhaps. Perhaps spouse or children or parents or close friends might all actually be our greatest gifts. And yet do not miss the way God demonstrates the glory of the divine goodness by sending us a teacher. This includes classroom teachers, but not just; I think also of writers whose works have altered my thinking, expanded my imagination and called me to repentance. I also think of those who have taught us skills: everything from how to drive a car to how to sell a product to how to ski. Our teachers deepen our lives and equip us for life. Indeed, life is inconceivable apart from these extraordinary gifts of God.

So it is no surprise to realize how significant this vocation is within the Christian and religious tradition. The book of Deuteronomy profiles the vital place of teaching in the lives of families and communities; Nehemiah highlights the work of Ezra and the scribes, whose teaching brought understanding and deep joy. In Proverbs we are reminded that wisdom is the fruit of teaching, the passing on of knowledge and understanding from one generation to the next. And then, of course, we come to the New Testament and recognize that our Lord Jesus was himself a teacher, commissioning his disciples to teach (Mt 28:19-20) so that teaching and learning are integral to congregational life.

Teaching leads to wisdom, and wisdom is the very stuff of life; we only mature as we grow in wisdom, and there is no wisdom without knowledge. And, there is no knowledge without teaching. So the longing for wisdom leads to a search for good teachers, who know how to engage heart and mind, who know how to teach for understanding, but specifically understanding that leads to wise living.

Some teachers are scholars who do original research; they are often found in universities and colleges, drawing upon the wisdom of previous centuries and with due diligence equipping us to make sense—to interpret—our lives, our communities and our societies. To them we are deeply indebted.

Other teachers take this research and translate it into curricula that are accessible to everyone from first graders to mathematics or history classes at the local university; these may not be original scholars, but they are equally crucial and vital to the teaching-learning process. I also think of those whose expertise as teachers is typically found in technical schools, in managerial schools, art schools, medical schools or institutions that teach carpentry, plumbing and how to drive a car or how to prune a tree.

They are all teachers, whether they teach us how to use our heads or our hands. They are God's gifts to us; each is a charism.

Yet, just as with both those in business and those called into the arts, it is so easy to dismiss them and fail to appreciate how indebted we are to our teachers. In our deeply pragmatic and short-sighted culture, including our religious cultures, we often do not have the patience to appreciate wisdom available to us through our teachers.

For example, in a recent article on the crisis brewing in Lake Erie, scientists discovered that the so-called recovery of Lake Erie is actually a misnomer because the lake has serious problems with "biological pollution," notably, the infestation of species that are destroying native fish. But the response of local fishers is captured by the following line: "There's not a damn thing wrong with the lake. It's just the yapping of a bunch of academics who have nothing better to do."

It is certainly possible that there is nothing wrong with the lake and that a "bunch of academics" could spend their time more effectively. But another alternative is that these academics are listening to both the lake and to those who fish the lake, and that those who fish should learn to appreciate that the academics are their friends.

This is not to say that all academics, scholars and teachers are a gift from God. Not for a moment; just as there are both business people and artists that misuse their skills and do their work out of misguided aspirations, the same is true for teachers. When teaching is done poorly, an opportunity is lost. Just as we love good teaching, teaching that informs the mind, strengthens the heart and fosters our capacity to act with wisdom and courage, poor teaching distorts understanding and discourages those who would learn. In the end it is nothing but a waste of time. I wonder if the same could be said of teaching as it is of art; no teaching is better than bad teaching.

So, how does the teacher, the scholar, do the work she or he is called to in a way that is faithful to that calling?

Three critical indicators. There are three key indicators of a good teacher. First, good teaching fosters wisdom and the capacity to act wisely. Teaching may foster reflection, and the teaching-learning exercise might spend extended time considering everything from the orbits of the planets to the causes of the Napoleonic Wars, but the goal is wisdom, understanding and the capacity to live well.

Second, all good teachers know how to engage both heart and mind. This is no different for the kindergarten teacher than for those who teach us how to play an instrument or who lecture on an arcane topic to a group of graduate students. Good teaching takes account of the emotional contours of the teaching-learning experience. Teachers that manipulate emotion or intentionally foster fear through intimidation violate their craft; the true master fosters joy and freedom for the learner.

Third, master teachers bring a gracious authority to their craft; yes, there is authority. When I want to learn, I want to learn from teachers who have mastered their topic and can teach without apology for their knowledge, their perspective and their capacity to communicate engagingly. But, I stress, it must be a *gracious* authority. Few things are so wearisome as the arrogant teacher whose credentials or whose access to the podium is nothing but an abuse of power and authority. The gift of the teacher is evident in the unique interplay of *gravitas* and humility; they are not taken with themselves but with the material of which they speak and the truth to which they point. Their passion and longing is to serve their students and to serve the truth.

Pivotal commitments for the teacher and the scholar. Beyond these three critical marks of the teacher, consider the following. Good teaching, like every other vocation, calls for excellence. Good teaching is a craft that can and must be developed. If you are called to teaching, do it with an attention to detail, with careful preparation (on both the content and the delivery); give attention to what students need to learn and how they are going to learn it. Practice the art of teaching so that you become a master teacher.

Beware of teaching for money. Just as the love of money will destroy the soul of those called into business and the arts, it is always a danger that we would teach for profit. Always remember that the greatest reward in teaching is that the student learns and grows in wisdom, and in time excels in life and work and surpasses the teacher. There is no greater wealth.

Keep alive the commitment to learning. Yes, of course, all of us are called to continuous learning. And yet, in no vocation or calling is this more crucial, so that we are inspired in our learning, than in the calling to teach. Just as those called to business always remind us of the economic parameters and those in the arts consistently keep us in the pursuit of excellence, the teachers in our midst keep us in a continual learning mode. This suggests they are always learners themselves. I remember a graduate school professor I had before the days of word processors who made it an annual practice to burn his lecture notes in the spring, at the end of the academic year. It was his way to keep himself from lecturing from old notes, from always pursuing the easier option. He insisted that he was first a learner and then only a capable professor, and this exercise kept him learning.

Finally, while we all need patience, and we need it from all of those around us, we need it most from our teachers. Inherent within the calling of the teacher is the resolve to teach at the rate and pace that the student is capable of learning, whether the student is a child struggling with numbers or a doctoral student wrestling with a disparity between two critical sources. Patience is an absolute prerequisite for teaching well. I have a vivid memory of attending a public lecture when professor James Packer spoke simply and clearly of meaning of the Holy Trinity. At the conclusion he took questions about the most elementary aspects of the doctrine that had clearly been presented in the lecture itself and did so with grace and clarity and patience. He took the inquiries without being patronizing, without a trace of impatience, and took us through that same part of the lecture again.

Thanks be to God for our teachers, those who have taught us with wisdom and patience, who have led us into greater understanding and given us courage to live well.

THE CALL TO RELIGIOUS LEADERSHIP AND PASTORAL MINISTRY

We all need those who are called into business; we cannot live without goods and services. The arts are essential to each dimension of our lives; we need artists. And we all need teachers. Now I will add one more: everyone needs a pastor.

Each vocation is God's gift to the world. God graces the world through the talents, commitments and energies of each, and this grace in and to the world is the grace of God manifested through the extraordinary diversity of callings—of the multiple ways people are called to make a difference with and for God in the world. Each is a gift; each is a charism.

However, it is also crucial to stress that while each is a gift, for each one the character of the *call* is consistent with the character of the *calling*. Those called into business and the arts are not called in the same way as those called into pastoral ministry. The character of the calling is itself consistent with the vocation. Thus we cannot expect someone to complete a vocational test of questions about aptitudes, talents and temperaments, and then turn to the back of the booklet and conclude, "Aha, this means I am to be an engineer!" Why not? Because each person is called *differently;* the way or character of the calling is congruent with that to which one is called.

Therefore, a critical way we can foster vocational discernment is to elucidate the particular *character* of a calling or vocation—by asking how a particular vocation or calling is a "gift." What is its unique charism? How is this way of life a means by which God graces the world? From this we can extrapolate and consider how then someone might be called. While we do not have examples in the Christian Scriptures of all vocations, we do for the artist, businessperson and scholar.

Each of these callings represents a distinctive gift from God: the gift of a solid economic foundation, the gift of beauty and the gift of understanding. Each charism given by God finds expression in the talents, passions and commitments of individuals who embrace this call. The calling of the pastor is also a gift to the church and the world, but it is not merely one gift among many "career options." Yes, a person needs to discern if this is his or her calling. And they may well do so against the backdrop of other possibilities. But the calling to pastoral ministry has a distinctive character and carries a particular weight of responsibility.

The uniqueness of this calling. I have more or less reflected on the callings to business, to the arts and to education in relative isolation from other callings. But this is simply not possible for the calling of the pastor, because the calling or vocation of the pastor can only be conceived of in relation to other callings. This calling is unique in that the very purpose or orientation of those called to be religious leaders is, to use the language of Paul in Ephesians 4, to equip others for the work to which they are called. This vocation is pivotal and basic, for the particular calling of this vocation is the vocations of others—to equip and support the others in the work to which they are called. Richard John Neuhaus comments:

> The vocation of the Church is to sustain many vocations. The ordained minister, the one set aside and consecrated, is to illuminate the vocation of the Church and the vocations of the many people who are the Church. That means that the ordination is not exclusionary but exemplary.[8]

This is, then, a *special* vocation. While our mothers rightly insisted that *everyone* is special and no one is more special than anyone else, this vocation is particularly critical because the fulfillment of all other vocations is in some way dependent on this one. Further, those called to pastoral ministry need to appreciate this dynamic: their calling does not make them more special—the proverbial top of the vocational totem pole. Instead, their calling is to be a means by which other callings are realized and fulfilled. Nothing is gained by an egalitarianism that seeks to level pastors or discount their role or significance in congregational life. While there have certainly been abuses of authority in the life and witness of the church, the solution is neither to eliminate nor disparage the ministry of the pastor, but rather to reaffirm its original intent.

Appreciating this distinctive character to the calling of the pastor then enables people to begin to ask whether this is their calling. In Wendell Berry's fascinating novel *Jayber Crow*, the chief protagonist wrestles with his own sense of calling, wondering whether he had a "call" to pastoral ministry, wondering if his own calling would be something like that of Samuel but also fearing that like Jonah he might miss his call. In the end we read his conclusion: "I decided that I had better accept the call that had not come, just in case it had come and I had missed it."[9] Coming to clarity about whether a person is called to pastoral ministry or not will never be an easy process. Jayber in the end was guided by a wise professor who helped him see that he was not likely called to be a pastor. But if Jayber or anyone is to appreciate the calling to pastoral ministry, they will necessarily need to give specific attention to *how* a person is called to this ministry. For everyone, regardless of their calling, vocational discernment is a two-dimensional exercise: one of recognizing their inner resonance with this charism and, second, of listening to the witness of the community. The community can ask: how do we experience this person as "gift." Does this correspond with what it means to be a pastor?

It is worth noting here that many feel called to pastoral ministry for all the wrong reasons (and, no doubt, there are many who feel they are *not* called, again, for all the wrong reasons). While we can easily identify the obvious misses when individuals seek pastoral office out of a longing to be loved or affirmed, or as a means to find power or influence, there are other less obvious misses that also need to be recognized. In other words, we need to help well-intentioned people discern well. Discerning vocation will always be a struggle, regardless of our call, if we live with a misguided or inordinate desire for wealth, or a misguided longing for power or influence. No one can discern well unless he or she is prepared to seriously engage the question of motives. However, what is needed is an approach to discerning vocation that assumes sincerity, an eagerness to do that which is good and a resolve to do what God is calling one to do.

Conventional wisdom allows that when a person seems to have religious propensities (an overt orientation toward spirituality or a sincerity in devotion), or if he or she is what is commonly called a "people person" (an enjoyment of being with, caring for and empathizing with others), or if the person seems to love truth and study, or seemly has a propensity to generous and sacrificial service, he or

she likely is the kind of person who would be a suitable pastor.
But *all* vocations are about God, people, truth and service. All are
called to their work in such a manner that they do it "as unto the Lord"
and for the sake of others. The cloistered nun is in prayer for the
world—for people. The carpenter works with wood, but with a passion
for quality that will ultimately serve others. The lawyer works as much
as the dentist, the social worker, the artist and the shopkeeper out of
reverence for God, a resolve to serve others with generosity and integrity and a commitment to truth. So these kinds of dispositions do not
necessarily mean that a person is called to be a pastor. To discern the
pastoral calling, we need to look at this question from another perspective, with a view that, as religious communities, we will have both
clarity on how we can dissuade those who seek religious leadership or
pastoral office for the wrong reasons and a good basis for inspiring and
encouraging those who are truly called to this work.

The elements of the pastoral vocation. One way of thinking about
the pastoral vocation is to posture it as having three fundamental
features: (1) the ministry of the Word, usually in teaching and preaching; (2) the ministry of empowerment—or as it is often found in
many translations of Ephesians 4:12, "equipping the saints," though
the role of the Word is central here; and (3) the ministry of oversight,
not as one who "rules" but as one who is alert to and attends to the
needs of the community of faith. Integral to each of these is the practice of prayer.

Insofar as this is an accurate portrayal of the ministry of the pastor—preacher-teacher, equipper, overseer—it is helpful to identify the
ability, intelligence and knowledge (the three words associated with
Bezalel in Ex 31:3) that make this ministry possible and effective.

Surely it includes ability in communication: the *capacity* to preach
and teach. Further, as Craig Dykstra has suggested, there is a particular imagination that is essential for "good" pastoral ministry—"a
distinctive kind of intelligence," "a particular way of seeing and
thinking that is particular to that profession."[10] And then, also, there
is a *knowledge* both of divinity but also of the way that congregations

work. Both dimensions of understanding are essential: insight into the Christian faith but also understanding of the character of congregational life and ministry.

Arising at the confluence of these responsibilities and capacities is a fundamental and essential charism that makes a pastor a pastor. Could it be the deep, underlying confidence in the power of Christ to, by Word and Spirit, make all things new? Is this not, at the heart, what this vocation is all about? This perspective, then, would elicit a deep underlying passion for the Word made plain to the people of God, and also a deep underlying patience that allows God to do God's work in God's time. And it must be both, for the confidence is in Word and Spirit.

Thinking back to the other three vocations identified earlier, it so happens that those called to these professions are often attracted to the pastorate. Artists are taken by the liturgical and aesthetic dimensions of pastoral ministry. Scholars are attracted to the elements of study and teaching. Those whose instincts are for business and commerce are often drawn to the pastorate too, for different reasons. Admittedly, sometimes they choose pastoral ministry because they are seeking something that they view to be more noble or sacred than the work of business. But sometimes it is out of a kind of frustration with how slowly and ineffectively churches seem to operate. They think their skills and capacities as businesspeople could fix things; they see in the office of the pastor a chance to make things happen, to "manage" things so that there are productive outcomes. While all of these are legitimate aspirations, good things in themselves, the result is a frustrated artist, scholar or businessperson. The vocation of the pastor is not their true métier.

The pastoral call is not, in the end, about beauty or scholarship or making things happen; it is fundamentally a matter of empowering others to respond to their respective callings. This requires a vision for the reign of Christ in the world that is oriented toward the world rather than the church. The pastor is servant of the Spirit and the Word, for in the end it is not so much the minister as it is God who enables his people to live out their callings in the world. A person called into pastoral ministry has a vision for the enabling of others, but also for *how* this empowerment happens—that is, through Word and Spirit.

The way in which a pastor is called, then, must be consistent with this vocation; it will be reflected in the inner impulses and desires of the heart, and the conversations with friends, family and mentors as the individual considers whether or not he or she is called to this ministry. Are one's passions, longings, aspirations (and frustrations!) consistent with this calling? Is there an appreciation of that which ultimately makes a difference? Does this find expression in the person's own experience? Is he or she taken not so much by beauty and scholarship and productivity as the mysterious Other—the intangible Spirit and Word—which while intangible finds concrete expression in the wonder of the liturgy and the ordinariness of congregational life? We can ask of the prospective candidate for pastoral ministry: Have you seen, understood and embraced the energy that makes congregations work? Do you appreciate that the key is not that of the proficient manager or pragmatist, the empathetic listener, or the artist or storyteller, and not even the scholar or teacher. However good and indispensable each of these roles is to a congregation, it is rather the Word and Spirit, not managed but aided and abetted by the gracious work of the person whose ministry is that of teaching, equipping and overseeing. A pastor, then, is not under pressure to be scholar, counselor, artist and manager—the superpastor who can be all things to all people! The pastor's orientation is to the Word and to the twofold question: How is the Spirit at work, in this place at this time, and How can I, as pastor, foster this attentiveness in our worship, our learning, our fellowship and our service to our world? A pastor is not a hero; a pastor is one devoted to prayer and the ministry of the Word (Acts 6:4), not to the exclusion of other critical and important activities, and not as the only one who assumes these roles (for we are hopefully cultivating the capacity to be partners with others on the pastoral staff and with gifted lay pastors), but as the one for whom this is at the heart of what a pastor does. When a person is considering a potential call to pastoral ministry, these are the inner impulses he or she needs to be attentive to; these are the dynamics that need to shape the conversation with one's counselors, friends and advisers.

CONCLUSION

I have identified four occupations that represent four distinct ways of being in the world in response to the call of God. They are offered by way of illustration; a similar exercise could also profile the work of the government official or politician, the lawyer and those who pursue justice, the journalist, and others. Further, I should also note that I am not suggesting that only business people do business and artists do art. To the contrary: all of us buy and sell, all of us have the capacity to do art, each one of us has opportunities to teach, formally and informally, and we all have avenues of ministry where we can speak the Word and encourage and equip others for their callings. I am speaking here of those for whom these "callings" are a divine *necessity*, that which they "must do," as examples of what it might mean for those called into these kinds of work and perhaps as an encouragement and guide to each of us as we discern our divine necessity.

8

COURAGE
AND CHARACTER

Turning from the Fear
That So Easily Entangles Us

Second Timothy 1:7 and Luke 10:41-42 are pertinent for one of the most crucial questions of all when it comes to discerning our vocations and acting on them. In 2 Timothy, the apostle addresses Timothy on a whole host of issues, but as the letter opens he gets to the heart of the matter rather quickly, saying, "God has not given us a spirit of [fear], but rather a spirit of power and of love and of self-discipline" (1:7). What he speaks to is not incidental or marginal: God has not given Timothy, and by implication God has not given us, a spirit of *fear* (variously translated as "timidity" or "cowardice"). Rather, God has given us a Spirit of power, love and self-discipline.

Then consider also the familiar story of Martha and Mary as found in Luke 10. Jesus comes to the home of these sisters after a day on the road. Martha is busy in the kitchen preparing a meal, no doubt. Mary in contrast is at the feet of Jesus, listening as an attentive disciple to what he is saying. Then Martha comes to them and rather than speaking to Mary with her concern she asks Jesus to tell Mary to help her. "The Lord answered her, 'Martha, Martha, you are worried and distracted by many things; there is need of only one thing. Mary has chosen the better part, which will not be taken away from her'" (Lk 10:41-42). In his response Jesus observes that Mary has chosen a "better part."

It has often been assumed that this account is given to profile the superiority of the religious or the contemplative life over the active life of service. Different groups or traditions have concluded differently: some that religious activities in general are superior, and others that specifically the contemplative life is the higher calling.

But in both cases, the point is missed. Yes, the way of contemplation and prayer and attentiveness to Jesus is essential and necessary, and, yes, this is the better way to live as a disciple of Jesus. Yet, because this story comes right after the parable of the good Samaritan, we cannot conclude that the contemplative life is superior to the active life. Could it be that the central point Jesus is making is captured by Jesus' first words in response to Martha's complaint: "Martha, Martha, you are anxious and distracted"—or "worried"— "about many things." This is the heart of the matter; rather than doing her work with focus and clarity, her heart was filled with anxiety and worry.

Taken together, we have two New Testament references that are particularly pertinent to our reflections on vocation. There is a growing chorus coming from diverse sources and contexts that is rightly making the observation that the greatest threat to the fulfillment of our vocations is not external to us but *internal*. The greatest obstacle to our vocations is not our family of origin, our culture or society, the economy or our company or our religious heritage or community. Yes, all of these could be obstacles and hurdles that impede us along the way. But could it be that the greatest obstacle is looking at us in the mirror: we are held back and dragged down, and we miss an opportunity because we are anxious and worried about many things. We see fear in our eyes. And the most crucial question when it comes to vocation is this: Will we have the *courage* to do what we are being called to?

It took courage for Clarence Jordan, in the late 1950s, to set up the Koinonia farm in southwest Georgia—to persevere with this community of racial reconciliation in the face of the threats of the Ku Klux Klan, to persevere when one of the farm's facilities was torched and the grounds strafed by machine-gun fire.

It took courage when Wolfgang Amadeus Mozart, who was brilliant on the piano and could have accumulated great wealth with the fees from his performances, made the choice to put his energies into composition, his true calling. (We are the beneficiaries today.)

It took courage for Dorothy Day, an unwed mother, a feisty social activist and journalist, to lead a movement to care for the poor and the hungry of New York City. Using her writing skills, she called all Christians, but particularly American Catholics, to live with more compassion. To do so, she had to confront the religious authorities of the day—with whom she was never popular.

It took courage for fifty-one-year-old Reynolds Price, American writer and novelist, to not only accept that he had cancer of the spine but to confront his sickness. Despite profound humiliation and horrible pain he refused to feel sorry for himself, but chose rather, in the healing that did come, to accept his new limitations. He works now from a wheelchair and has published thirteen books—novels, plays, memoirs and collections of poems and essays.

It took courage for Albert Benjamin Simpson, senior Presbyterian minister, pastor of a prominent congregation in New York City, to see, when his congregation refused to accept Italian immigrants, that there was no choice, that he had to step aside and start something new, a movement that would emphasize both evangelism and social concern, a movement that would affirm a doctrine of sanctification that incorporated both soul and body. Eventually he began the first Bible institute and missionary training center in North America, in Nyack, New York.

It took courage for Nelson Mandela to refuse to be victimized by his oppressors, to refuse to take a course of revenge against the white authorities of South Africa. As a civil rights advocate for all residents of his country, he had been imprisoned for over twenty years, often in solitary confinement. Yet his generous spirit was never broken; neither was his resolve that he would seek to overcome racial tensions. In 1995, a year after Mandela had become president and South Africa was hosting the World Cup of Rugby, and his fellow black Africans were refusing to support their own, primarily white, South African team, it took courage to don the team uniform. Nelson Mandela put it on! He wore it to the stadium, and dramatically the whole country, it seemed with one voice, cheered for this team which till then was associated with white South Africa! It was a powerful symbolic action, but it represented the courage of this man in his commitment to racial reconciliation.

Benigno ("Ninoy") Aquino had been first jailed and later exiled from the Philippines because he was a political threat to then dictator Ferdinand Marcos. But after several years in the United States he resolved that he could no longer stay away. It took courage for Ninoy to board a plane in Boston, in August 1983, knowing that his life was threatened and that Marcos would most likely once more put him in jail. He had, after all, made the point in a public speech in 1980 that the Philippine people were, in his words, "worth dying for." Tragically, he was assassinated on the tarmac of the international airport in Manila, an airport that now bears his name. And his courage inspired his wife, Cory, and thousands of others to take to the streets in February 1986 and stand in front of tanks and armored vehicles, and refuse to move until Marcos and his wife, Imelda, fled the country.

All the virtues are sustained by courage. We are not women and men of virtue unless we learn to overcome our fears and live in courage.

But celebrating courage does not mean that we praise any act of bravado regardless of motives or outcomes. Many foolish things have been done in the name of courage, conviction and principle. There were white leaders in the American South in the 1960s who refused—courageously, we might say—to allow African American students into the public schools and into the universities. But this was bigotry, not courage. And there are religious zealots, people who in the name of a religious cause will maintain that they see the truth and demand that others agree, who seem courageous, but true courage is also generous.

Here is the irony: these people are not courageous but fearful. They are driven by the fear of losing control, fear of people who are different, fear that their positions, security, comforts or influence will be lost.

So, will we have the courage to do what we are being called to be and do? As we consider this, it is important to note that true courage has several notable qualifiers.

COURAGE AND WISDOM

First, for example, true courage will always be qualified by wisdom. Sometimes we are profoundly impressed with grandiose schemes—people with visions of some remarkable future. We think they must be courageous people indeed to have such an extraordinary vision. Leadership takes vision, but sometimes we lose our capacity to distinguish between a grandiose scheme and a courageous vision. With all such aspirations, we need to ask: Is this truly a courageous vision or is it nothing but hubris and presumption?

When we are tempted to be miracle workers—turning stone to bread—or heroes who can leap from the height of the temple, it helps to be reminded that our Lord rejected this path and chose the way of the cross. Earlier in this chapter I identified some prominent people who had grand visions. But what marked them as women and men of courage was not a great scheme; it was the courage to do what needed to be done and said.

True courage always involves risks—of loss of reputation, that not everyone will praise you or that you will lose influence. But you take the risk because you choose to live by conscience. True courage might actually mean backing away from something with a resolve to quietly leave and move elsewhere.

In other words, wisdom and courage are partners. If an action is cavalier and perhaps even irresponsible, we do not call it courageous. True courage is marked by prudence.

MORAL INTEGRITY

Another qualifier of true courage is that it is rooted in moral integrity. When the apostle Paul calls his readers to think of themselves with sober judgment (Rom 12:3) he has already urged them not to be "conformed to this world" (v. 2). His assumption is that they already have moral integrity and commitment. This includes financial honesty; it assumes sexual integrity—faithfulness to one's spouse, or celibacy for those who are single. Moral integrity also incorporates consistency of speech, care in what we say and how it is said, including the refusal to participate in a lie or to flatter another.

In other words, our private lives and our work in the world are part of a whole. If we have clarity of thought and heart when it comes to our vocation, it will be because of purity of heart. Vocational integrity—living consistent with who we are—is only possible when there is a commitment to moral integrity.

GRATITUDE AND HUMILITY

But true courage, while founded on moral integrity, is also qualified by gratitude and humility. Without these virtues, moral integrity is nothing more than moralism and judgmentalism. When the apostle Paul advises Timothy that God has not given us a spirit of fear but of love, power and self-discipline, we are reminded of a crucial and vital qualifier: true courage is always matched by humility, grace, forgiveness and compassion. Genuine courage is always complemented by a teachable spirit.

Gratitude and humility are two cardinal virtues of the spiritual life—the two from which faith, hope and love spring, the two virtues or graces that make courage life-giving.

Gratitude is the virtue of celebrating the goodness of God and living with a fundamental conviction that God is indeed good. It represents a fundamental posture of life: to see the good, the noble and the excellent, and to receive it as sheer gift. The alternative is the posture of complaint, of constantly assuming that we deserve better, that we are getting the raw deal in life and, of course, that God is not really good.

Humility is the soul mate of gratitude, and both are the heart expressions of those who have experienced the mercy of God. Humility is evident acceptance of who we are—the grace to embrace our own identity and calling rather than live by pretense. And this means that we refuse to envy another. This humility frees us to celebrate the gifts and abilities of another rather than feeling diminished by them. Further, this humility is probably also evident in a sense of humor, a sign that we are not taking ourselves too seriously.

PATIENCE

Genuine courage is also qualified by patience. When it comes to vocation, one of the great temptations is thinking that we should act immediately on what we are called to do. The sooner something happens the better, and we feel rushed, pressured and intent on accomplishing "great" things quickly.

But God works slowly; his ways are often subtle and almost imperceptible. He is never in a hurry. The shepherd David was anointed to be king of Israel. He had God's blessing and he knew he had the position; his call was clear. But, remarkably, it was years, many years, before he actually sat on the throne. He had to wait patiently until the throne was given to him by God. And in his waiting he refused to take things into his own hands or force the hand of God. He refused to kill the incumbent king, his archrival and enemy, when he could easily have done so. He chose to wait on the timing of God.

Then there is Nelson Mandela, president of South Africa. If ever there was a person destined to be the leader of his people, it was he. Yet he spent most of his adult life in prison, waiting. He did not fulfill his call (at least in terms of the role as president and leader of his people) until he was past "retirement age."

True courage is matched by patience—with God, whose work is often imperceptible and slow; with others, being generous with them; and with oneself.

Patience means recognizing that our vocation will be fulfilled *eventually;* we do not need to grasp after it or jump at opportunities prematurely. We can eagerly engage in a study program in the present knowing that opportunities will open up in the future. It is very unwise to cut short an education program now because of some opportunity, unless it is clear that the opportunity is itself chosen as an act of patience.

If we are the parents of small children, we can wait, knowing that opportunities will come in the future, but for now our priority is to care for these children given to us by God. In other words, with patience we can accept that our options are necessarily limited during this time. And we do not resent this (which the children themselves would feel) but embrace it with grace and patience.

By patience, I do not mean that we do nothing but rather that we trust our future to God and take full advantage of the present to enjoy the moment, learn from it and serve in the opportunities that *are* given to us rather than sitting around waiting.

Nelson Mandela, for example, established an extensive system of study and learning in the prison system, preparing himself and others for the day they would have to provide leadership for their country.

A parent can be fully present to her or his children but also see the child-rearing years as a season for reflection and study as well as a time to form substantial friendships. A person who feels called to be a professor can eagerly engage the opportunities for service that *are* given while awaiting for an opening. Patience means that we wait with grace, without bemoaning lost time or assuming that time is somehow being wasted.

Courage must be characterized by wisdom, moral integrity, gratitude, humility and patience. But the bottom line remains *courage*.

THE COURAGE TO BE

It is what Paul Tillich called *The Courage to Be*. Though Tillich spoke as a theistic existentialist, the principle has validity even for those who do not accept this philosophical presupposition. Do we have the courage to be—the courage to be who we are and do what we are called to do?

Theologian Paul Tillich makes the case that courage is essentially the courage to be *oneself*. "Courage," he says, "is the affirmation of one's essential nature."[1] Because we often fear this, Tillich notes that fear is not only the fear of dying but also of *living*. His question really is, Do you have to the courage to live? When we do, we find joy, for "joy is the emotional expression of the courageous Yes to one's own true being."[2] This affirmation is rooted in a basic assumption: that our essential nature is good—something we can and must affirm and accept. God created us good. And while we have certainly had that essential nature distorted and confused because of sin, the effects of sin are not so great that we are incapable of coming to terms with who God has made us to be. Our redemption includes accepting God's creation and embracing the grace that enables us to live consistent with this creation.

Jackson Bate, in an extraordinary biography of Samuel Johnson, celebrates the courage of this English man of letters. He observes that central to Johnson's courage was his honesty.

> We have a hero who starts out with everything against him, including painful liabilities of personal temperament—a turbulent imagination, acute anxiety, aggressive pride, extreme impatience, radical self-division and self-conflict. He is compelled to wage long and desperate struggles, at two crucial times in his life, against what he feared was the onset of insanity. Yet step by step, often in the hardest possible way, he wins through to the triumph of honesty to experience that [which] all of us prize in our hearts. . . .
>
> One of the first effects he has on us is that we find ourselves catching, by contagion, something of his courage. . . .
>
> His honesty to human experience cuts through the "cant," the loose talk and pretense, which all of us get seduced into needlessly complicating life for both ourselves and other people.[3]

Johnson was a man of profound moral sincerity. He detested false piety. He refused to be a victim and blame his circumstances and his limitations on anyone. For him, envy was a waste of energy. But most of all, what made him a man of courage was his honesty about himself. Bates calls it his "massive honesty."

Courage begins with honesty about our fears. The wise know that fears haunt us from within and cripple us if we do not face them with honesty, "massive honesty."

When government officials operate out of fear, they shut down the opposition or run from criticism and accountability to the people. When religious leaders live in fear, they "lord it over [the] flock" rather than leading by example (1 Pet 5:3)—however legitimate or noble we make our "fear" appear. When parents are afraid, they become controllers and manipulators of their children.

We rationalize and say that we did what we did in order to keep peace, or because we did not want to hurt the feelings of another, or because we are concerned for the well-being of our families, or some other high and noble spiritual aspiration. Our rationale or reasons may sound legitimate, but if we are honest, they are often nothing more than rationalizations. We are really motivated by fear.

We don't speak the truth to the boss, saying what we know we need to say because we fear the implications for our future job prospects. We don't speak the truth in love to a friend because we fear that he or she will strike back at us in anger or will reject us.

We don't venture into a new opportunity because we fear failure and so would rather continue in mediocrity rather than truly strive for excellence. We allow people to call us to submission when they really mean compliance, and they persuade us of the lie that compliance is the same as spiritual submission. We don't do our best at something because we fear success and the responsibility that it brings.

Just because we acknowledge our fears does not somehow make us courageous or justify our actions. But it is a start. When we acknowledge our fears, we can ask if these are legitimate and whether we are really living in faith, hope and love, or if our fears are nothing but a rationalization for actions that are actually less than noble. We can at least begin to move toward massive honesty—an honesty with our fears that enables us to cast our cares upon our Father in heaven and become, truly, a courageous people.

Only with courage will we have the capacity to move beyond convention, compliance and imitation, and truly be who *we* are called to be. This takes courage in the face of pressure from family. It takes courage to choose our vocation in light of our own expectations and in a cultural context that encourages us to seek comfort, fame and power. Our hearts, our fallen hearts, that is, have a natural propensity toward the comfortable, easy and secure. But often, if we are to fulfill our vocations, we will have to run counter to these superficial propensities. The longing for wealth, comfort and security will inevitably undermine our capacity to know and respond fully to our vocation.

The longing for fame is also a great threat to vocation. Men in particular are prone to seek or accept positions that raise their profile and feed their egos. But this is a false satisfaction. I know that for myself I need to embrace my vocation even if it means that I go through my life in obscurity. I cannot choose an occupation or even fill my time with projects and tasks that either explicitly or subtly are done to gain recognition. In so doing I am undermining my capacity to know and fulfill my vocation.

It takes courage: the courage to be, the courage to be true to who we are, even if it means living on the edge, living with risk, living with less security, less influence and less power, because it means that we have chosen the way that is true to who we are, true to ourselves, true to our call.

When we make the transition to our senior years, it will take courage to let go of our roles, our occupations and the outward forms of influence and power. Many of us will feel that we have been pushed aside and are no longer valued. The great danger at this transition is that to sustain a sense of our personal dignity and worth, we will cling to our titles, our roles, our "influence" for fear that if we let go, we lose everything that has mattered to us. This is particularly a danger for those whose personal identity has been wrapped up in their work, their company or the organization they have poured their lives

into. When we are feeling the loss of influence and significance, it
will take courage to let go and accept that our role will be very different. But only in letting go, the critical act of courage, do we become a
source of blessing and wisdom. By fearfully clinging to our influence,
we actually lose it; through the courage of letting go, we actually gain
influence.

We will only be able to live with this degree of courage, reflected
in focus and passion, when we are clear about who we are and what
we have been called to do. As Parker Palmer notes, this is only possible if we live "connected" rather than disconnected lives.[4] If we feel
disconnected from our work, from the organization we serve with or
from those we serve in our work, the resolution must come through
a renewed connection with ourselves. Only as we live with this connectedness are we at peace with ourselves. Our words and our deeds
have integrity because they are consistent with the fundamental
character of who we are. We are not living by pretense; we are not
living a lie.

This means, almost more than anything else, that we come to
terms with our fear. We can only live connected lives of focus, courage, intentionality and purpose, if we are honest with ourselves and
come to some level of resolution of the fears that so easily hound us,
sap our energies and undermine our capacity to be all that we are
called to be.

Palmer thus observes: when we blame others—responding as victims—rather than taking responsibility for our lives, it is invariably
the case that we do so because we have failed to be honest about our
fears and what is really driving us to a particular pattern of behavior.

Thus, will we be consumed by our fears, or will we be able to confront them honestly and somehow tame them? I suspect that in this
life they will never go away completely, but in God's grace they can be
kept at bay. Yet this is only the case if we are honest about our fears
and find friends and supporters who enable us through their encouragement to rise above them. Only then do we live "connected" lives—
lives that find integration from the very core of our being.

THE GRACE OF GOD AND
THE ENCOURAGEMENT OF OTHERS

In a fascinating study of mysticism and vocation, Canadian philosopher James R. Horne makes the observation that mystics (those who have had a profoundly emotional experience of an external, perhaps transcendent, authority) and those who make a good vocational choices have two characteristics. They are certain of themselves and are prepared to take risks.[5] It is a matter of both courage and calling, the courage to accept the risk that inevitably comes with embracing our vocations, but a courage that is rooted in a confidence that we know ourselves and have no desire to be anything other than who God has made us to be. This is never absolute self-knowledge, but we are able to have a meaningful degree of self-knowledge from which to act with courage.

If we are honest with ourselves and with what is in our hearts, we know and feel that this world is too much for us. We are in over our heads. We live and work in a discouraging world—at home, at work, in our studies, in the church, in contexts and settings that insidiously undermine our capacity to be people of courage. Consequently, our only hope is to appreciate that we are not in this alone.

First, our confidence is that God goes with us and fills us with his Spirit. When the apostle Paul speaks of the extraordinary peace of God that guards our hearts and minds (Phil 4:7), he speaks of an inner serenity and connectedness that frees us to live, work and speak with courage. Our only hope for acting with courage is to acknowledge our fears before God and receive this consolation.

Second, we are also called to encourage one another. When the apostle Paul says that he does not lose heart, meaning that he remains en-*couraged*, he does so in virtually the same breath in which he says: "But God, who consoles the downcast, consoled us by the arrival of Titus" (2 Cor 7:6). Paul speaks of the encouragement that comes through a man much younger than himself.

There is hardly a more powerful ministry than that of encouragement. When we encourage others, we pass on that quality and virtue to them, that intangible inner strength which enables us to rise above the fears that so easily cripple us and to have the strength we need for this day, this hour, this moment to do what we know we are called to do, to follow conscience and to agree with Paul that we have not been given a spirit of fear. We do not walk this road alone; the grace of God consoles us; and we walk together. Thus it is vital that we find encouragement and make it a point to en*courage* others, for few things are so crucial to our capacity to fulfill our God-given callings.

THE CAPACITY FOR CONTINUOUS LEARNING

The Way We Stay Alive and Engaged

There are at least five points of leverage that enable us to be all that we are called to be as stewards of our gifts, opportunities and potential. The first has already been discussed: character, particularly *courage*. Each of the others is the subject of the four chapters that follow:

- continuous learning
- our capacity to live and work through difficulty and disappointment with emotional resilience
- the organizations we are a part of
- the routine and rhythm of our lives, particularly the interplay between solitude and community

Each is a point at which we can invest time and energy in ways that will bring a good return: equipping us to discern and fulfill our vocations. This chapter will focus on the first, the potential impact of always being a learner.

CONTINUOUS LEARNERS

It is not an overstatement to say that our potential for long-term vocational growth and vitality is in direct proportion to our capacity to learn. Learning is one of our principle points of leverage as stewards of our gifts and opportunities. But further, change is a fundamental feature of the world we work in, and critical to our capacity to respond and adapt to change is knowing how to learn. Learning enables us to embrace change effectively.

Furthermore, we cannot assume that we will have one occupation for the whole of our careers. Thinking just *occupationally* rather than vocationally, futurologists were suggesting only recently that the average person in the West would experience five significant occupational or career changes in the course of a normal lifespan of work. But now those same writers are observing that the trend has continued and now the average is *seven*. And the obvious conclusion to this is that only those who are learners—continuous learners—will be able to survive and thrive.

When we ask, What will enable us to, in the words of the apostle Paul, "fan into flame the gift of God" (2 Tim 1:6 NIV), there is no doubt that a key means by which this happens is through intentional, mindful, continuous learning. As Peter Senge insists, people who have "personal mastery" are those who "live in a continual learning mode." He speaks of this as a lifelong discipline and notes that "people with a high level of personal mastery are acutely aware of their ignorance, their incompetence, their growth areas."[1] Mary Catherine Bateson aptly says, "Learning is the new continuity for individuals, innovation the new continuity for business."[2]

It is imperative that we view the learning process as pertinent to the *whole* of who we are, not just the work that we are trained to do. Formal, academic study is just one part and perhaps even a small part of all that it means to be a learner.

Sharan Merriam and Carolyn Clark, in their fine study *Lifelines*, effectively show that life is fundamentally about two things—our work and our relationships. And maturity is found in having the capacity to (1) work well and effectively, and (2) to live in relationship—to know how to love and receive love. We define our identities by our work and our relationships, and Merriam and Clark contend that maturity is found in the interrelationship between work and love, and that the key to this interplay is the capacity to learn.[3] I would add that failure in either of these two areas—work or relationships—invariably affects the other. Though they are distinct, they cannot be polarized or compartmentalized.

Further, each of these areas offers opportunities for growth and personal development. The first is task oriented, with a focus on achievement. The second is people oriented, with a focus on feelings and relationships. The challenge of true personal maturity is to develop the capacity to be complete and effective in both areas. And Merriam and Clark contend that "learning is the linchpin in this process." In other words, our lives are structured around work and relationships, and learning is the means by which we develop our capacity to work well and live in loving relationships.[4]

We learn from family, from work and from friends. We learn from failure as well as success, we learn from being let down but also by being affirmed and loved. We learn from the complexity of daily life—from the dilemmas we face, from the problems we encounter, from the situations that inevitably cross our paths. If we learn well, we grow in our capacity to work and love—to achieve something but also to live in healthy relationships. The goal then is to be effective at what we are called to do—to become a master of our craft, you might say—but also to be people of highly fruitful and meaningful relationships, in marriage, family, friendship and community.

But it must be stressed that this is not merely a matter of mastering each aspect individually; maturity is found not only in and through each of these but also in the capacity to resolve the demands of both—to be effective in both respects simultaneously. I am an academic administrator who is a father of two sons. These represent distinct areas of my life, but I am not the one without the other. I am an academic administrator shaped by being a father. My effectiveness as a father is profoundly significant to my capabilities as the executive director of nonprofit agency. And as a father, part of my sons' formation includes living out my call and responsibilities as an administrator. My work is not isolated from my life as a family member.

I grew up as the child of missionaries to Ecuador, South America. And one of the perpetual debates among mission societies in the 1960s was whether it was good and appropriate for children to be sent away to boarding schools. The justification for this kind of action was twofold: children needed an American-style education, and their parents needed to be freed to give themselves full time to their missionary responsibilities.

The rationale is flawed on both accounts, but it is the second that intrigues. I was away at a boarding school for my initial grade-school years. But later my parents made the courageous decision—for which I am profoundly grateful to them—to confront mission authorities. They resolved that they would keep me and my sister at home, and that we would attend a local school—even if this meant they would have to resign from the mission organization. There were many reasons for this decision, but one of them is captured in my mother's words when she noted that she was both a mother and a missionary, and that her effectiveness as a missionary was directly linked to the fact that she was a mother. My mother insisted that she was not going to judge others who chose otherwise; many people she has very high regard for sent their children to boarding schools. But for her it made no sense to have a ministry to women, young women with young children, while she sent her children miles away! It made no sense that somehow her children were an *obstacle* to her ministry as a missionary. To the contrary, she ministered as a whole person, as a mother who taught women who had children. And her very mothering gave integrity, character and depth to her teaching ministry.

In looking at the two dimensions of work and relationships, it is probably fair to say that, on the whole, men have been more prone to emphasize the first, mastering work; women the second, mastering relationships (at least in Western societies). But men are becoming more aware of the importance of relationships; we are beginning to see that relationships are an end in themselves. Relationships cannot and need not be sacrificed as a means to be complete in work. Indeed, if they are neglected, our work suffers. And women are increasingly conscious that they have unique vocations, and the call to work is an essential dimension of their personal identity and fulfillment.

It only makes sense, therefore, that as a fundamental orientation of our lives we nurture a love of learning in *both* of these dimensions of life: in our work and our relationships. Learning is empowering: it frees us to serve more effectively. It enables us to respond to problems and challenges with minds and hearts capable of improvisation. If we are learners, we are less intimidated by changes in the home, in the workplace and in our social environment. And if we are confident that we know *how* to learn, we are more likely to have the necessary courage to tackle things we have never done before. If we are learners, we are growing in our capacity to live in authentic relationships, in family and friendship, within the context of congregational life and in our places of work as we learn to work with others.

Indeed, in the end, learning trumps intellect. We all have different IQs. No doubt some among us are smarter. And yet intelligence is of little value if it is not matched by learning. Learners will always go further, do more and make a greater difference; wise women and men are always asking, What can I learn in this situation? What do I need to learn to respond to this new development or opportunity?

Peter Drucker suggests that we should always sustain two streams of learning and self-improvement. And though he is speaking specifically about work and career, what he says is equally applicable whether we are speaking of learning that enables our work or our relationships. The two streams Drucker suggests are (1) "do better what you already do reasonably well," and (2) in response to change— new opportunity, new responsibility—learn a *new* skill.[5] In other words, continue to improve in an area where you are already effective. If you are a teacher, even a very good teacher, continue to grow in your capacity to teach. This may be through learning a new approach to teaching, or in adapting your teaching to new or different situations. Second, Drucker rightly calls us to develop new skills in response to new circumstances or opportunities—whether learning a language, how to be a parent or a new computer program.

In each case, think of learning as a way to mature in the expression and fulfillment of your vocation and relationships.

HOW WE LEARN

It is imperative that we step back at this point and affirm that learning happens in a wide diversity of ways for different people. Some thrive in classrooms; some don't. Some find it easy to learn from books. Others would never learn by reading a manual; they learn by observation. Yet others cannot learn except in the context of relationships and conversation.

Consequently, it is helpful both to identify the *different* ways people learn and also to affirm that we each have our *preferred* way of knowing. Yet some things are best learned or only learned in particular ways. This suggests we need to recognize two things. First, we are wise to affirm our preferred way of learning and exploit it to our benefit. Second, we also need to be attentive to each model or style of learning, for, indeed, some things that matter to us can only be learned by one approach or style.

Though there are complex and sophisticated analyses of the different styles of learning, I have found it helpful to identify four approaches, which are summarized as follows.

- Some learn best cognitively—through lectures and reading. Here the emphasis is on *intellectual* understanding as the key to learning. It is assumed that the learner then applies and lives out the principles and implications learned.

- Some learn best socially—through small group discussions. *Conversation* is the key to this kind of learning. The actual learning comes *with* others as wisdom, insight and perspectives are shared. Learning happens together.

- Some learn best *by doing*. Learning occurs while doing the very thing that is being taught. This kind of learning often, but not always, takes place under the direction of a supervisor. In this approach an individual develops a capacity to learn from trial and error, from seeing and sensing both what works and what does not work.

• Some learn best through *observation*. These people are most comfortable approaching a concept or skill by standing back, outside of the focus of the event, and watching from a safe distance before actively engaging the issue at hand or the skill being taught.

Consider all four approaches in more detail. Some love books, libraries, classrooms and lectures, and they thrive on the formal structures and patterns of an academic life. Some struggle with this approach, not because they are not smart or intellectually capable, but because this is not their preferred mode of learning. The fact is that this is the best way for assimilating knowledge and information, of appropriating wisdom—whether from a teacher or from an author. In other words, if I want to know what Karl Barth taught and thought, I need to read his books. I need to find the quiet space for reflective or thoughtful reading; I need to take notes and consider what he says in the light of what others say about the same issues. Attentive listening—to lectures or teaching—and thoughtful reading are an essential means by which we appropriate much that is critical to a full practice and program of learning. While not everyone will gravitate to this mode of learning, it is a mode that we all need to incorporate into our learning patterns because there are some things that can only be learned in this way.

For those who love conversation, learning happens not so much by listening to a wise or competent teacher or through reading a text or book, but through reflective conversation, which they usually find to be most fruitful with peers—others who are at similar stages in the learning process. They love to learn *with* others. But more, these people discover truth through the very interaction they have with others, who may see things differently or may have experienced the very things being learned.

When I use small groups in my teaching, I consistently notice that some students immediately gravitate to a group. They have been listening to a lecture, and now they are eager to talk—not to dominate but to share their perspectives in a safe environment where they can thrive on the give-and-take of conversation. Others, in contrast, wish that the lecture would go on. They wonder why they have to talk with others when they enrolled in this course to hear this teacher. What value is there in talking about this topic with their peers who know no more about the subject matter than they do?

But conversation is a vital means by which we learn. This requires the capacity to listen and appreciate that others see things differently. Further, through listening and conversation we sharpen and help one another clarify our thinking, and then begin to live in light of what we have learned. The first approach to learning—the more cerebral model, through lectures and books—is usually highly individual, which makes it easy to learn something but then not live it. This second approach to learning is communal and thus often includes an element of accountability. Do you live in light of what you have learned and discovered; do you live by the principles you have discovered *with* us, in our group?

Some of the best learning is done by teams—people who work together need to learn together. Rather than each reading something and then applying it to the workplace, why not read and discuss and debate and learn together? When we learn together, through conversation, we are more likely to be able to work together effectively. Conversation, then, is a critical means of learning.

Nevertheless, there are some things that cannot be learned through a book or lecture, and for which no amount of conversation will make much difference either. These things are only learned by *doing* them. For some, this is the preferred way of learning, but we all need to appreciate this approach because much that is important can only be learned in this way.

We cannot learn to drive a car by hearing a lecture or discussing it with peers. There is no other way to learn than by *driving*. And this principle is even more apparent when using a manual transmission.

No amount of discussion or lectures will give us the *feel* for that clutch. We can only learn how to release the clutch by feel—by doing it ourself.

The same applies to prayer. We can learn to pray only by praying. Again, while there is certainly a place for lectures and group discussions on prayer, if we are going to learn contemplative prayer—the practice of being in and responding to the presence of Christ—we learn by doing it. This does not eliminate the value of a teacher, a mentor who comes alongside. But this mentor does not lecture or even teach, per se; rather he or she comes alongside to help explain what is happening and why it happened. But the learning takes place through trial and error, by fleeting moments of success that incrementally lead us to some level of mastery. This is how we learn to play a musical instrument or master a sport.

Finally, the most fruitful way of learning for some is through *observation*. Usually those that learn best this way have a heightened ability to see what is happening and imitate it. They prefer to learn by watching what someone else does and then doing it themselves. When shown how to do it, they can do it.

Again, though some prefer this mode of learning, all of us can enhance our learning skills through careful observation. Much of what I have learned about teaching has come by watching master teachers—not just learning through their lectures but by observing how they manage the class and respond to students. Athletes learn much by watching the premier athletes in their chosen sport. But they will only learn this way if they develop powers of observation, of being attentive and seeing what is new, what is different and what is significant.

Observation is a critical means by which we learn about people—especially those who are different. Here, travel can be very formative in enabling us to see others and to appreciate the human differences and the diversity of human experience. But a traveler is not the same as a tourist. To travel is to be with and among a people. A tourist is the center of attention; a traveler intentionally stays to one side and does not draw attention to her- or himself.

We learn about the organization we work in through observation, by watching and sensing what makes this institution unique, what defines its culture, its ethos and its way of doing things.

While my description of these four ways of learning may not be sophisticated or exhaustive, it is enough to urge us to do two things. First, recognize your preferred way of learning and exploit it. Build on it, celebrate it, and without apology enjoy learning that way. If you love libraries, then enjoy them. If you learn best through conversation, then don't let anyone minimize your capacity to learn because you are not drawn to quiet libraries as they are!

Consider this an integral part of self-knowledge. Observe how you learn, how you have approached new situations in the past, and how you have learned new skills or responded to new opportunities. How have you adapted to changes, regardless of how well you have done it? In particular, ask yourself how *you* enjoy learning, and what learning situations have brought you the greatest joy. The way you enjoy learning is probably the most fruitful mode of learning for you. Then, honestly identify where you struggle to learn, where learning is a chore for you. This does not mean that you should avoid this approach to learning, but you recognize that learning will not come easily to you this way.

Second, recognize that you need to master *each* approach. There are some things that are either learned best or only learned through one of these approaches. And if you are going to grow in wisdom and maturity, and in your capacity to thrive in your vocation, you need to learn through each approach.

LEARNING REQUIRES PATIENCE

I need to stress, though, that learning always takes time. True and good learning is the fruit of patience. There is no quick way to learn how to play the flute; it is learned by *doing*, and it takes practice and years of patience before it is mastered. This applies to each way of learning. Those who are masters of child psychology have spent countless hours watching children. There is no way to do it quickly.

Those who discover new asteroids have mastered the ability to observe the heavens, and because of their patience they know when something in the sky is new or different.

Each way of learning requires time and patience; there is no such thing as instant education.

EVALUATION AND REVIEW

Further, each way of learning is strengthened when we appreciate review and evaluation, when we welcome and learn from critical assessments of our work, our accomplishments and our efforts. Many, unfortunately, are threatened by evaluations. They fear the judgment of others and feel diminished by any critique that calls for change or that points out an area meriting improvement. But if we are going to master anything—literally anything—we need to learn through others' observations and critiques. We learn from those who have already mastered our craft, from our peers, and from those we serve. In their eagerness to serve better, good companies regularly solicit comment from their customers.

Remember also that there is little value in flattery. The book of Proverbs warns against those whose words might inflate our heads but actually do us harm. It equates flattery with lying. We all need affirmation, but we do not need the empty praise of flattery. We can only learn and grow if we are not crushed by criticism and if our heads are not inflated by praise; we can take both in stride and learn from both.

Ask: Where and in what way do I need to give myself to the task of learning, and which approach will most foster where I am in my vocational journey? For some, regardless of age, the need is for formal education, for a program of study in an academic environment that might lead to an academic degree program. Many young people need a formal program of study. But not all. We should not so idolize formal education that we minimize the value of other forms of learning and their significance in a person's long-term vocational development.

Many in midlife gain clarity about their vocation when they recognize that to thrive in their calling they need to go back to school—or to some form of formal study, whether long- or short-term. We do this because we want to learn. Many return to school in midlife to prove that they already know what they need to know and only need the "paper" to confirm it. This attitude wastes everyone's time, most of all their own. If we go back to school, we go to learn.

We need to ask, What would strengthen my capacity to thrive vocationally? Perhaps you have a Ph.D. in physics, but you do not know how to teach. The challenge, then, may to be leave the physics department and find out how to teach—either through reading or attending a seminar or by having someone critique your teaching. But resolve to learn how to teach! You might be gifted in sales, but if you decide to start your own business, you may need to learn how to do some basic accounting.

MENTORS

In all of this we need to affirm the significance and potential of good mentors in our lives. When I recognized that I did not know how to pray and resolved that I must learn to do so, I sought out Alex Aronis, a pastor in the city where I lived, and asked him to teach me. He taught me a great deal but eventually suggested that I approach another person, Father Thomas H. Green. The degree to which I know how to pray has come largely through the generosity of these two men, who have given me many hours of conversation about my own prayers, not about prayer itself or the phenomena of prayer, but about *my* prayer and how it was progressing. They were mentors or coaches. They were on the sidelines while I did the learning. But I could not have learned without them.

I learned as much about how to pastor a church from a monthly afternoon meeting with Rev. Ronald Unruh, a senior pastor in the same city where I first pastored, as from any other source or book. What a gift he gave me—one afternoon each month for conversation and encouragement. This does not minimize the importance of my seminary education but rather affirms that some things cannot be learned except in the actual context of ministry. It has become commonplace in recent years to berate theological schools for all that they are *not* doing; some have even published books listing all they did not learn in seminary. But such a posture is simplistic; there are some things a person can learn only in seminary and some only while in ministry. I learned much more about preaching while in a regular routine of preaching than I could possibly have learned in seminary, but this does not mean that what I learned in seminary about preaching was not essential to my capacity to learn how to preach while preaching. We need both—the capacity to learn in the context of formal education and the capacity to learn while on the job.

For the latter, what we need to learn often will be given through another, a teacher, a guide, a counselor or spiritual director. They are gifts. Most of all, they bring hope. This is the genius of good mentoring—the capacity to bring hope and encouragement. Believing in people enables them to learn, grow and embrace all that they are called to be. To truly learn from a mentor we must have a posture of eager attentiveness, which reflects a longing for wisdom and learning. Unfortunately, some are so confident in their own wisdom, or are incapable of admitting they do not know all they need to know, that they never experience the joy of being mentored.

LEARNING AND WISDOM

We learn skills. We learn how to be effective in relationships. We learn history and theory. It is easy to summarize all the things and the different ways we might learn. But we need to find a center, something that integrates and gives focus to our learning, and ultimately enables us to mature as individuals through our learning.

Wisdom gives us this center and brings focus and integration to our learning. Surely our deepest longing is to be wise women and men who can bring depth of character, understanding and skill to our work and our relationships. It may well be that nothing else matters vocationally as much as becoming wise. In the book of Proverbs we find these words:

Get wisdom; get insight: do not forget, nor turn away
   from the words of my mouth.
Do not forsake her, and she will keep you;
   love her, and she will guard you.
The beginning of wisdom is this: Get wisdom,
   and whatever else you get, get insight. (4:5-7)

In the end, no one will care how successful you were, how much you accomplished, how important you were or what roles you had. All that will matter, the older we get, is whether we are wise women and men.

The pursuit of wisdom provides focus and integration to our learning, for the wise person is mature in both relationships and work. But wisdom also provides depth, the conviction that what we long for is not merely knowledge or information, but learning which enables us to mature. By wisdom I do not mean abstract principles or profound truths so much as the capacity to respond to the developments around us with strength, to have the skills to embrace change and new challenges with ingenuity, and to grow mature emotionally through the ups and downs of difficult setbacks and disappointments.

For the LORD gives wisdom;
   from his mouth come knowledge and understanding;
he stores up sound wisdom for the upright;
   he is a shield to those who walk blamelessly,
guarding the paths of justice
   and preserving the way of his faithful ones.
Then you will understand righteousness and justice
   and equity, every good path;
for wisdom will come into your heart,
   and knowledge will be pleasant to your soul;
prudence will watch over you;
   and understanding will guard you. (Prov 2:6-11)

Wisdom enables us to live and work, to sustain meaningful relationships and work with integrity, focus, and balance in our lives. It includes the grace of accepting that we are growing older, which means embracing the implications of the transitions of our lives, both the possibilities and the limitations.

In our pursuit of wisdom we attend to history and stories—for the wise see the present in light of the past. In the pursuit of wisdom we seek depth of understanding in order to be people in whom there is both depth of conviction and an understanding that is not self-centered or superficial. Finally, the pursuit of wisdom is eminently practical, for a wise person longs to make a difference. In other words, the pursuit of wisdom keeps us from learning theories that have no practical application. The pursuit of wisdom integrates mind and heart, for a wise person is not interested in knowledge that does not inform the whole person and enable us to live in truth. That is, wisdom is not just cerebral or analytical; it includes emotion and even the body. To grow in wisdom demands that we learn to think and act holistically. Consequently, it is helpful to always keep wisdom as a central and defining focus for our lives and our learning.

WISDOM, LEARNING AND EXPERIENCE

One of the key means by which we grow in wisdom is through the discovery, understanding and application of truth or knowledge. But another key means of growth in wisdom and thus growth in learning is through *retrospection*. As already suggested in chapter six, retrospection is a means by which we think vocationally. Part of the reason for this is that retrospection is a critical means by which we *learn*. Wise people know that in both work and relationships, growth and development lie in our capacity to make life itself the curriculum. By this, of course, I am thinking of the power of lived experience and the ability to reflect on our own story as well as that of others. C. S. Lewis aptly says:

> What I like about experience is that it is such an honest thing. You may take any number of wrong turnings; but keep your eyes open and you will not be allowed to go very far before the warning signs appear. You may have deceived yourself, but ex-

perience is not trying to deceive you. The universe rings true
wherever you fairly test it.[6]

Learning from experience requires that we develop two skills: *observation*, to see what is going on around us and in us, and *improvisation*, to adapt what we have learned form experience to a new life
situation. But all the while we are learning. Learning is continuous in
that it is threaded throughout the whole of our lives. New circumstances regularly and consistently require that we adapt, experiment,
adjust and change. Education is then less and less a *preparation* for
life and work, and more and more a matter of life and work *itself*. To
live is to learn—to grow in wisdom as we draw from experience and
make sense of and respond to new circumstances. The only way we
can adapt to new circumstances and do better what we already do
well is to learn from past experience.

The bottom line is this: never grow complacent. Never grow tired
of learning. As soon as we stop learning we lose the capacity to grow
and mature in our work and our relationships. This continual learning enables us to grow in wisdom, which is to say that through learning we experience personal transformation. We acquire skills through
learning. But more, we discover ourselves through learning and develop a more expansive and holistic life perspective. And we can
learn from everything, every day—whether through the human responses in a doctor's waiting room, through the people around us on
the bus or through the morning newspaper.

By this I do not mean that we draw simplistic insights or that we
become reductionistic, deducing a moral from every last thing that
we come across. Sometimes our own experience or observations only
begin to make sense years later, when we draw on a previous experience or a range of observations to respond with courage and wisdom
to a new situation. It is merely that we are *attentive* to life and people
and circumstances, and most of all to ourselves and our own responses and reactions along the way.

In all of this I am assuming that whenever we learn, we are expanding heart and mind, and that through learning we become people with depth and breadth of soul. For example, when I began to learn how to pray, though it only represents one skill, it was part of a radically new way of understanding God's work in my life. For others, it is in learning a language that they enter into another world; a new language gives them another way of seeing life and people and relationships. And how do we begin to calculate what a gift is given to children or adults when they learn how to read?

Mary Catherine Bateson puts it well:

Learning is perhaps the only pleasure that might replace increasing consumption as our chosen mode of enriching experience. Someday, the joy of recognizing a pattern in a leaf or the geological strata in a cliff face might replace the satisfactions of new carpeting or more horsepower in an engine, and the chance to learn in the workplace might seem more valuable than increased purchasing power or a move up the organizational chart. Increasing knowledge of the ethology of wolves might someday replace the power savored in destroying them.[7]

But, as Bateson also implies, this requires that we increasing come to see knowledge as a source of delight rather than as a means of power. We enjoy learning because we enjoy discovery and the expansion and growth of heart and mind in wisdom, not merely because it might become a means to accomplish something.

Consequently, we must nurture a love of learning. This begins by recognizing how we prefer to learn, but we must stretch beyond where and how we are comfortable in our learning. Further, our capacity and desire to learn will enable us to overcome our fear of change. If we are learners, we can take on any challenge or change in our circumstances without fear.

Finally, through learning we know personal growth and transformation. For this reason I suggest that your potential for vocational growth and development is in direct proportion to your capacity to learn.

10

THE CROSS WE BEAR

Difficulty and Emotional Maturity

It is a simple fact of life: there will be difficulty, setback and disappointment. For some there will be rejection; for others there will be tragic losses. For others—there is no other word for it—there will be *suffering*. No one is immune from pain; it is part of the package that comes with life. This is a broken and cruel world. God is good, but life is unfair. God is good, but the sheer fact remains that whether we fulfill a vocation in the world or the church, neither the world nor the church is fair. All will experience the brokenness of the world intersecting their lives in multiple ways.

Consequently, two things must be stressed. First, we should not be surprised by difficulty. We should not be derailed or overly perplexed when it comes. Some people respond as though very surprised when difficulty hits them, and I wonder if their mother never told them that life is not fair. Difficulty surprises many First World people because their lives are so comfortable; this lulls them into assuming that things should and will always be this way. But it is illusionary, and we must remember that most of the world lives with difficulty and suffering daily.

Second, not only should it not surprise us; it is also clear that we need to make *some* sense of it and see what significance it has for our capacity to fulfill a vocation. There is hardly anything more critical to personal and vocational development as the nature of our response to difficulty, setback, rejection, disappointment or suffering. The evidence of this is that we develop emotional maturity and resilience.

MAKING SENSE OF PAIN

We need a sustaining theology of pain and suffering. Without one, we will never be able to live with sanity in the midst of the setbacks and disappointments that we will inevitably experience. We need a theology of suffering that is biblical, but more, we need one that is congruent with our experience. In this regard, I find three texts of Scripture to be particularly helpful.

First, in Romans 8:17 the apostle Paul makes an extraordinary statement and assumption: that our identity in Christ assumes that we will experience difficulty, setback and disappointment. It is inherent in what it means to be a Christian. If we are heirs with Christ, we will suffer with him. It is as simple as that. We cannot conclude from Scripture that if we are Christians we will have an easier road with less difficulty.

Though Christians suffer, and thus experience the same pain that others encounter, there is a difference for the Christian: we suffer with hope. This is the fundamental difference being a Christian makes. Our faith gives us a different perspective by which to live through those times when pain intersects our lives. In Romans 8:19-25, Paul uses the image of the woman in childbirth. He makes the observation that all creation is groaning as though in labor pains, which is a reminder that our own pain is but part of the pain of a broken and fallen world. But the image of labor and childbirth give us perspective on suffering. Imagine a woman in the pain of childbirth who has no idea what is happening to her body! In contrast, for the woman who understands, the pain is no less, but she experiences it as one who longs to see and hold her newborn child. In the same way, we cannot despair when pain and difficulty intersect our lives; we experience suffering as those who see the big picture, and thus as those who know that in the end all will be made well.

Second, in 2 Corinthians 4–6 the apostle makes another assumption: that our capacity to be life and grace to others comes through our experience of difficulty. We are "clay jars" (2 Cor 4:7). And in our vulnerability he outlines a remarkable series of ways he has and continues to experience the pain of this world, speaking of this as "carrying in the body the death of Jesus" (2 Cor 4:10). And then, building on this thought, he concludes that though death is at work in him, life is at work in those he serves (v. 12).

In others words, our ability to make a difference for God in a broken world, in society or in the church, comes through our capacity to be life in the midst of death, to be people of hope in a discouraging world.

Paul himself spoke of this as his weakness. In speaking of weakness, indeed of boasting in his weakness and the glory of God evident in this weakness, he was not speaking of toleration of mediocrity. Rather, as is clear in 2 Corinthians 12, Paul's "weakness" was the difficulty, obstacles and setbacks that were inevitably a part of his ministry. Clearly, his conviction is that this difficulty is the very locus by which God brings life and grace to others.

Third, in Romans 5 we are reminded of the simple principle that suffering, setback and disappointment are the means by which we are formed into people of maturity and strength. We might wish it otherwise. And there is also no doubt that suffering has broken many people and left them disenchanted, bitter and lifeless. But the fact remains that through the stress points of life our character is tested and proven. As the apostle puts it: "suffering produces endurance, and endurance produces character, and character produces hope" (Rom 5:3-4).

Everything depends on our response. Suffering and pain either break us or make us; through it all we either become angry, bitter and cynical, or through grace we become people of character and signals of hope in a dark and dispiriting world.

Consequently the real test of vocational and emotional maturity lies is our capacity to handle difficult and painful times. Through these stressful events—whether in relationships or in our work—we mature in faith and grow in self-knowledge as we come to greater clarity about what really matters to us and what priorities must guide our life choices. In the end we learn to love and be loved even in the midst of difficulty.

The choice is always ours. As a Canadian who has spent half of his life overseas—first as the child of missionary parents, then in the Philippines as the dean and professor of theology of a seminary, and later as a pastor—I am impressed by a characteristic of my culture and society: an inclination to feel *victimized*. John Ralston Saul identifies "victimization" as a kind of *Canadian* sin or propensity. He uses the example of the political movements that are more regional than national and describes how they are nourished on the idea that their region of the country is victim of another region or the federal government. He notes, then, that we should not be surprised that we have little vision for the whole country. Then, powerfully, he notes the dangers and foolishness of this posture: "All of us, it can't be denied, are victimized from time to time. But this is quite different from believing ourselves to be victims all the time."[1]

There is a great line, attributed to Robert Orben, which, tongue in cheek, captures this feeling of victimization: "Sometimes I get the feeling that the whole world is against me, but deep down I know that's not true. Some of the smaller countries are neutral."

By *victimized* I mean that we get lost in a sea of self-pity, live with a martyr complex and then carry this hurt around like a chip on our shoulder, becoming ever more cynical, having lost the capacity to live with grace, humor, compassion and patience. It robs us of life.

Viktor Frankl has helped me see that suffering is the real test of whether we transcend self-absorption and "live for others." Suffering imparted meaning and purpose to Frankl's life.[2] The genesis of a person's values are to be found in a person's suffering. That is, life has meaning and values, but these are discovered, attained and sustained by the ways an individual confronts and responds to evil and the suffering that entails.

So we begin to realize how critical it is that we learn to respond well to difficulty, setback and disappointment. We need to learn how to respond positively. At essence the issue is one of perspective, of living with and accepting the simple reality that God is good but life is not fair. The genius of our response ultimately rests on whether we allow ourselves to be victimized or allow our difficulty and suffering to become means of grace to ourselves and to others. Social critic Stephanie Golden makes the astute observation that a great deal of self-help recovery groups actually encourage the victims of abuse to focus so much of their attention on the abuse and the abuser that their primary sense of identity becomes the very fact that they are victims. The principle fact of their lives becomes their identity as a victim, and this posture disables them from getting past the abuse. She draws on the insights of others who note the irony that victims of abuse begin to see themselves as special because of the abuse. The power of the victim image blinds them to their own imperfections and failings. Golden notes:

> This grandiosity, compounded by self-righteousness and fueled by anger, often characterizes people who present themselves as victims. It is easy to fall into it, for when you feel powerless, the virtue accorded the victim seems the only route to some form of respect and to a feeling of entitlement. . . . The sense of being righteous and special is part of what makes the role of the victim so attractive.[3]

So attractive, she suggests, that some actually go so far as to create a kind of bogus victimhood that, ironically "provides a reliable, ongoing sense of virtue."[4]

The bottom line, then, is how we respond. Are we consumed by ourselves and filled with self-pity and anger, or does our encounter with pain become a vehicle through which we are a means of grace to others. The issue is not whether we experience difficulty; that will inevitably happen. We will not be treated as we should be. We will not be thanked as much as we should be. We will not be affirmed or appreciated as much as we deserve. Less competent people will get positions for which we are more qualified. We will be overlooked and not appreciated because of false perceptions. We will be misunderstood, underappreciated and wrongly accused. This will happen.

The great danger is not only self-pity or, worse, a martyr complex. These are pathetic, no doubt. No, the great danger is bitterness and cynicism. Far better to go into life and engage the work that God has called us to with the assumption that no one owes us anything (and that God will affirm and bless us in his time). Only then can we begin to respond positively to setback, difficulty and disappointment.

RESPONDING POSITIVELY

What does it take to respond with grace to difficulty and pain?

Forgiveness and the resolution of the past. First, we can only respond positively to current developments after we have come to terms with our past and resolved the ways that pain has intersected our lives. For this, we must practice forgiveness.

We begin by forgiving our parents. This is fundamental. By this I do not necessarily mean that we have been grievously wronged—though for many that is the case. However, no parent has been perfect; no parent has been all that we hoped for in a parent. Consequently, we must forgive and in compassion let go of any resentment we might have against father or mother.

For some, this will mean coming to terms with deep wrongs: they may have been abandoned by a father or mother they have never met; worse yet, they may have been physically or emotionally abused by a parent; or a parent may have, in ignorance, not given the child all that might have been given. Most did their best, but as every parent knows it is never good enough. My wife and I can easily look back and see how we might have done things differently. But there is no changing that; there is no going back to assure that every hurt and pain is removed from the consciousness of our two sons.

We will remain forever locked in resentment if we do not begin with forgiving our parents. This is one of the most important lessons and actions of our lives. We need to forgive what was wrong in our parents and childhood, but more, we need to appreciate and affirm what is *good*, what is of God, in our parents and their generation.

As I am intimating, this resolution of our childhood involves more than just forgiving our parents; it also includes reconciliation to all that our parents represented—the spiritual, cultural and social heritage that shaped us as children. For some it will be a religious or denominational heritage. In many cases it is easy to look back and resent, deeply, the wrongheadedness or the narrowness of a fundamentalistic perspective. And while we must move on and embrace a broader notion of truth and life, we can never sever our roots. We have to come to terms with them.

Some are lost nostalgically in the past. Others are eager to cut the past off as so much garbage. But to do so is to discard both the good and the bad, and the truth is that we are only able to make a lasting contribution, regardless of our vocations, when we celebrate and embrace the good, and gently, though firmly, discard what is less than good. This demands a *gracious* discernment that includes fundamental gratitude for all that was and is good. Only with this discernment can we build on what is positive in that heritage.

Second, this forgiveness must also be extended to others. One of the givens of life is that we will be wronged. We will be wronged by family, by coworkers, by our boss. It is not merely that we will not be treated as we deserve; rather, we will be *wronged*. People will take advantage of us. Others will speak ill of us and through gossip or slander seek to destroy our credibility. I could easily go on and list a multitude of ways we could be wronged. But the point remains: our only hope for vocational vitality over the long haul is that we learn to let go of resentment.

If we are wronged while working for one organization and carry that resentment on to the next place of work or ministry, we will infuse our work with resentment, and it will destroy our capacity to live and work well. We may cover it up for a while and with a pleasant temperament and quiet resolve seek to be gentle people who carry on.

But unresolved resentment in our hearts will come out in ways that deeply undermine our capacity to thrive. The most telling signal is that we will express our anger in inappropriate ways. One of the sure signs of unresolved resentment is anger that is disproportionate to the wrong. When a colleague blows up over something that, while wrong, simply does not deserve that response, I can only assume that there is something in the past that is still lurking in the dark shadows of his or her mind and heart.

Third, the resolution of the past also needs to include self-forgiveness. It is so easy to look back with regrets and wish we had done things differently. We may regret that we cut short a study program or perhaps that we are living with the consequences of a profoundly foolish pattern of behavior. Or maybe it is no more than regret that we were not all that we could have been—to our children, to our friends, our deceased parents or to our coworkers. This is only possible, of course, as we come to accept God's forgiveness. Further, I have found that my own experience of forgiveness has been most significant when I was able to confess sins to a trusted spiritual adviser or director, and heard the other declare aloud, "In Christ you are forgiven; go in peace." I cannot help but wonder if something was lost when the Protestant tradition moved away from oral confessions and the personal, one-to-one assurance of pardon given and received.

But the bottom line is that we must forgive ourselves. Nothing is gained by living with regret. Nothing. Forgive yourself; learn from what has happened and what you have done. Move on, embracing the new moment and the new opportunity. Regret is so easily nothing but self-pity, another form of self-centeredness and self-indulgence.

Seeing and accepting our limitations and our losses. To respond positively to the pain of life, we need to forgive. But further, we need to come to terms with losses and limitations. We will have at least three major transitions in our lives—when we move into adulthood, when we move from early into midadulthood and when we move into our senior years. It is probably safe to say that with each of these transitions we make the transition well when we recognize and see our limitations. That is, each transition includes seeing, accepting and then actually embracing our limitations. In different ways each transition makes us conscious of those limitations. Parker Palmer reminds us:

> Each of us is given a nature by God. To have a nature is to have both limits and potentials. We can learn as much about our God-given nature by running into our limits as by experiencing our potentials. . . .
>
> The truth is that I cannot be anything I want to be or do anything I want to do. The truth is that my created nature, my God-given nature, makes me like an organism in an ecosystem: I thrive in some roles and relationships within that system, but in others I wither and die.[5]

But often our encounter with these limits is painful. We are rejected in a job application, or we are fired where we simply lack the necessary abilities or potential for a job. In other cases pain comes from the dashing of our expectations and hopes. We long for a position that we realize is *beyond* our abilities or perhaps not *aligned* with those abilities.

Further, if we are honest, we usually realize that our dashed expectations were really rooted in a desire to impress others. We had dreams and aspirations that were unrealistic. It is not so much that we failed but simply did not achieve what was really unachievable. We have been confronted with our limits.

For some this happens early in life; for many it comes closer to midlife, when it dawns on us that we are not going to achieve all we had hoped to. We will not be millionaires, or we will never get a Ph.D., or perhaps we will never have children. Whatever the hope or aspiration, it is dashed, and we are confronted with limits.

For others it may be a physical limitation—the recognition that he or she does not have what it takes to be a professional athlete, or the realization that because of a serious accident the rest of life will be spent in a wheel chair.

Either way, we will not live with joy unless we learn to accept with grace the losses we experience and choose to live in peace *within* the limits of our lives. Again, Palmer says it well: "The truth is that every time a door closes behind us, the rest of the world opens up in front of us. All we need to do is stop pounding on the door that is closed, turn around, and see the largeness of life that now lies open to our soul."[6]

The way to joy and vocational vitality is to accept what is—regardless of the pain that it may represent for us—and embrace the opportunities that *are* before us rather than bemoan what might have been. When we do, in ways that can be simply uncanny, "the world opens up in front of us," to use Palmer's words. And this only makes sense if we live with the assumption of God's providential care. God is over all and cares for all. And though we can accept that God allows evil, our fundamental theological posture is one of living in the confidence of his love, provision and direction. But more, our confidence also rests in the assurance that God's grace is greater than sin and that he is always working by his gracious power to bring good from evil. Further, it is essential to remember that God's time line is never the same as ours; he works to bring about his purposes. Our confidence in his providential care frees us to trust God to do in his time what only he can do.

I am regularly reminded of the story of Nelson Mandela and his twenty years in prison. He could easily have come out of the experience bitter, angry and dispirited; instead he came out with more life in his eyes than when he went in. He quite simply chose to accept what was rather that beat his head against the limitations that were forced on him. He lived with hope that one day change would come, and in the meantime he would make the best of the situation he found himself in.

Accepting the pain inherent in our vocations. First, we come to resolution about the past. Second, we accept graciously the limits and limitations of our lives and our circumstances, including the losses that this may represent. But we need to go further.

If we are going to thrive in our vocations, we also need to accept that some form of difficulty or pain is actually *inherent* in what we are called to do. Jesus began his public ministry with a clear sense of call (Mk 1), and he was able to say at the conclusion that he had finished the work given him by the Father (Jn 17). But he could not finish that work unless he accepted the cross, the way of Calvary. Further, in speaking to his disciples, Jesus advises them that they are to take up their cross and follow him. In other words, when we follow Jesus we follow him to the cross; we bear a cross. Consequently, it is reasonable to conclude that in some form or another the cross (or a cross) will mark *every* vocation; there will be some way that the pain of a broken world intersects our call.

In some cases we need to accept with grace the fact that difficulty is part of what it takes to *achieve* a particular end. The cost of being a first-class athlete or musician is rigorous training, practice and work. Many talented individuals who might well be very good musicians or athletes never become accomplished for the simple reason that they were not prepared to pay the price—the hours and hours of training, rehearsal and practice away from any kind of affirmation or praise. In this sense the pain or cross may be the discipline—what it takes—to accomplish our goal.

In other cases the cross may be that which *attends* the role or responsibility. For example, we should not be in administration if we need to be affirmed and recognized every time we do something helpful. It is inherent to the job, much like in the role of mothering or homemaking, that a great deal of the work that a person does goes unnoticed and unappreciated. If we cannot accept this with grace, we are better off staying out of administration.

An artist will never find the support and affirmation needed in a culture that is fundamentally pragmatic. A businessperson will always live with the ups and downs of the market and of consumer trends. A teacher will be amazed that people who seemed to understand what was taught never really got the point, or if they did, they did not appreciate everything and do not live consistent with what they learned. Jesus faced this also, as we see from Philip's question in the initial verses of John 14. This is *never* an excuse for poor teaching, but the recognition of the inherent difficulty that attends good teaching. A surgeon will save many lives, but will also lose some—some that could have been saved. A politician will never be able to satisfy all constituents, and many who might have supported him or her at one point can so quickly turn and condemn this leader because he or she dashed their hopes, and they will never understand the art of compromise.

In other cases the reality of the cross may come through the unique circumstances in which we are seeking to fulfill this particular calling at this particular time. That is, the cross may be that while we know our calling, we have limited options to do what we feel called to do because we have to sustain a waged job to sustain our livelihood. Or it could be that we have a dual identity (e.g., as a both an administrator and a writer, or as a teacher *and* a mother), and it seems that the two sides of our life and work are always in tension and competition. But in fact the two are probably in some significant way essential for the other. But any way we come at it, the point is that difficulty is inherent, in some form or another, in every line of work and at the heart of every vocation.

Where this difficulty intersects our lives and our work is not incidental; it is central and significant for at least two reasons. First, here is where we encounter our own need for God and to grow in dependence on God. It is, then, a means of grace to us. The place we feel the mark of the cross in our vocation is where we grow in dependency on God for his all-sufficient grace. And note, the book of Hebrews speaks of the cross as something that Jesus endured "for the joy that was set before him" (Heb 12:2 NIV). It was something, in other words, that was a necessary means for the fulfillment of his vocation and of his joy. The cross then marks each vocation not as a limitation but as the very *means* by which God enables us to know the joy through the calling and work that he gives us. We must then learn to accept graciously the way this pain intersects our lives, our work and our vocations.

Second, the intersection point of the cross is the very place where we are grace and life to others. As Paul says, at the point of our weakness, where we feel "death" at work in us, we are life to others (2 Cor 4:12).

The place where the cross intersects our lives will only be a means of grace to ourselves and others if we reject any propensity we might have to feel self-pity for ourselves because others do not see, feel or appreciate our difficulty. The cross becomes a means of grace through the very fact that it is accepted with patience, grace and submission—the quietness of a meek heart. This is not weakness, in the end, but strength, and herein we are women and men who truly live and bring life to others.

It should also be noted that many fall into the trap of attributing their difficulty to the evil one—to some form of demonic opposition or attack. In some missionary newsletters and business reports I have read I sometimes get the sense that every difficulty they have is due to the direct work of evil one and his demonic host! While in principle this is certainly possible, most of the difficulty we experience is part and parcel of what it means to live on planet earth, or it is something inherent in our vocations—something clearly allowed by God. Attributing this difficulty to the evil one is giving evil more credit than is due. And then we fail to embrace it as a cross through which God is bringing grace to bear in our lives and in the lives of others.

Responding positively to failure and setback. Finally, we will only suffer with grace when we learn how to handle failure and setback. One of the most crucial capacities of vocational development and expression is to respond positively, with emotional resilience, to setback, failure and rejection.

On a personal level, it would be very easy for substantial health problems or a major family problem—with a spouse or with children—to leave us feeling profoundly sorry for ourselves. Few things cut the nerve of joy and vocational vitality quite like self-pity. Invariably, those who thrive in life and work learn the power of gratitude, hope and faith in the midst of darkness and pain.

There is no doubt that if we do not develop the capacity to accept with grace the setbacks of life and work—whether from our own failures or through the actions of others, justified or not—we will become nothing but angry, bitter, hard people.

In some cases our sense of failure is based on unrealistic expectations. We failed ourselves by failing to be all *we* had hoped to be. All that is really suffering is our wounded egos. But it still hurts!

In other cases we were living with false notions of success. Rather than being content in our work—in this place, at this time and with these people—we had hoped to be heroes and solve all the problems. We struggle with accepting our limitations; we struggle in the realization that we cannot do everything, that we cannot be responsible for everything that happens in the organization; we can only be accountable for our work and our situation. Sometimes our potential for success is limited by the performance of others. Wisdom demands that we accept this with grace.

But in other cases, we *have* failed. As we look back, we can see the things we did that with more foresight we might have been able to avoid. Humility, in this kind of situation, demands that we accept that we are not all that good at something, or that at least on this particular occasion we did not do good work—that as a preacher you did not preach a good sermon and there was no particular excuse, that as an investor you made a bad investment and either you or your clients have lost money, or that as a mechanic you did not do a good job on that car repair assignment and the customer is right to demand that it be corrected. There are no excuses, no extenuating circumstances and no way to avoid the simple fact that what happened is failure.

To thrive vocationally we must accept this with grace and move on. We do not need to be defensive; we do not need to dig for excuses. We can acknowledge that we are not perfect, that we will learn from our mistakes, that even though we failed it does not mean that we tolerate mediocrity. We can press on with faith, hope and love.

It is important to acknowledge failure. Often the unwillingness to acknowledge failure means that we remain in a situation that can only get worse—and all we do by staying is to reinforce the failure. Further, failure is probably not as bad as we are inclined to think. We tend to be crushed by failure, when we should probably merely close that door of our lives, cut our losses and move ahead. When we do there is probably more ahead of us than we could possibly have imagined, and in time, especially if we learn from our mistakes, we will look back on what increasingly becomes a distant memory.

SUFFERING AND CAREERISM

There is something implied in all of this discussion about the cross and difficulty that needs to be made explicit. This is but one point at which reflection on vocation parts ways with careerism. The great danger of thinking in terms of career is not only that we might miss our vocations but that we would fail to appreciate the significance of suffering. When we think in terms of career, we are so easily inclined to assume that our lives and our work will represent a single, rising curve, as we "climb the ladder" and move up the ranks. We are so easily caught up in the trap of thinking that what we are doing will position us for the next slot we hope to fill.

But the fact of the matter is that people lose their farms, lose their jobs and experience major setbacks. Pastors, good pastors, who over the long haul will be very effective, are released by a congregation. Missionaries find that all their training seems to be meaningless in the face of intense difficulty and opposition. People in business experience great losses; gifted and capable politicians lose elections.

Thinking vocationally means we can accept that difficulty is not an aberration in our career development; rather, it is an integral part of what it means to accept our vocations.

EMOTIONAL DEVELOPMENT AND RESILIENCE

The capacity to handle difficulty, suffering, disappointment and setback is an essential element of long-term vocational development. How we handle a major setback, failure or loss may be one of the most critical factors in our lifelong vocational effectiveness. This applies equally if it was our fault, the fault of others or both.

Fundamentally, though, emotional maturity and resilience is at stake. That is, the difficulty is not so much the issue but whether we mature in our capacity to respond *with* heart and *from* the heart to the ups-and-downs of life, work and relationships. Only as we come to terms with our joys and sorrows can we be all that we are called to be. Indeed, nothing so represents maturity as *emotional resilience*. We remain perpetually adolescent if we fail to develop emotional maturity. Further, this emotional maturity or resilience is our primary resource when it comes to vocational identity and development. Emotional resilience will enable us to respond to the changes and challenges that will inevitably come and which will enable us to respond with strength to setbacks and disappointments.

It is tempting at each of the major points I am making in the second half of this book to say that *this* is it—this particular item is the most critical factor in our vocational development and is the most significant factor in our capacity to achieve our potential. Some will say that nothing matters more than character, and others that nothing is so critical as our capacity to learn, and yet others will raise either the capacity to suffer with grace or the ability to work within and through organizations. But increasingly I am impressed that emotional development may be *the* factor that determines whether we will become all we are called to be. Somehow it is the thread that runs through each of the points of leverage to our personal and professional development.

In other words, lack of emotional maturity and resilience will sabotage our lives and vocations. Intelligence, giftedness, hard work, dedication and opportunities will all be forfeited and wasted. This may well be the most critical factor in our vocational development.

I grew up within a Christian subculture that viewed emotions as incidental or secondary at best. People who were emotional were in some way suspect. If someone was cerebral or rational, we tended to view him or her as deep, profound and trustworthy. But if someone was deemed emotional, he or she was not to be trusted and was generally viewed as superficial. Part of the horror of this is that as often as not gender stereotypes were also involved. Frequently women were portrayed as more emotional and therefore less competent or rational and thus less dependable or trustworthy.

But I have come to learn that this is completely backward. The force of emotion within Scripture has helped me to see this: the powerful emphasis on joy in the ministry of Jesus and his explicit assumption that he came that joy might be made complete in us (Jn 15:11); the marked emphasis on emotion in the writings of the apostle Paul, who speaks of a peace that transcends understanding and guards the heart and mind in Christ (Phil 4:7). But this is only a brief sample of what is probably *most* explicit in the Psalms, the prayers of the Old Testament that are obviously rooted in the heart, arising out of the depths of human passion, and thus preeminent demonstrations of emotion.

We have come to see that people of depth are those who have learned to live from the heart—from the core of their being. They have learned the power and truth of responding emotionally to God, to his creation and to others. As such, it may well be that there is nothing more crucial to our call to become Christian, to mature in our faith, to love God and others, as reflection on our emotions.

This means, then, that a person is weak and immature not because they are emotional but rather because they have lost the capability to express a whole range of emotions and to express them in a manner that is appropriate to the occasion. Feelings are erratic; great anger is expressed over what is really a minor inconvenience; and an unreasonable fear undermines the capacity for elemental human joy and comradery. I have come to see that only those who are emotionally mature are capable of responding to the ups and downs of life and work, and the crises that inevitably come our way. In my experience it is men who often fall short in this regard, who come completely unglued when they are suddenly overwhelmed with a crisis or a problem. But all of us, men and women, urgently need to learn and grow together in our capacity to live emotionally, but more to the point, to live with emotional maturity.

THE SIGNS OF EMOTIONAL HEALTH

What then are the signs of emotional health? What would be the goal we should reach toward, a goal of emotional maturity and resilience that would enable us to grow in faith and wisdom but also grow in our capacity to fulfill our vocations?

I will put it this way: you are a person of emotional health if

1. You know your feelings and are able to draw upon them in making significant decisions (rather than having those decisions sabotaged by your emotions). You are able to manage your emotional life so that you are not paralyzed by worry or swept away by anger. You manage your emotions; you are not managed *by* your emotions.

2. You are able to persist in the face of setback and disappointment, able to channel your emotional energy toward worthy goals. You are willing to live with delayed gratification.

3. You are able to empathize with others and recognize the feelings of others; you are able to handle the emotional aspects of relationships with grace. This means that your own emotional state does not undercut your capacity to listen to and identify with others. It also means that you can speak openly and frankly, with grace, patience and tact, and say what needs to be said even if this means that it will stir up the emotions of others. This includes the capacity to handle another's anger with grace, even when that anger is expressed toward you. In other words, you are not paralyzed by the fear of another person's response—*anger*, if you have a difficult thing to say, or *mourning*, if you have sad news to share. This does not mean you are uncaring. Not at all. You empathize. But you are not fearful or sabotaged by the emotions of another.

On an organization or group level, you have a sensitivity to the group process that enables you to be alert to emotional responses and dimensions of community life.

4. You are able to express honestly your emotions in appropriate settings: whether ardent devotion, anger or disappointment, whether to God, spouse, friend, child or colleague. The emotional response is

appropriate: for example, the anger corresponds to the wrong. You do not lose your emotional keel; you do not lose your temper when angry; you do not, in your anger, take it out on your spouse or a child, or in your anger cast another in the wrong light. The feeling of discouragement is aired where there are confidants who can work through the disappointment with you and where your comments will not be misunderstood or misread.

5. You do not use emotional blackmail to get your way—by threatening to resign or quit if you do not get things as you want them, or by withholding favors or good will because someone is not fulfilling your expectations. This means you respond with openness and honesty, but also with grace toward those you differ from, particularly family and coworkers. But more, it means that the fear of hurting your feelings does not keep others from acting according to their convictions or conscience. They are not straightjacketed by a fear of your emotional reaction—whether your anger, the loss of temper or just the fact that your feelings would be hurt.

6. You are able to respond to both praise and criticism with grace. You are not crushed by criticism; your head is not inflated by praise. You do not crave praise; you do not respond to criticism with undue defensiveness. Neither do you deflect the criticism by blaming another or blaming the one who brings the criticism. If you do, you neither hear nor benefit from it.

7. Finally and most critically, the sign of emotional health is the capacity to respond with sorrow—anger, mourning or discouragement—when pain intersects your life. But you always come back to an emotional center of *joy*. The person of emotional maturity is the individual in whom the dominant emotion is joy, which is rooted in the confidence in the goodness of God, trust in the providential care of God and hope in the ultimate triumph of justice and peace.

One of the signs of emotional immaturity is that we are not able to distinguish between genuine difficulty and suffering, and the vicissitudes of life. Bad weather is not suffering; traffic delays are not suffering. These are just part of life. On the whole, emotionally immature people are irritated or frustrated with things that we merely need to take in stride. They find minor inconveniences to be great injustices. We need to bear with these elements (e.g., the weather) and live from a fundamental posture of gratitude, humility and patience.

THE WAY TO EMOTIONAL HEALTH

How do we get there? How do we become people of emotional maturity? It comes quite simply through the same "massive honesty" I spoke of in chapter six—honesty with what we are feeling, with what is happening inside of us and with what this means. Only with this honesty can we accept that we are emotional beings. But more, only with honesty can we live in truth and then, through that truth, come to joy.

If we are *angry*, we are angry. Anger itself is not a sin. But it is a sin if we lose our temper or if in our anger we do something that clearly violates the call to love or justice. Anger is a sin and destroys us when we carry the anger in our hearts from one day to the next. For some reason, when we sleep angry, the anger scorches our souls and becomes a bitterness from which it is very difficult to recover. In this I seek to consistently remember the words of my father: "Keep short accounts with God," which has such an immediate application to anger. We will be wronged; nothing can stop this. But we can decide if that wrong will fester in our hearts and ultimately destroy us, or whether we will let it go. Note then that we lie to ourselves when we deny that we are angry. To feel emotional hurt while insisting that we are not angry is nothing but a denial of what is happening in our hearts. Emotional health comes through acknowledgment and then the letting go. It is both; we acknowledge the anger, but then refuse to live in the anger.

We will become *fearful*. This is so for the simple reason that we are vulnerable. Only someone entirely out of touch with life could suggest that he or she never feels anxious. But we walk the way of death when we allow anxieties to consume and overpower us. Our only hope, again, is to honestly confront our worries and fears, and accept with grace that all we can do is trust in the providential care of a good and almighty God.

We will become *discouraged*. We live in a discouraging world. But if we remain locked in discouragement, it becomes a cynicism that leaves our hearts in a perpetual state of gloom. There is nothing wrong with getting discouraged per se, but then we must receive the encouragement that comes—whether through the glory of a new morning, the words of kindness of a friend or colleague, the testimony of Scripture, the witness of the Spirit to our hearts, a dog frolicking in a park or the smile of a child. For those of us who are prone to become discouraged, the grave danger is that we would get lost in self-pity and cynicism, a pit from which it is so difficult to climb.

We also will all experience *loss*. And our only hope is to mourn the loss honestly. Denial is self-defeating. It saps energy and keeps us from moving on. We become locked in the past and live falsely. I recently read that it probably takes a year to recover from a major loss—the death of a parent, for example, or the loss of a job. It takes time, and the only hope for emotional recovery and strength is to accept this, mourn the loss and allow God to heal our hearts in his time. In the end, if we have the capacity to be grace to others in their pain, it is because we have learned to mourn our own losses and then serve or minister to others out of consolation we have received from God. The apostle Paul speaks of this in 2 Corinthians:

> Blessed be the God and Father of our Lord Jesus Christ, the Father of mercies and the God of all consolation, who consoles us in all our affliction, so that we may be able to console those who are in any affliction with the consolation with which we ourselves are consoled by God. (1:3-4)

Many people have experienced great losses, but it has left them unchanged; they have managed to shelve the experience or push it aside so it cannot touch them. They have not been changed by it; they have not mourned. When we know someone has experienced a profound loss, we are prone to say that they are doing very well if they are composed, dry-eyed and carrying on with a "stiff upper lip." But the danger is hypocrisy. Does this really reflect what is happening in our hearts? Further, the danger is a hardened heart—the heart of one who has experienced the loss but has not been changed.

It is far better that the one who has experienced loss is actually in deep mourning, overwhelmed by the pain—not self-centered but feeling deeply the loss. This should encourage us, for then we can be fairly certain our friend will come to emotional strength; they we know they will have a capacity for joy.

In other words, we only know emotional maturity and resilience when we learn to open our hearts to God and to one another. There is no other way to discover and sustain emotional growth and health than with a strong *vertical* connection to God and a vital *horizontal* connection to others. The first speaks of the priority of solitude, the individual, private encounter with God. The second speaks of community and conversation. We need both, and I will speak to both in chapter twelve, but first it is important that we also consider what it means to fulfill our vocations in the company of others, as part of organizations or institutions, the subject of the next chapter.

11

WORKING WITH AND
WITHIN ORGANIZATIONS

Leveraging Our Work with
the Work of Others

We fulfill our vocations in partnership with others. The most obvious form or expression of this is found in the organizations in which
we work and through which we invest our lives and our energies.

By an organization I mean any formal association of individuals
who are working toward a common end. They have a mission they
hope to accomplish together. This applies to congregations as well as
businesses; it includes everything from volunteer associations to
educational institutions. An organization could include something
as large and as complex as the American government to something
as small as two people who have agreed to work together on a common cause—perhaps just a short-term project, perhaps to start a
business together.

The assumption that underlies organizations is simple: we are
more effective working with others than functioning as hermits. It is
easy to think of organizations as agencies that limit us. There is a
boss or a board that seemingly restrains our potential or restricts us.
Some are inclined to think of organizations as necessary evils. But

organizations are the appropriate context in which we fulfill our calls. It is helpful to recognize a fundamental principle—when people work together, the end product is greater than the sum of the parts. Synergism allows us to do greater things together than any one of us could conceivably do alone. Organizations, at their best, empower us by granting us the opportunity, the encouragement, even the training to excel. Organizations, at their best, force us to stretch beyond our perceived limitations and enable us to discover our own potential, something we would never have seen or discovered if we were hermits. It helps to think of organizations as gardens where we are able to flourish because of the husbandry of the gardener. Indeed we can only hope to fulfill our vocations if we learn the grace and strength of working with others in partnerships that enable us to be stewards of our gifts and opportunities.

Even when organizations are not at their best, we still need them. No matter how gifted we are, we cannot achieve our potential in isolation from others. Wayne Gretzky is the greatest hockey player ever—a remarkably gifted athlete. But if he were to compete alone, even a group of young teenagers would undoubtedly win a game against him. It would be sheer foolishness for him to suggest that he could do it all alone. Part of Gretzky's genius is his capacity to work with others, and this is largely what has made him an extraordinary athlete.

The greatest musicians need coaches, mentors, composers and orchestra halls managed by others. Writers need editors and publishers, and publishers need writers! No one can fulfill a vocation alone; we all need associations, partnerships and structures that enable us to work collaboratively with others.

Consequently, if we are going to be all we are called to be, and respond with skill, courage and grace to the call of God on our lives, we must develop the capacity to work with others in the context of organizational life. Further, we need to see how our individual vocation can fit within specific organizations. That is, we need to develop the capacity to recognize the organizations where we are likely to be most effective.

But we also need to see the dangers; organizations have particular qualities that can actually undermine our capacity to be true to who we are and who we are called to be. Thus the call for discernment and, of course, courage. We need to know when it is wise, vocationally speaking, for us to resign or at least accept that we are leaving an organization. The goal, of course, is to discover and join an organization that most enables us to fulfill our vocational identity, and in the end such an organization does not serve us but rather provides us with an avenue to be of service to Christ and others.

HOW TO BE EFFECTIVE WITHIN AN ORGANIZATION

An important place to begin, as we consider how we fulfill our vocations in partnership with others, is to examine how we can develop the capacity to be effective *within* the organizations we work in, or with which we worship, fellowship or serve together. In this regard the principles or practices are simple: they represent, essentially, the capacity to live in community, which will be the focus of chapter twelve. But when considering organizations, we are wise to identify and embrace the qualities that specifically enable us to work with others toward a common goal or mission. These principles are equally applicable to a large business or to a group serving as volunteers in a small nonprofit organization.

Character qualities. Character is the most critical characteristic that enables us to work effectively within organizations. Character includes the humility and courage to live by one's conscience, and the ability to live and work with others with grace, patience, kindness and humility. Certain character qualities that can be nurtured and strengthened are directly related to our capacity to be effective in partnership with others.

First, regardless of what role we have within the company or congregation, we are most effective when we are good *listeners*. This is true of the president, an assistant manager, a board member, a plant caretaker, a salesperson or a donor. Our capacity to be effective is directly related to our capacity to listen. Effective leaders listen to their constituents; effective donors hear what the organization is or hopes to do; effective salespersons listen to what a potential buyer is saying; effective companies are attentive to their customers, seeking as much feedback as possible. They listen.

Further, effective organizations demand *dependability*. The people who work with us, whether supervisors, peers or those we manage, know that we can be counted on to do what we say we will do. We are people of our word. We do not overpromise because of a misguided generosity. At the same time, our colleagues can relax when something is on our desk; it will be done on time. We are dependable. We will be there, whether it is for a meeting, an appointment or a project deadline.

My observation of organizational life and work make this quality—dependability—a constant, living illustration of the words of Jesus when he notes that those who are faithful in small things will be entrusted with much. Many people take lightly "small" issues or responsibilities and then wonder why they do not get promotions or other opportunities. The reason is often simple: they were not diligent and careful in what they viewed as "secondary" matters.

Character also relates to how we *respect others* and sustain the dignity and reputation of one another. People who thrive in organizational life work with a fundamental assumption: each person I live and work with is a person of worth, dignity and value. They are treated as such regardless of their actual competency or effectiveness. Even if a person needs to be released because they did not perform their duties well, or because they violated trust—whether by theft or through sexual harassment—they still deserve to be treated with grace and dignity. Those we report to deserve the dignity and honor appropriate to their roles or offices; those who report to us are never merely pawns; they are partners without whom we would be helpless. Each of our colleagues deserves to know that we will not speak ill of them behind their backs or slander their character through innuendo or unfair criticism.

Nurture these three character qualities: develop your capacities to listen; be faithful and dependable in whatever is given you, big or small; and resolve to treat all with whom you work with grace, dignity and honor.

Think globally, act locally. Character is fundamental. But if we are effective, this is also reflected in the way we approach our work. In this regard, people who are effective within organizations have learned to *think* globally and *act* locally.

We are most effective, regardless of our particular role within an organization, when we do our *own* work well—acting locally—in a way that takes account of the big picture. We do not do our work in isolation but with the whole organization in mind. This principle intersects everything we do within an organization.

The most effective labor union leaders are those who recognize that the company must make a profit and that it must have a president who is able to lead. Only then can they be effective. But just as surely, the most effective management knows full well that the company is utterly dependent on a quality group of employees and colleagues who know that their rights, benefits and working conditions are cared for.

Most literature on effective organizations is addressed to those in management. Yet what I am suggesting is that all of us, regardless of how we contribute to the organization, need to think about how we can work together effectively. The center on a football team may never carry the ball and may never score a touchdown, but if his team wins it is because he knew and executed the plan; he knew what his role was within the big picture, and he knew that without his contribution no one else would be effective.[1]

All of us are effective, then, when we think in terms of the whole. This requires that we think and act in terms of three distinct but interrelated components of organizational life: (1) the organizational mission, (2) the organizational budget and (3) communication. First, few things are so critical as thinking in terms of *mission*. What is the purpose of this organization—not just what is on paper but what exactly is this group of people seeking to accomplish? And how does what I do to contribute toward that mission? What are the underlying values of the organization and how can I function in the light of those values? Know the history of the organization, whether a church or business, for that is a primary insight into its mission, its values, its character and its potential.

First and foremost know the mission and work toward it. But always remember that the mission is not *your* agenda for the organization. A mission is always the commitments of those who work together toward the common objective. The mission will evolve and develop, but it consistently will be a reflection of the organization's character, history and fundamental values. A leader will almost certainly fail if, for example, she imports a vision that does not fit this organization at this time. And as the organization evolves and its mission adapts to new possibilities and opportunities, the leader is almost certainly doomed to frustration if he remains in the past, nostalgic for what the organization used to be. Rather, we must embrace and work with others toward what God is calling this organization to do today, in response to current circumstances and possibilities.

Second, work conscientiously in light of financial realities of the organization. We must ask how *money* functions in this company, church or school. And the heart of the matter is that those who have the "big picture" realize that budget issues affect everyone. One person or department cannot hope to be effective in the long run if they maneuver funds for their individual agenda or department in a way that does not take account of the whole. We need to consider what is strategic and recognize that our own areas of responsibility may not, at all times, legitimately demand new money. We can grow in our appreciation that if there are budget cuts, we work with everyone to keep the whole organization healthy. Most of all, perhaps, we learn to be stewards of the resources that are made available to us, exploring ways we can creatively do more with the limited resources available to us. Nowhere is there more danger for selfish patterns of behavior than when it comes to money. Here, more than in any other area of organizational life, we need to regularly check our hearts and motives, and consistently turn toward a posture of both humility and service.

Third, we are effective in fulfilling our vocations within organizations when we live and work with a commitment to effective communication. When we have the "big picture" and are seeking to work toward a common mission, we need to communicate well and attend well to what others are seeking to pass on to us. Ask yourself regularly how you can *communicate* well and be attentive to the communication of others. If we are partners, we need to listen; we need to speak. We need to hear what others are saying, whether through formal pronouncements, memos or communiqués, or through casual conversations in the hallway.

This principle applies to what *we* are doing as well. To be effective, communicate! This does not merely mean that we need to advertise our product if we are in business. It applies to all of us, such that we ask regularly, Who needs to be informed about what we are doing or what we know so that we can be effective together? Who needs to know about this, and how can we make sure they know in a timely manner? Do others need to know what we are doing—for their sake and ultimately for our own? And our leaders need to appreciate that the rest of us are most effective when we are well-informed; good leadership requires effective and thorough communication, not communication that shows off what they are doing but that enables all of us to be see the big picture.

Usually, the more people know, the more effective they can be. Organizations that withhold information sometimes do so unwittingly; they are either careless or simply do not appreciate how important it is to keep their people informed. But in some cases they do so as a means of sustaining control (a fundamentally parental posture toward colleagues); it is, in subtle ways, an abuse of power. My wife and I sometimes worship with congregations where an order of worship is not printed, and we find it perplexing. We wonder, *Why do they withhold the simple information about where we are and where we are going in the worship service?* Certainly we would worship more effectively if we did not have to wonder what is coming next. If the information is withheld, is it a subtle form of control? This is certainly not always the case. In many congregations it has never been the practice to provide an order of worship. Nevertheless, this is an example of areas where communication might be helpful. The main point is simply this: If we work well with others—whether in worship or in business—we need to communicate so others are informed.

Big-picture thinking demands attentiveness to *mission*, to *finances* and to *communication*. But the flip side of this equation is that we *act* locally. Think "big picture," and act with a commitment to effectiveness and quality within your own sphere of responsibility; pour your energies into where you can make a difference, to your own assignment.

Everyone has the capacity to be effective within his or her own sector, own department, own area of responsibility. Few people are content with everything that happens in every part of the organization. But nothing is gained by complaining or fretting or belaboring the point about those things we cannot fix or that are really not our responsibility. Rather, we must focus our energy and say, "I will do what I do well. I will establish an island of excellence—in the areas I am responsible for." And that excellence will be defined in terms of the whole organization—its mission, its finances and the need for effective communication.

Think in terms of complementary capacities. Third, we are most effective within organizations when we learn to think in terms of *complementary* competencies and capacities. We enter into the formal associations of companies and organizations because we need one another in order to achieve a common goal or purpose.

We are most effective when we see, appreciate and rely on the complementary strengths, abilities and perspectives of others. We can only do this if we have a clear sense of who we are and the gracious humility to *accept* who we are. But it also comes in celebrating the strengths and abilities of others. We are not threatened and we refuse to feel diminished by the character strengths and abilities of others; rather, we celebrate them and depend on them.

Most literature that urges people to stop working so hard and delegate more fails to address this fundamental question: have we learned to trust and depend on others? It is not merely a matter of delegation but also a question of the way that we think. Do we see ourselves as threatened by others or as working to complement others? Do we permit others to fulfill their role, to fulfill the responsibilities that have been given to them? Do we accept the necessary role that leadership plays within the organization? To accept the role of leadership requires trust; to accept the decisions of others that affect your work requires trust—whether those in leadership are making decisions on behalf of everyone.

We will live with perpetual frustration if we seek to control everything in the workplace and fail to freely allow others to function in ways that inevitably affect us. I am also reminded that board members of not-for-profit organizations need to be board members; that is, they should free leaders and staff to do their work, the very thing they were hired for. This too requires trust. To think in terms of complementary capacities demands that we learn to depend on one another, and this means that we grow in our ability to trust others.

Learn how to share power. Everyone in an organization has power. Everyone. This includes the customers of a department store, whose power is most evident when they refuse to buy something. It includes the secretary who manages the flow of information to and from an office. Traditional organizations work with the assumption that power flows one direction—from those in power to those without, and this flow is viewed as not only unidirectional but also as coming from the "top."

Increasingly, though, we are seeing that those who are effective learn to work *collaboratively*, using the power inherent in their role in the organization as a means to enable others to be effective. I am convinced that effective preaching is never merely the fruit of diligent preparation and careful delivery; good preaching happens when there is a congregation of attentive listeners who, through their demeanor and the posture of their response, elicit an effective ministry of the Word. Boards and presidents of academic institutions are profoundly naive if they do not realize that faculty have a powerful and influential voice (and it is right that faculty have this power). Thus, to be effective together, boards, presidents and faculty need to share power. But in each case it is a matter of affirming the character of the power that the individual or the group has. As constituents we have the power to elect our national government officials, but then we must free them to do their work (with appropriate structures of accountability). As members of a congregation, we have the power to elect our lay leaders, but then we need to free them, within appropriate structures of accountability, to lead the congregation.

Effective organizations thrive where there is a pattern of *shared* power. In congregations, leadership can and must come from both the lay church council as well as from the paid pastoral staff, but it is a different kind of leadership, where power is shared, where each leads in a different way. In academic institutions, all parties have a leadership role, but it is different and complementary, as faculty and administration, for example, affirm the role of the other and work together to a common end. And there is no reason why sales personnel cannot be a major source of genuine leadership within a department store, since they have the eyes and ears that can give management a read on what customers are saying and how those customers can be served most effectively.

We will only thrive in this environment if we are not threatened by the real power of the other, and if we know how to work collaboratively with others regardless of where we fit in the hierarchy of the organization. This means that we treat others first and foremost as colleagues rather than as people who report to us or we report to. Further, it means that we need to be able to function where it is not clear who has the final word and where there is no need for the buck to stop anywhere. That is, it means we have learned to work effectively with others in a peer relationship, where no one involved has positional authority over the other, or if they do it is not a significant point of reference as we work together.

We will thrive through our capacity to listen well, depend on complementary strengths and our resolve to negotiate a win-win outcome for all parties. Most of all we will thrive when we come to our working relationships with a commitment to empower others— to have the capacity to see how we can help another be effective in *his* or *her* work. This means, of course, that we refuse to abuse power or use the power we have to undermine the effectiveness of another or to bypass this person's voice and input into the decision-making process. It means that whether we are acting individually or corporately we always ask, How can we make others more effective through our actions, and how can we do this in a way that enables us to achieve our goals?

One of the most valuable means of fostering effectiveness within organizations is by being a person who can *learn* with others. This may take time and patience with one another since the patterns of working (and learning) independently sometimes run deep. But when we learn *together*, our propensity to compete with or blame one another for problems is torn down, and in our learning together, we grow in our capacity to adapt to and depend on one another in the midst of change.

Working together includes being honest with what is happening and learning to respond openly without being defensive or protective of our "space." Very critical in this respect is our capacity to work together as women and men. Increasingly these kinds of cross-gender partnerships will characterize workplaces. Whether on a church board or in business partnerships, the strengths of both men and women will enhance our decision-making processes. But these partnerships will not work if our conversation is patronizing, defensive, manipulative or filled with innuendo. We work together when we learn to converse well together.

Everyone has power. Those who thrive in an organization find ways to use their position and influence to enable others. In other words, they are servants. This is merely one dimension of what our Lord means when he says that if we are going to be "great"—that is, individuals who fulfill powerfully who they are and who they are called to be—we will learn to be servants (Mk 10:43-44).

Accept and work within the limits and strengths of the organization. We thrive within organizations when we work in and through the actual circumstances of our situation rather than fighting the limits or boundaries that we invariably meet. We accept the limits and build with and on the strengths of the organization.

This means *accepting* the limitations inherent in a situation, but more, it also means seeing the potential within those limits. Sometimes an organization lives with self-imposed limits that are bandied about because of fear or lack of vision. That is, we must not overstate the limits; to do so, is to limit the potential we have together to accomplish something significant and lasting.

It is equally imperative that our vision of possibilities is rooted in what is prudent. It is not wisdom or courage or true vision when we have aspirations not congruent with the *actual* situation and the *actual* potential of the organization. Wisdom, courage and vision are all partners; true visionaries are wise people.

This does not mean that we tolerate mediocrity; it means rather that we pursue excellence within the context of our *particular* situation and its potential rather than complaining about our situation. In this I am reminded of the insight of two great sources of wisdom in the history of the church: St. Francis of Assisi and G. K. Chesterton. St. Francis is famous for the prayer that beckons us to accept what we cannot change, to have the courage to take on what we can do with excellence and the wisdom to know the difference. This is not fatalism; it is humility. More than that, it is wisdom.

But Chesterton gives us the spiritual framework to think through this Franciscan model of response. Chesterton wrote the remarkable introduction to the Charles Dickens novel *David Copperfield* in the Everyman series. When I began reading Chesterton's comments, I could not help but wonder why the publishers asked him to write it, because he carries on at some length—two to three pages—about what he calls Dickens's "monstrous errors!" I had the impression that

Chesterton was not at all inclined to recommend that anyone read the book! But then he writes:

> Any fair critical account of Dickens must always make him out much smaller than he is. For any fair criticism of Dickens must take account of his monstrous errors, as I have taken account of one of the most monstrous of them during the last two or three pages. It would not be honest to conceal them. But no honest criticism, no criticism, though it spoke with the tongues of men and angels, could ever really talk about Dickens. In all of this that I have said I have not been talking about Dickens at all. . . . I have been talking about the gaps of Dickens. . . . I have been talking about the omissions of Dickens. . . . In one word, I have been talking not about Dickens, but about the absence of Dickens. But when we come to him and his work itself, what is there to be said? What is there to be said about earthquake and the dawn?[2]

Here is what strikes me so deeply in the words of Chesterton: it is easy to be a critic. It is easy to identify what is *not* present, what is *not* good and what we wish would make an organization better. But true genius has the capacity to identify the strengths and work from them, build on them, celebrate them and be grateful for what is there rather than complaining about what is *not* there. It is not—not for a moment—that we are passive in the face of obvious problems that need resolution. Rather, we work constructively for change *within* the specific horizons that we have within the organization, building on the strengths that are there rather than constantly complaining or berating leadership or bemoaning that things are not as we think they should be.

To function effectively within these strengths requires that we live with a fundamental posture of gratitude for those very strengths. This posture of gratitude empowers individuals and groups to be catalysts for positive change in the organizations they work in—or, in the case of congregations, in the fellowships where they worship and serve.

Learn to be effective in the midst of change. People who are effective within organizations are prepared to adapt to and be effective through change. Only those who are effective in the midst of change will have long-term vocational vitality. Change is a constant in every organization. Effective organizations are those with high capacities for flexibility, adaptation, innovation and change. Thus, those who thrive *within* organizations have a high capacity for adapting to change.

When I was a college dean, I remember patiently listening to a board member complain that things were not as they used to be at the college, like they were in his days as a student. While there is no doubt that some change can be less than positive, his complaint was sentimental nostalgia; it was rooted in unreality. Organizations change. We either accept and embrace this, or we will live with an unrelieved burden that is reinforced with every change.

We thrive in change when we maintain a fundamental flexibility—the capacity to adapt to changes and see them as opportunities for growth and learning. Some changes mean that we will have to leave the organization. But most changes call us to adapt, to adjust the way we exercise our strengths in this organization at this time, to consider how we can thrive in an ever-changing environment.

FINDING CONGRUENCE

To thrive vocationally within an organization we must find congruence between ourselves and the organization we serve. I was involved in an extensive 1996-1997 study of the vocational vitality of professors in Canadian seminaries; senior faculty members in Roman Catholic, mainline Protestant and evangelical schools were interviewed. The results of our research left us with several fascinating insights. One of the most notable for me was that the faculty members over age fifty-five who were viewed as vital and alive by colleagues and students felt a fundamental congruence between their own and their school's values and vision. And at some point in midlife the majority of them had left one place where they taught for another.

They were seeking a setting where there was a high congruence between themselves and the theological school.

That is, those who possess vocational vitality are in organizations in which they own the mission and identify with its values. Herein lies an important vocational principle: to thrive in vocation we need to seek this level of congruence, we need to find organizations we can closely identify with. There is no need to hurry this when we are young, but as we come into midcareer, we must give this serious consideration. (I am inclined to say by our late forties, though in all these things we remain flexible and respond to opportunities as they become available to us.)

Some will never find this congruence. In some cases this lack of congruence is a character problem: it is nothing more than a lack of willingness and resolve to work with others. Some people move from one organization to another, through one crisis after another. Each time they leave one organization (or change jobs within the same organization) they hope to find the perfect place to invest their energies or to finally get the level of affirmation they think they need to be effective. But no organization is perfect; every group, company or institution has its problems; and many times when we move to get away from problems we merely exchange one set for another.

Sometimes the lack of congruence means we need to explore the option of change. The inability of some to find congruence reflects a call to become entrepreneurial—to start their own business where they can have direct influence on the vision and values, or to plant a new congregation rather than inherit a parish that is the fruit of another's work. Perhaps they should leave the newspaper where they work and become a freelance writer.

This is not me; I am not entrepreneurial in this sense. I am inclined to identify with organizations in which I can build on what has already been accomplished or strengthen an organization that is working through change. But vocational fulfillment and integrity of others will only come when they embark on a journey of their own.

Which leads me, then, to discuss a distinct and notable danger when it comes to the organizations we work in, a danger and a threat to our vocational identity or fulfillment. While we are called to fulfill our vocations in partnerships with others—through formal associations or organizations—there is the danger that we will align our own identity too closely with the organization itself.

An example is the person who cannot envision any possibility of working anywhere else. This person is, in a sense, married to the company. We will never come to full vocational integrity until we define ourselves as *distinct* from our work, our occupations, our careers and from the organizations we serve. That is, we are never truly ourselves unless we maintain a fundamental distinction or *differentiation* from the organizations we work in.

When we fail to sustain this fundamental differentiation we almost invariably find that we get caught up in an unhealthy dependency on the organization. Some people see an organization—a church, mission or business—as a kind of parent. They find in their workplace the love, acceptance and community they never received from their parents. They look to their fellow workers for the emotional support that can only come from family, friends and church. Love and unconditional acceptance are basic needs, but we cannot look for these in an organization. We cannot look to the organization we work in to find support, security or affirmation.

Those who seek this level of affirmation and security from an organization almost always find that they are underappreciated, so they come away disappointed and sometimes resentful of the organization. The reason is simple: the workplace will not provide this support.

Often the language of "family" is used to describe those who work together. But these organization are not families, and they cannot be *family* to us. Families, for example, can never reject one of their members. But the workplace includes evaluation, review and even terminations. Terminated people who thought of the organization as family are then emotionally crushed. They wonder how they could be asked to leave their "family."

We should find significant and meaningful friendships in the workplace; our work is more effective when we know that at least one other in the organization is a friend. But we cannot depend on the workplace to meet all of our needs for community, friendship and emotional support. It is an unrealistic expectation. Consequently, it is essential to find a breadth of emotional support *outside* the workplace. This is a key means by which we keep a balance in terms of our institutional loyalties. But more to the point, it is critical that we develop our sense of vocation with *reference* to the workplace but not in *dependence* on the workplace. Jobs are not secure, and our workplace colleagues are not and cannot be our main source of emotional support.

Further, if an individual is in need of constant affirmation, he or she will drain energy from the organization rather than strengthening it. When we so long to be affirmed and supported by the organization, we almost invariably begin to behave in ways designed to bring about this approval, and the consequence is simple: we are no longer true to ourselves and to our vocations.

A key indicator that individuals have an unhealthy dependency on an organization is that they are at a loss when the organization does not tell them what to do, or they are left helpless when the organization does not take them into account in its plans for the future. They have placed the responsibility for their lives in the hands of an organization—essentially giving that organization a parental role—and they have failed to take responsibility for their lives. Many times this is justified by an appeal to faithfulness, perseverance or dependability. While these are noble virtues in themselves, they are not mature virtues when they are not coupled by personal responsibility, courage and conscience.

The ideal may be captured in the principle noted earlier: We can be 100 percent present, but we need to be present while holding a primary commitment to our own vocational identity, which is defined in terms of our loyalty to God. We can be 100 percent present— eager and generous participants in the organizations we serve—but we need to hold our institutional loyalties lightly, for they are not family. For most people, especially in this new economy, God's direction in their lives will lead them to resign at least once in the course of their careers. And each time that choice will be one of vocational integrity—a resolve to be true to their own call.

I need to make an additional comment about what it means to be 100 percent present. This does not speak of an unhealthy emotional dependency; we hold our institutional loyalties lightly. Nonetheless, it does require the commitment to give our energies to these people, this mission, this organization at this time. I have over the years spent a great deal of time in recruitment interviews and hiring new personnel for the organizations I have worked for. And one of the things I have learned is that some people give themselves to the minimal level because they are "ladder climbing"; they seek this position only until they can find what they are *really* looking for. This is odious. When I hire, I am not suggesting that people are making a lifelong commitment to this organization. When I hire good people, chances are that down the road they will move on to another challenge. But while they are here, it is reasonable to expect that they will be 100 percent present, giving themselves to *this* mission and to *these* people at this time.

TO RESIGN OR NOT TO RESIGN: THE TOUGH DECISION

We need to come back to the question of resignations. It is helpful to consider when and under what circumstances it would be appropriate to resign from the organization we work for.

First, our fundamental bias should be *against* change. The virtues of perseverance, patience, faithfulness and dedication are essential if we are going to fulfill our vocations. When we change organizations, we as often as not merely exchange one set of problems for another. And the character of many is never adequately developed because they have not worked through a situation, a problem or a crisis, but always run from difficulty.

There *are* times, though, when we should resign. In the new economy it is highly unlikely that an individual who lives in faithfulness to their vocation will not resign at least once during the course of a career. The reason must be rooted in conscience and calling; it must be an act of *courage*.

Some will recognize that they have completed what they came to the organization to do. Their strengths no longer match the needs of the organization. God called them to this church or that business to match their strengths and vision with the particular needs of the organization. Now, before God, they have the courage to see that they have completed what they came there to do. Part of the genius of effectiveness is knowing when to persevere and when to leave, when to work through the difficulties and when to recognize that we have reached the limits of our effectiveness.

Do not stay when you are no longer effective. In some cases you see that what you have to contribute could best be used elsewhere. In other cases, you see that you can no longer be effective because you do not have the necessary level of support from others to be effective in your work—the person you report to or the board you are accountable to.

No situation is inherently hopeless. But in all situations we must ask if our strengths are needed in *this* place at *this* time. Will our strengths be complemented by others to produce a common vision? Remember the genius of Winston Churchill who in war came to see that there is nothing gained by reinforcing failure. Surely this has significance for our commitment and involvement in organizations. For example, too many people begin a business venture only to discover that it really will not work, or they accept a call to missionary service only to discover that this is *not* really their call.

For others, it will be a matter of conscience. There have been changes in the organization, which they can no longer in good conscience support, or there are expectations placed on them that are either unreasonable, debilitating or unconscionable. Perhaps they are being asked to perform duties they cannot in good conscience do. In some cases a resignation follows an unethical demand; in others, it may be an unreasonable expectation. Either way, the decision to resign is a matter of conscience. My parents, for example, offered their resignation to their mission group when they were required to send me and my sister to a boarding school.

Unfortunately, fear of the consequences could keep us from making a wise choice to resign. There are at least three reasons why people are fearful of resigning. First, some fear that they will make a mistake. This is understandable. We probably recognize that our motives may not be entirely pure, and we may, with good reason, question our own judgment. When we do hesitate, it is wise to have a bias against change and an intentional inclination to stay with a situation, however problematic. While we should not delay unnecessarily, the fact is that in most cases a person who should resign stays much longer than he or she should have. Sadly, they are either released or terminated long after they should have taken the initiative, or they end up resigning when all those around them have known for some time that they should resign. Think about it this way: decide that when it comes time to resign you will be the *first* to know, not the last.

The second reason people do not resign when they should is fear of financial insecurity. We must be wise when it comes to financial management and the care of family and our basic needs. But often when this fear keeps us from resigning we have unrealistic expectations of what financial security is, or we have placed our lifestyle expectations ahead of matters of vocational integrity. That is, our sense of financial security or insecurity has more to do with our heart commitments than with how much money we actually have.

It is more important for us to resign a well-paying job, or a job that provides financial security, than to compromise our conscience. The courageous thing to do may be to accept with grace a simple position, just to pay the bills, rather than continue in a better paying position where vocation, conscience or family responsibilities are being violated.

The *International Bulletin of Missionary Research* has an interesting series titled "My Pilgrimage in Mission." In one article William A. Smalley describes his journey of faith and ministry. At age fifty-four, with a Ph.D. in anthropology and linguistics, he realized that he needed to resign his post with the United Bible Societies. He and his wife sold their home and moved into a low-rent apartment, and Dr. Smalley paid the bills by working as a clerk in a discount toy store. But he nevertheless speaks of it as "a time of learning, growth, and liberation for" him and his wife, until he found an academic post a couple of years later.[3]

The grave danger is that we will make career choices solely in terms of financial prosperity or security, and essentially identify our self-worth with our capacity to make money or with the amount of money we have. But money is so elusive.

Third, people hesitate to resign because they fear that they will be *perceived* as lacking the will, the fortitude, the perseverance and the grace to stay with a difficult situation. They fear they will be branded as quitters and face a loss of reputation. But when it comes to vocational matters, with integrity we must accept that at times we will make others unhappy and that they may well take out their unhappiness on us. This is the bottom line: if we are not quitters, then ultimately our conscience is our guide and we are ultimately accountable to God.

It is virtually impossible to make a major vocational step, to embrace what we are being called to do, without some powerful sense that we are letting go or losing something else. It will be a "small death"; sometimes it may mean that we let go of and lose the respect of certain people. That may be the price, but it is a small price if we walk away from a situation with a sense that our personal integrity is intact.

When you are inclined to quit or resign from a work situation, there are some fundamental questions you need to ask or consider. Why would I *not* quit? Is it because of fears that are not legitimate? Am I hesitating because of nothing more complicated than a desire for financial security? Am I hesitating because of my fear of what people might say?

What is motivating the move? Is it anger, frustration, discouragement or a hurt ego? Is it because I cannot work with others, or that I am running from problems or unresolved relationships? Ask yourself, Am I inclined to resign because I do not want to accept the limitations of this organization, or work with others who will critique my work?

A sure signal that we should probably *not* resign is when impatience is driving our inclination to resign. We need to distinguish impatience from a gracious recognition that we can do no more in this situation; we have accomplished what the Lord brought us to this organization to do.

Finally, when we are inclined to resign, we need to ask, Is the fundamental reason for leaving that I know I have to be true to myself? Is it motivated by the recognition that I must live the truth about my own identity and that I must live in the truth? When we consider whether we are running from difficulty, it is entirely appropriate to ask if this is a cross, a difficulty that I am being called to bear. God will unquestionably lead us through difficult valleys. But it is always reasonable to ask if this is something that he is calling us to. Gethsemane was an extraordinary experience for our Lord; he was confronting the Father to verify whether the cross needed to happen. It was not that he was unwilling to go to the cross but that he needed to know that this was what he had to do—that this was *his* cross. Sometimes God calls us to stay with a difficult situation, and sometimes he graciously calls us on. This is why it is so imperative that we consider the matter of difficulty and suffering *before* we explore what it means to fulfill vocation within organizations, lest we think that difficulty automatically means it is time to move on.

I have heard an observation made by a number of persons in different spheres of work: we should embrace new work, or find a new way to approach the work we have already been doing, every six to eight years. A university president, for example, has suggested that the shelf life of a senior executive of an academic institution is likely about this long, and that after this it is perhaps best to let someone else have a go at it, someone who brings complementary strengths that will build on the work already done. None of us has all that is needed for a particular role, so we do it for a season and then let another, with different capacities, take the responsibility for the next chapter in the life of the organization. Is this perhaps what rightly lies behind the limit of two four-year terms for the U.S. presidency? There may be something to this, but this does not necessarily make these transitions any easier.

Often it is so difficult to know what is right. Indeed in my life no decisions have even come close to matching the tough choice of whether or not to resign. Each time it brought me to another level of radical dependence on God and on others. And through each of the transitions I have been impressed by how difficult it is to know when to persevere and when to resign. Rarely is this an easy choice. James Fowler captures this tension well when he notes:

> There is likely no area of potential self-knowledge where we are more subject to self-deception and more tempted to resort to self-serving rationalizations than in accounting for our efforts to influence and determine the social collectivities of which we are a part and the lives of those involved in them.[4]

How can we do it? How can we resign with conscience and courage as well as wisdom? How can we be people who are fully and generously engaged in our places of work, but not in unhealthy dependency on them? How can we sustain a differentiation that will, when the time comes, give us the freedom to step aside and move on to another challenge.

We have a twofold hope: that we have a vital connection with God through *solitude*, and that we have a vital connection with others in *community*. Solitude and community. Our only hope is a pattern of solitude that enables us to live with the peace and serenity that comes from God, and second, that we have a pattern of intimate relationships with others with whom we converse about what really matters—conversations in which the questions I have just outlined can be discussed with ease.

We now turn to the pattern of solitude and community.

THE ORDERED LIFE

Between Solitude and Community

There are several leverage points available to us by which we can strengthen our capacity to know and embrace our vocations. One of the most critical is the way that we order our lives.

THE FREEDOM OF ORDER

Order brings freedom. Without order our energies are dissipated and our focus dimmed; we are caught up in hectic, confused activity, or we are left purposeless and confused about our identity and what to do next. Through order, a gracious routine and rhythm to our days and weeks, we live with strength and freedom.

Without order, deadlines become burdens and time becomes an enemy—something we constantly struggle against and feel threatened by. With order, time is a friend. But it is important to stress that order is not synonymous with regimentation or rigidity. The order for our lives is an order that *fits* our lives—that is customized to *our* vocations. It is a pattern of life that enables *us* to thrive; it suits our temperament, the character of our relationships, the focus of our work and our life circumstances. The order that brings freedom to an artist or a homemaker will be quite different from that of a dentist or school teacher. But each will find freedom through order.

Through order we find the freedom that comes with regular sabbath rest and thus the joy of a life in which both work and rest are embraced, where the sabbath is indeed a sabbath rather than just a "day off" from work.[1] Through order we come to accept, with grace, both our responsibilities and our limitations. The order of our lives frees us to respond with grace and compassion to needs along the way without being derailed from our fundamental call. Without order we are left confused and bewildered by competing demands and expectations, by an overwhelming sense of the needs around us, and by our own egos that drive us to be heroes, busy people who though busy accomplish little.

It is helpful, as we order our days, to remember and work with three guiding principles. Some may read these principles as another form of "time management," and to some extent they are. But the ordered life is the fruit not so much of time management (whatever that means) as the management of self. What follows are not time management techniques—though there are no doubt techniques that might enable us to live with more order to our lives—but rather the root principles that give us freedom from disordered lives.

The principles of an ordered life presuppose the three levels of understanding of vocation outlined in the introduction to this book: the fundamental call or vocation to be a Christian; the specific or unique call on each life, our purpose for being; and the daily duties and responsibilities we are each called to this day, our immediate priorities.

SUSTAIN CLARITY ABOUT WHAT IS IMPORTANT

First, to live an ordered life we have to sustain a clear sense of what really matters and what is truly important. Invariably, a disordered life is but a symptom of a lack of clarity about priorities and purpose.

A to-do list is not merely a random identification of things that need to be done; it should reflect priorities—what is most important and what, over the long term, needs attention, that which will never be accomplished if we only think and act in terms of the urgent and immediate.

Our sense of what is important is rooted first and foremost in the fundamental call to be Christian. Nothing is more important than our growth in faith, hope and love. At the center of our lives we must sustain a pattern of spiritual discipline and nurture that enables us to be thoroughly Christian.

Further, what is important must be reflected in what we are called to do, both in the present and in the immediate future—whether it is the priority of raising children, of keeping a house clean or of writing a paper. While this may not in itself reflect our fundamental call, it is important. When my sons were in their pre-adult years, they of necessity were a priority. While this did not mean that I would not attend to career or ministry, it was essential for me to sustain a sense that for now, at this stage of their lives (and my life), they were a priority for me.

Nevertheless, our daily agenda should consistently reflect what we are being called to do in this place at this time. In other words our to-do list can and must include both what must happen today—reflecting our immediate priorities—and what needs to happen today because it reflects a long-term priority for us. For example, in my daily work patterns I must be attentive to multiple agendas: What meetings are coming up for which I need to prepare reports or agendas? What needs to happen today and this week even though the benefits or fruit of these actions may not be evident for weeks or even months. I am always impressed as a professor that students complain when assignments for my course are due on the same day as that of another professor. Why, I wonder, should that make any difference? All through our lives we have to live with agendas that intersect, and so we have to learn to do today both what is immediate and also what is due several days or even weeks from now.

Finally, many have found the dictum of "first things first" to be a helpful way to prioritize a to-do list. It is a way to cut the propensity to procrastinate, which leaves so many scrambling with deadlines at a later date.

ACCEPT WITH GRACE THE LIMITATIONS OF LIFE

Another way that order brings freedom to our lives is through the gracious acceptance of our limitations. We cannot do all that we wish we could do, and we cannot be all things to all people. With that, then, we can stop trying. We can learn to depend on others—either by delegating when we have the possibility of so doing or by simply accepting that others can and will do things well.

Further, accepting the limitations of life includes living with the grace that there will be interruptions, delays and unforeseen developments in our day. As we are often reminded: life is messy. This means, of course, that we cannot respond with frustration or irritation every time we get caught in a traffic delay. Life is messy; traffic delays are part of the package, part of owning and driving a car, a normal element of urban living. It means that we choose, in an ordered life, to remain flexible, to maintain our sense of humor and to be patient with ourselves, with others, and with life itself.

Then, of course, the freedom to accept our limitations is evidenced in the ability to say no. The lives of so many are one continual burden for the simple reason that they are trying to do too much. We accept more than we can possibly do well; we respond to the requests or needs of others when we know that we are being driven not by a spirit of love, power or self-discipline (2 Tim 1:7), but by some other propensity.

It is helpful to at least know what keeps us from saying no. For some, it is the fear of rejection; our longing for acceptance drives us to do more than we should attempt to do. For others it is the longing for importance. When they are busy doing many things for many others, these people feel worthwhile, important and in control; they feel needed. Still others do not know what they are called to do, so they assume that if they do as much as possible, they might hit on what they *should* be doing!

The inability to say no inevitably leads to frustration. We can never do enough to gain acceptance or to feel important. It is hopeless. Our only hope is to come back to a clarity of purpose and call, a sense of who we are and what we are being called to do in this place at this time. We need to be clear about what is important. And there will be many days when that is all that we do. But at least we did what was important.

Therefore, we must, before God, resolve that we will not take on more work or responsibility than we can fulfill with a calm and serene heart, without rushed busyness. This resolve is liberating and will keep us from much grief. More to the point, it will free us not only to live an ordered life but to live a life that is ordered around who we are and what we are called to be and do.

CREATE AND EMBRACE THE SPACES IN YOUR SCHEDULE

Finally, an ordered life includes spaces, times in our days and weeks that are unscheduled and uncommitted. We can intentionally create these spaces, but we can also learn to accept the spaces that inevitably come our way—waiting times over which we have little if any control.

First, create the spaces in your schedule. Create margins in the day between daily activities—time for thinking, planning and conversation. Arrive early to appointments so that you are centered and at peace with yourself as you attend the meeting. If you are in charge of a meeting, plan to end early, before the scheduled adjournment time, so that there is space at the end that frees others from feeling they need to rush on to their next appointment.

Begin the day with space for prayer and reflection, and find the spaces during the day to collect your thoughts, quiet your heart and respond to something unforeseen.

Embracing the spaces of the day also includes the grace to accept the waiting times we do not choose but are part of life. We can accept them as gifts rather than as burdens or interruptions. We can, with grace, accept that waiting is part of life—whether in traffic or in the waiting room of a dentist or if someone is late for an appointment. We can allow impatience and irritation to filter into our hearts, or we can accept the time given to us as a gift: an opportunity to read something that we have been carrying with us, or to pray, or to observe life around us. Or we can wait and allow our thoughts to settle on that which is true, honorable, just, pure, pleasing, commendable, excellent and worthy of praise (Phil 4:8).

These are three simple principles. If practiced they will enable us to live in the freedom that comes with an ordered life: sustain a clear sense of what is most important and what takes priority; accept with grace the limitations that come in anyone's life; and create and accept spaces in our schedule

TWO ANCHORS

But we must go further. However helpful these three guidelines might be, we still need anchors to our lives if we want to live ordered lives that enable us to respond with strength and grace to the call of God and the actual circumstances we face.

We need two very particular anchors if we are going to grow in self-knowledge and have the courage to see and the humility to accept who we are. These anchors enable us to come to terms with our fears, to make sense of the difficulty and pain that intersects our lives and respond with heart—with emotional resilience to changes and trials of life and work, living and working with a life-sustaining joy.

There are no exceptions. The ordered life is structured around and is anchored in two realities: community and solitude. One without the other is of little value; it must be both community *and* solitude.

Community as conversation. We need the grace of community. We discern our vocations in community and fulfill them as individuals anchored in mutual interdependence with others in community. Further, all vocations are negotiated with others: with our spouses, with the community of faith, with the actual needs and circumstances of those we live and work with. No vocation is fulfilled in a vacuum apart from the needs and experiences of others. Having a vocation never means that we are freed from the obligations and responsibilities of communal life—whether the duties of making and sustaining a home or the needs that inevitably rise as we live and work together. *All* vocations are communal in character.

This is not all good news; the community, even the community of faith, can be oppressive. The traditions, expectations and cultural patterns of family and community can so easily undermine our capacity to be our true selves and to discern our vocations. Some may wonder, when they consider their own contexts, whether it is even possible to genuinely discern vocation in their communities; they may think that their only hope is to get away to find solitude, strength and encouragement elsewhere. The community can be oppressive. We easily can get caught up in the expectations of others. We must beware of parents, pastors, authority figures and all who have something to gain if we would fulfill their expectations, people who all too easily equate their expectations with the expectations of God. There may be times that we do need to make a break, if and when we conclude that personal integrity is impossible because of the oppressive character of a community. But it will nevertheless be community in some form that grants us the capacity to discover ourselves and embrace vocation.

This is where solitude is so critical. In solitude we encounter the One to whom we owe our *ultimate* allegiance and who alone can give us security, identity and purpose. This is why we cannot merely live in community; when we do, the community becomes oppressive. We are consumed by communal expectations rather than living in response to the voice of God.

But in recognizing the dangers of community and affirming the need for solitude, we must come back to our critical need *for* community, for life in the company of others. We are not and cannot expect to walk this road alone.

By *community* we mean the grace that enables us to live in communion with others. This communion is a means of grace and the very stuff of life. It is remarkable that God would say, as we read in Genesis 1, that the creation is very good. But he also stated that the solitary Adam was "not good." In other words, Adam needed more than God! He needed the company of others, and only through this company could the radical aloneness of the human soul be overcome.

Through community we learn to honor one another—to honor without flattery, with a love informed by truth. In community we learn forgiveness—the capacity to bear with one another as Christ has accepted our sins and forgiven us. And in community we learn how to serve and be served, how to give and receive. In other words, we love and receive love in community. Without this, we remain fundamentally alone, one-dimensional, disconnected from others, from ourselves and from God.

Ultimately it may be that *conversation* is the greatest gift of community and the fundamental means by which community in the Spirit is attained. Conversation sustains marriage, friendship and congregational life; conversation enables us to work together effectively.

Most of all, though, it is the conversation of friends—between spouses, between parents and children, between peers or between the older and younger—that we grow in wisdom, grace and strength. We are en-*couraged* (we fill one another with courage!) through conversation. Encouraged, we able to overcome our fears or at least keep them at bay.

Conversation involves two simple acts or elements. First, conversation involves the discipline and grace of *listening*. There is probably no greater service that we give others. For in listening we attend to them, honor them, accept them and respond to what matters most to them. Nothing so demonstrates that we love others than listening to them.

We listen, of course, only when we resist the temptation to say something, to teach something or worse, to use the word *should* before we have really heard the other. The death of conversation comes when we speak before we listen, when we speak before the other has really spoken, when we jump to conclusions or make premature assumptions about what they are going to say.

Second, conversation includes *speaking*. But it must not include innuendo, complaint or sarcasm. It is spoken without pretense or posturing, the truth plainly given without exaggeration, without flattery. Some, it would seem, cannot speak without being patronizing; their speaking is either controlling or is a means to cover their own fears. Patronizing speech is a pattern, a habit of speaking, for some people. And it undermines any possibility for genuine conversation; their words are no longer connected to their eyes, let alone their hearts.

When genuine conversation happens, it brings us life. In listening and speaking we develop the capacity for intimacy. Through conversation we discover the honesty and humility to accept who we are, confronting our innermost fears, forcing them into the light and finding that they are probably not as terrible as we imagined.

Through conversation we come to terms with our joys and sorrows, and acknowledge and live through the pain of anger, mourning and discouragement. Without this conversation we are alone in our fears, but worse, alone because we are disconnected from ourselves. The irony is that we are only connected to ourselves when we are connected to others; we are only capable of true self-knowledge, the knowledge that enables us to know and accept the call of God, when we are in communion with others.

When we are consistent in the quality of our conversation with all—spouse, family, colleagues and others—God in his grace and wisdom grants us the special friendship of a few, perhaps only two or three. We cannot find intimacy with all; we cannot share our greatest hopes and deepest fears with all. But in the grace of God we can respond intentionally to a few with whom conversation becomes increasingly honest and true, without pretense or posturing. My closest friends and I can pick up where we left off even if we have not see each other for a year or two. Second only to the joy I have in family life, I count these friendships—just three or four along the way—to be among the most precious gifts God has given me.

Solitude. We cannot live in genuine community unless we know solitude; without solitude community becomes oppressive.

I have already made reference to the text of Mark 1, where Jesus is pressed by Peter and the others disciples to return to Capernaum because of the needs of that city. Without equivocation he advises them that he must go to other villages also, that he might preach

there, for that was why he had come. That is what he had to do. But
lest the disciples conclude that he is heartless and lacking in compassion, we read in verses 40-42 that when he comes upon a desperately
ill man who calls out to Jesus, the Lord, filled with compassion,
reaches out, touches the man and heals him.

Here is what makes this so remarkable. Jesus had a clear sense of
purpose. He knew who he was and what, fundamentally, he was
called to do. He was not derailed or overwhelmed by the needs of
Capernaum. Neither was he caught up in the emotional pleas of his
disciples. As Glyn Owen, the great Scottish-Canadian preacher, put it
so well, "It was more important for Jesus to *be* a servant than to be
thought of as a servant."

But then we are brought up short with the power of his encounter
with the leprous man. He was *filled* with compassion. The Father did
not call Jesus (and God has never called us) in such a manner that he
could not respond with compassion along the way. No one has a call
that precludes responding with grace to the needs around us, whether
it is toilets that need to be washed, children who need attention or a
colleague who needs an empathetic ear.

Is this not what we want? Do we not long to be people who have
clarity of vision and purpose, and a clear sense of who we are and
what we are being called to do? But do we not also long to be people
of compassion, who without pretense or posturing engage with care
the lives of others? Some, of course, are so clear about their call that
I wonder if they are aware of the people around them and the real and
immediate needs that beckon. Others are like sponges, uncritically
absorbing and responding to the needs around them, but with little
sense of purpose. In both cases what really drives them is ego—first,
a desire for accomplishment; second, a desire to be needed.

The question then is how can we be both people of purpose, with
clarity of vocation, as well as people of compassion? The answer is
found in Mark 1:35. Early in the morning, while it was still dark, Jesus
went to a solitary place to pray. When his disciples found him, with
frustration they exclaimed that everyone was looking for him.

Solitude is fundamentally a place of prayer—of personal and individual encounter with God. To be in solitude is to be intentionally present to God. Solitude, then, is not the act of being alone but the event of being alone *with God*. It is therefore the fundamental and most essential act of Christian spirituality. It is the emotional and spiritual *space* where we give our unqualified and undivided attention to the One who calls us. The prayer of solitude is the prayer of conversation. It is the place of honesty before God and the place of the open heart—of responsiveness to the prompting of the Spirit.

Solitude is essential for vocational clarity and integrity, because in solitude we are enabled to sustain a connection, a relationship, with the very one who has called us. Through the encounter with God in solitude we are able to see ourselves in truth, to think honestly and critically about who we are, without pretense or misguided aspirations. In solitude we can come to terms with our emotional ups and downs, be honest about our joys and sorrows, know grace for the times of difficulty and disappointment, and accept and confess our own failures and shortcomings.

Without community, solitude is nothing more than escape from people and the pressures and stresses of life and work. Stepping aside like this may have its time and place. But the danger is that it might become nothing more than self-indulgence. When we are people who live in community, solitude is the critical spiritual discipline that enables us to draw on the strengths of the conversation we have in community and avoid oppressive community ways.

While *conversation* is the critical means by which we know the grace of community, *journal writing* is the equivalent exercise in solitude. Journal writing is really nothing but the written record of our prayers—of what we are saying to God and what we sense God is saying to us. In my experience, the journal is an indispensable means by which we (1) make sense of what is happening in solitude, (2) develop vocational awareness, (3) monitor our emotional development, (4) process the transitions of our lives, and (5) keep track of the critical choices and decisions we make in response to the prompting of the Spirit. It is, then, so much more than a mere diary; it is the account of our prayer, of our encounter with God.

Tolstoy, I believe, once wrote that between the lines of what we write in a journal is the outline of our future. But this is only the case if when we write, we write as though in conversation with God. A journal is not something we write in with a view toward one day publishing our memoirs! Rather, it is a private space in which we can respond with "massive honesty" to God, to others, or to our circumstances and to ourselves.[2] The journal enables us to see things as they are. Few things are so effective as a journal to enable us to live mindfully, to respond intentionally and keep our hearts from illusion on the one hand and despair on the other.

Each person will approach a journal differently. But I recommend the following approach. Take time at least once a week, perhaps even daily, to identify first, simply and concisely, what is happening in your life. This is not the most important thing you write, and this is not a diary, so it is best kept brief. Second, describe how you *feel* about these events and developments, and what you are *learning*. That is, identify what is happening to you emotionally, including how, when and to whom you have felt angry or if you are feeling discouraged or if you are feeling a major loss. But also identify what you are learning and how it is enabling you to grow and develop either in your work or your relationships.

What you have written so far is essentially *your* perspective on your life, your side of the conversation, so to speak. This is what *you* see and feel, and this is what *you* bring to God. But then it is imperative that you also record what you sense the Lord is saying or impressing on your heart in the midst of this. The record of this *conversation*—the journal—is a record of your personal encounter with God. To the degree that we write with massive honesty and listen with open hearts to the prompting of God, the journal is one of the most valuable resources we can have for vocational discovery and development.

COURAGE AND CALLING

We seek the freedom that comes with order. It is found with careful attention to our priorities, a gracious acceptance of our limitations and the intentional creation of spaces in our daily agenda. But what gives us stability in the midst of the turmoil and pressure of daily life are community and solitude, and the grace that we find through conversation and a personal journal.

We do not seek order as an end in itself. Order enables us to live with courage and hope in the midst of a confusing and broken world, and to be people with a clear sense of call in the midst of so much change and so many uncertainties. The two poles—community and solitude—are the means by which we know the grace that enables us to live with faith, hope and love. Community and solitude enable us to be mindful, intentional and purposeful. These are the two anchors that enable us to confront our fears and live and work with hope. Through the grace of conversation in community and the encounter with God in solitude, we can increasingly become people of courage, even in a disheartening and broken world. These anchors enable us to know and embrace with courage that which we are called to be and to live and work with integrity. They give us centered lives that find their focus, purpose and strength in Jesus Christ. Our ultimate goal is not so much to accomplish great things as to be women and men who know, love and serve Jesus. Our final concern is not career or ministry or reputation, but whether through the course of our lives we grow in the saving grace of Christ.

Some of the deepest longings of our hearts will *not* be fulfilled in this life; they await the reign of Christ when justice and peace will embrace. In this life we have to set aside much that we long for, in some cases because expectations are dashed, in others because even if we have a life rich in opportunity and a highly supportive community, the sheer fact of life in a broken world is that we will not be all that we hope to be. I suspect that many if not most of these longings, fulfilled and unfilled in this life, are a foretaste of how we will live and work in the new heavens and the new earth. That is, I have a

suspicion that somehow our vocation is not merely for this life but for
the life to come.

But in this life, we will have unrealized expectations and longings.
This is not to minimize our life and work now; human life has extraordinary possibilities, even in a broken world. It is appropriate
that we should long to make a difference through what the apostle
calls "fruitful labor" (Phil 1:22), and these chapters are offered as
encouragement that we might be all we are called to be. But in the
end, our freedom comes in joining the apostle as he seeks the ultimate vision—salvation and the glory of Christ. All that matters, in
the end, is knowing Christ Jesus (Phil 3:7-8).

This vision can and must give perspective to the disappointments,
frustrations and setbacks of our lives. But in the light of what matters
most of all, the experience of a life ordered around solitude and community can enable us to embrace our vocation in the world and free
us in Christ and with hope to act with courage.

NOTES

Chapter 1: Stewards of Our Lives

[1]Wendell Berry, "Toward a Healthy Community: An Interview with Wendell Berry," *Christian Century* 114, no. 28 (1997): 912.

[2]Gary D. Badcock, *The Way of Life* (Grand Rapids, Eerdmans, 1998), p. 30.

Chapter 2: The Meaning of Our Work

[1]Matthew B. Crawford, *Shop Class as Soulcraft: An Inquiry into the Value of Work* (New York: Penguin, 2009).

[2]Bruce K. Waltke, *The Book of Proverbs: Chapters 15–31* (Grand Rapids: Eerdmans, 2005), p. 529.

[3]Ibid., p. 521.

[4]Ibid., p. 523.

[5]John Calvin, *Institutes of the Christian Religion* 3.10.6, trans. Henry Beveridge (Grand Rapids: Eerdmans, 1979).

Chapter 3: Seeking Congruence

[1]Parker Palmer, *The Active Life* (San Francisco: Harper & Row, 1990), pp. 64-68.

[2]David Kiersey and Marilyn Bates, *Please Understand Me: Character and Personality Types* (Del Mar, Calif.: Gnosology Books, 1984).

[3]Brian J. Mahan, *Forgetting Ourselves on Purpose: Vocation and the Ethics of Ambition* (San Francisco: Jossey-Bass, 2002), p. 114.

[4]Ibid., p. 120.

[5]Peter Block, *The Answer to How Is Yes: Acting on What Matters* (San Francisco: Berrett-Koehler, 2002), pp. 4-7.

[6]Ibid., p. 137.

[7]Ibid., p. 22.

[8]Ibid., p. 1.

[9]Ibid., p. 79.

[10]Ibid., pp. 86-88, 21.

[11]David Whyte, *Crossing the Unknown Sea: Work as a Pilgrimage of Identity* (New York: Riverhead, 2001), p. 132.

[12]Ibid., pp. 133-35.

[13]Ibid., p. 165.

[14]Henri Nouwen, *The Road to Daybreak* (New York: Doubleday, 1988), p. 3.

Chapter 4: Chapters in Our Lives

[1]Maynard Solomon, *Mozart: A Life* (New York: HarperCollins, 1995).

[2]An earlier draft of this paragraph noted that if we make a good break from parents "the next transition will come more easily and more naturally." But in revising this chapter I realized that at least for me the midlife transition was not getting any easier! And now as I work on the second edition of this book I am aware that the move into our senior years is every bit as challenging as the earlier transitions.

[3]Ralph Waldo Emerson, "Self Reliance," in *Selected Essays, Lectures and Poems of Ralph Waldo Emerson*, ed. Robert E. Spiller (New York: Washington Square Press, 1965), p. 241.

[4]Jackson Bate, *Samuel Johnson* (New York: Harcourt Brace Jovanovich, 1975), p. 235.

[5]Maxine Hancock, "The Chafing Collar: George Herbert's Uncomfortable Vocation," *Crux* 38, no. 3 (2002): 2.

[6]Tim Stafford, *As Our Years Increase* (Grand Rapids: Zondervan, 1989), pp. 62-64.

Chapter 5: As Unto the Lord

[1]Thomas Merton, *New Seeds of Contemplation* (London: Burns & Oates, 1961), p. 16.

[2]Simone Weil, *Gateway to God*, ed. David Roper (New York: Crossroad, 1982), p. 83.

Chapter 6: Thinking Vocationally

[1]James Fowler, *Becoming Adult, Becoming Christian* (San Francisco: Harper & Row, 1984), p. 103.

[2]Ibid., p. 104.

[3]A. W. Tozer, *The Pursuit of God* (Harrisburg, Penn.: Christian Publications, 1948), p. 114.

[4]Maynard Solomon, *Mozart: A Life* (New York: HarperCollins, 1995), pp. 285-305.

[5]Parker Palmer, *Active Life* (San Francisco: Harper & Row, 1990), p. 66.

Chapter 7: Four Callings

[1]Henri J. M. Nouwen, *Reaching Out: The Three Movements of the Spiritual Life* (New York: Doubleday, 1975), p. 27.

[2]Annie Dillard, *Teaching a Stone to Talk: Expeditions and Encounters* (New York: Harper & Row, 1982), pp. 11-16.

[3]The insightful spiritual writer and one-time bishop of Geneva Francis de Sales (1567-1622) suggested the following as a spiritual exercise: "Be just and equitable in all your actions. . . . Always put yourself in your neighbor's place and him in yours, and then you will judge rightly. Imagine the seller when you buy and the buyer when you sell and you will sell and buy justly" (Francis de Sales, *Introduction to the Devout Life*, trans John K. Ryan [New York: Doubleday, 2003], p. 203).

[4]H. R. Rookmaaker, *Art Needs No Justification* (Downers Grove, Ill.: Inter-Varsity Press, 1978).

[5]I am thinking here, for example, of the work of Hans Urs von Balthasar and the strength and depth of his writing on theological aesthetics. See his magisterial multivolume *The Glory of the Lord: A Theological Aesthetics* (New York: Crossroad, 1991).

[6]See the whole conclusion of Lewis Hyde, *The Gift: Creativity and the Artist in the Modern World* (New York: Vintage Books, 2007), pp. 356-64. For many of us there is no finer comic strip than Bill Watterson's *Calvin and Hobbes;* thus an essay by E. J. Park caught my eye when he spoke of how Watterson refused to allow for the commercialization of Calvin and his equally famous tiger friend—no T-shirts, movies or coffee mugs, though this would have been highly lucrative for Watterson. Rather, Park quotes Watterson as noting that this would have cheapened his work and he asks, "Who would believe in the innocence of a little kid and his tiger if they cashed in on their popularity to seek overpriced knickknacks? . . . Who would trust the honesty of the strip's observations when the characters are hired out as advertising hucksters?" And thus Park speaks of the artist who stays true to his or her medium (E. J. Park, "The Tale of Two Kitties: Lovers

of Aslan Should Heed the Warnings from the Creator of Hobbes," *Christianity Today*, February 1, 2006, pp. 68-70).

[7]Rainer Maria Rilke, *Letters to a Young Poet*, trans. Stephen Mitchel (New York: Vintage Books, 1984), p. 6.

[8]Richard John Neuhaus, *Freedom for Ministry* (San Francisco: Harper & Row, 1979), p. 228.

[9]Wendell Berry, *Jayber Crow: A Novel* (Washington, D.C.: Counterpoint, 2000), p. 43.

[10]Craig Dykstra, *Initiatives in Religion* 9, no.1 (2001): 1-2, 15.

Chapter 8: Courage and Character

[1]Paul Tillich, *The Courage to Be* (New Haven, Conn.: Yale University Press, 1952), p. 4.

[2]Ibid., p. 14.

[3]W. Jackson Bate, *Samuel Johnson* (New York: Harcourt Brace Jovanovich, 1975), pp. 3-4.

[4]Parker Palmer, *The Courage to Teach: Exploring the Inner Landscape of a Teacher's Life* (San Francisco: Jossey-Bass, 1998), pp. 35-38.

[5]James R. Horne, *Mysticism and Vocation* (Waterloo, Ont.: Wilfrid Laurier University Press, 1996), p. 58.

Chapter 9: The Capacity for Continuous Learning

[1]Peter M. Senge, *The Fifth Discipline: The Art and Practice of the Learning Organization* (New York: Doubleday, 1990), p. 142.

[2]Mary Catherine Bateson, *Peripheral Visions: Learning Along the Way* (New York: HarperCollins, 1994), p. 83.

[3]Sharan B. Merriam and M. Carolyn Clark, *Lifelines: Patterns of Work, Love and Learning in Adulthood* (San Francisco: Jossey-Bass, 1991), pp. xi, 1.

[4]Ibid., pp. 1, 3.

[5]Peter F. Drucker, *Managing the Non-Profit Organization* (New York: Harper-Collins, 1990), p. 223.

[6]C. S. Lewis, *Surprised by Joy* (London: Collins, 1955), p. 143.

[7]Bateson, *Peripheral Visions*, pp. 74-75.

Chapter 10: The Cross We Bear

[1]John Ralston Saul, *Reflections of a Siamese Twin: Canada at the End of the Twentieth Century* (Toronto: Viking, 1997), p. 26.

²Victor Emil Frankl, *Man's Search for Meaning : An Introduction to Logotherapy*, trans. Ilse Lasch, 3rd ed. (New York : Simon & Schuster, 1984).

³Stephanie Golden, *Slaying the Mermaid: Women and the Culture of Sacrifice* (New York: Harmony Books, 1998), pp. 233-34.

⁴Ibid., p. 234.

⁵Parker Palmer, "On Minding Our Call—When No One Is Calling," *Weavings* 9, no. 3 (1996): 18-19.

⁶Ibid., p. 22.

Chapter 11: Working with and Within Organizations

¹There are few resources as helpful as those produced by Peter Senge and his associates, most notably: Peter M. Senge, *The Fifth Discipline: The Art and Practice of the Learning Organization* (New York: Doubleday, 1990); and the sequel, Peter M. Senge et al., *The Fifth Discipline Fieldbook: Strategies and Tools for Building a Learning Organization* (New York: Doubleday, 1994). These helpful volumes identify the kinds of practices and perspectives that enable individuals to thrive within organizations. As Senge and his associates emphasize, we need to think *systemically*. We are effective when we see ourselves within a system—a whole and complex network. Senge's work is valuable in large part because it is written for all who work within organizations. Clearly the leadership and management have a critical part to play. But to thrive in our common efforts, all of us need to see what makes for effective organizations. Many of the principles that follow are based, in part, on insights from these two works.

²G. K. Chesterton, introduction to Charles Dickens, *David Copperfield* (London: J. M. Dent, 1907), p. xii.

³William A. Smalley, "My Pilgrimage in Mission," *International Bulletin of Missionary Research* 80, no. 318 (1991): 70-73.

⁴James Fowler, *Becoming Adult, Becoming Christian* (San Francisco: Harper & Row, 1984), p. 109.

Chapter 12: The Ordered Life

¹Note the distinction between a "day off" and a genuine sabbath rest as described in chapter five.

²See W. Jackson Bate, *Samuel Johnson* (New York: Harcourt Brace Jovanovich, 1975), pp. 3-4.